THE CROFTING WAY

Other books by Katharine Stewart include:

A Croft in the Hills
Crofts and Crofting
A Garden in the Hills
A School in the Hills
The Post in the Hills

All available from Mercat Press

THE CROFTING WAY

Katharine Stewart's Country Diaries

KATHARINE STEWART

Foreword
by
IAIN MACASKILL

MERCAT
PRESS

First published in 1999 by Mercat Press
at James Thin, 53 South Bridge, Edinburgh EH1 1YS

© Katharine Stewart 1999

ISBN: 1873644 99X

Set in Marigold and Garamond at Mercat Press
Printed and bound in Great Britain by the Cromwell Press

Dedication

For the crofting people of yesterday, today and tomorrow

CONTENTS

I
Crofting Days

II
After Crofting

III
The Land

IV
An Ending,
A New Beginning

ILLUSTRATIONS

FOREWORD

By Iain MacAskill,
Chairman of the Crofters Commission

In the 1970s, while enjoying a leisurely family tour round one of my
favourite areas by Loch Ness, we decided to stop at the small museum
at Abriachan. I shall always retain fond memories of this visit mainly
because of a charming lady who enthralled us all with her enthusiasm
and knowledge of the exhibits, their purpose and of the lifestyle of the
people who used them as tools of their trade. She had a gift of quickly
making friends and a love and appreciation of the heritage and culture
of the crofting community with whom she had been so actively involved. This was my first meeting with Katharine Stewart.

All of the qualities that so impressed me on that far-off day at
Abriachan shine through in her latest book *The Crofting Way*. The
same keen eye for detail, a love and appreciation of the environment,
a closeness to nature and all its creatures, and an understanding of all
its bounties and hardships. She enjoys the support of friendship, the
sense of sharing that is a key feature in small Highland communities.
Perhaps most of all she has an understanding of the value of her culture and heritage which has created so much of what we cherish today.

The Crofting Way covers a period of rapid change over the years
from the immediate post-war period to the present. A time of labour-
intensive, largely self-sufficient units, gave way to a more machinery-
driven age. We move through the years during which hydro-electricity
was introduced and when improved infrastructure and other key services reached remote communities. On the negative side depopulation
continued, with the inevitable closing of schools, shops and other services so vital to the continued existence of a thriving community.

The daily records of crofting activities throughout each season provide a fascinating insight into crofting family life over the decades covered
in the book. The crofting system has helped retain population and communities in the Highlands and Islands. The book will help increase our awareness
of the important role that crofting plays in our rural and remote Highland
communities and in the proper management of our environment.

Today there is an increasing recognition that our land resource must be
protected and sensibly used. Crofting provides the ideal model for achiev-

ing this with its environmentally-friendly system and ability to help provide a population base. There is now an increasing demand for crofts from young people and with prospects for land reform and other developments the future of crofting looks more promising than it has done for a considerable time.

There has also been a revival of interest in our culture, in the language, music and heritage of our Highland areas. There has already been a reversal of the tendency to depopulation in some of our communities, and by building on the many positive things that are currently happening I would be hopeful that this movement of people back to the Highlands can be accelerated.

To preserve the unique and valuable heritage and culture in the Highlands and Islands we need vibrant communities with people who understand the value of the very special environment which we currently enjoy, and are able to help preserve it. By preserving what is best from the past and taking advantage of new technological developments we can, I am sure, realise many of the hopes that Katharine Stewart outlines in the conclusion to her book.

My thanks

go to Mr Iain MacAskill, Chairman of the Crofters Commission, for kindly writing the Foreword to this book. His work and that of the Commission are vital factors in the promotion of crofting. I should also like to thank Mr Brian Macdonald, Information Officer of the Commission, for his valued help in providing documentation and ideas.

I have happy recollections of working with editors of the *Scotsman* publications, now departed, from Mr Robert Yeats of the *Weekly Scotsman* to Mr Alastair Dunnett of the *Scotsman*, who all encouraged me in writing for their papers. Mr Tom Johnstone of the Mercat Press has, as always, been my skilled and helpful editor.

I
CROFTING DAYS

The croft in winter

1954

We came north in 1950. Before that the hills we walked were the lowland hills. There was lark-song and the scent of heather. But always in the inner eye were the hills of the north, vast hills under a white sky. And the distant curlew calling.

With the aftermath of war and its effects slowly seeping away, we began to think... a tangle of thoughts which began, slowly, to take shape... We each had close links with the land. Jim's forebears had been crofters and weavers in Atholl, mine had farmed further south, in Galloway. A spell in the Women's Land Army had taught me to milk a cow, to stook corn, to drive a tractor at the tattie-lifting. We had grown vegetables and fruit, had kept chickens and bees. So it was that we came, quite naturally, it seemed, with our small daughter Helen, to live and work on a croft, close on 1,000 feet up, in the hills above Loch Ness.

The house stood, four-square and solid, its walls of granite and whinstone, its roof of fine blue slate, facing the morning sun. Cleared fields surrounded it, rough grazing stretching west, and in the distance those vast hills, and the white sky, there, in reality. Nearby stood the ruin of the original house on the holding, a small single-storey structure, and a good steading with stable, barn and byre, with traces of the old horse-driven mill.

It is not always realised that crofting, as we think of it today, originated only about some 200 years ago. The word 'croft', from the Gaelic *croit*, means a small piece of enclosed land. This is significant. Until the latter part of the eighteenth century, the people had lived in 'townships', small clusters of houses, working the land on the 'run-rig' system, that is, as joint cultivators, the arable apportioned in strips, the good alternating with the poor. Their mainstay was the cattle which they grazed on large areas of hill-ground. In these close-knit communities there was much interchange of ideas, discussion, debate.

When the chiefs who, in the movement of the time, had become landlords, set out to make their estates profitable by the introduction of large flocks of sheep, many of the people were cleared from their holdings in the glens and given small plots of land, or crofts, to provide some sustenance for their families, with a share in a common hill-grazing and the possibility of finding some paid employment. For those sent to the coast this meant work at the 'kelping', the burning of sea-weed to produce alkali, or in developing the fishing. Some, as in the area we had come to, were given a few

3

acres of barren, shelterless land with the possibility of obtaining some seasonal employment at draining, ditching, wall-building, with a small wage paid by the estate, which, of course, obtained the ultimate benefit. It was at this time that there were many emigrations, some willing, many enforced, to the developing colonies in America, Canada, Australia, New Zealand.

The people who remained, eking out a living as best they could, seeing the land they craved turned into sheep-walks or deer forests, these people began to realise that to fight was the only way to solve their problems. This time the fight was to be, not with their chiefs as in former times, but against them, against those who had abandoned them. From some of their supporters, men who had travelled in America, they heard stories of the troubles of the native people there. Broken promises, reservations…? There were riots in many places, rents were withheld, summonses burned, ricks destroyed, fences pulled down, police attacked with sticks and stones. Eventually, after several years hearing evidence from crofters, a Royal Commission set up to investigate the situation reported its findings. A crofter was defined as 'a small tenant of land, with or without lease, who finds in the cultivation of his holding a material portion of his occupation, earnings and sustenance and who pays rent to the proprietor.' In 1886 the Crofters' Act was passed by the Government. This gave crofters security of tenure in their holdings but still did not restore the land they needed. Since that date many more measures have been adopted to improve the lot of the crofting community. We had always known something of the background to crofting. We were to learn more as we experienced the actuality.

Our place was one of a small community scattered over this upland strath known as Caiplich, the 'place of horses'. In former times the ground had been fit only for the rough grazing of the many horses needed to work the surrounding areas. Quite soon friendly and helpful hands were stretched to us by members of the families all born and bred in the place. We were to value their skills and their wisdom, their companionship and help over the times to come.

The first years were hard but rewarding—seeing good ground bearing sturdy crops, sheep and cattle thriving, producing most of our foodstuffs, sharing the warmth of the old way of life. Schooling for Helen was in the best tradition, with the added benefit of new friends, new ploys. If spending money was hard to come by there was always the possibility of earning something from a spell of paid employment in a nearby town—Inverness or Dingwall. The crofter has always had recourse to something similar. But to have to split up, even for a short time, was not a happy thought. Then came a fresh idea. There must be many Highland people in the towns of the south who would like to hear about life as it was still lived in the *uplands, I thought. I had always written diaries, letters, had had one or two things published...*

One bleak afternoon in the January of our fourth year on the croft I sat down at the kitchen table, a large blank sheet of paper in front of me, a pen between my fingers. Jim was outside, shifting loads of muck from the yard, Helen was not due home from school for a couple of hours. The writing came quite naturally. It was simply a description of a quiet January on a hill croft. Rejected by one editor on account of 'lack of space' it quickly found a home in the pages of the Weekly Scotsman *and was to be the first of many welcomed by successive editors of that paper. This was the start of a record of our life and that of our neighbours in the crofting lands of Caiplich, part of Abriachan. Today, this may seem to many to be almost the stuff of legend, to us it was the reality of our daily lives. It began like this:*

January 23rd

On the croft we are now well into the New Year and the last of the ceilidhs is over. Festivities are prolonged where friends are separated by hill and glen and where snow and storm may mean the postponement of a call of greeting. But now we have settled down to normal life again.

On January 12th, the date of the 'old' New Year, there is an hour on the day, it is said. How eagerly we seize on that extra hour, which lets us get one more job done before the lamps are lit.

As though to brace us for coming once more to grips with reality the weather has turned chill and bitter. 'Very cold' is once more the greeting when neighbours meet.

The cows are glad to stay all day in the byre, generating what heat they can and waiting patiently for the armfuls of straw and pailfuls of chopped turnips that are carried to them. Even Charlie the horse, that tough old Highland warrior of nearly thirty summers, we think, who dearly loves his freedom to glean what he can, though it be from frozen shoots of heather—even Charlie is glad to be lured into his stable at night with a tasty sheaf of corn.

The pullets, bless them, are still turning out their daily quota, encouraged by a warm mash each morning, and the cold has put an end to the determination of some of them to sit on their eggs.

Shortly before Christmas a neighbour's hen, which had been missing for a while, came proudly home with a family of nine chickens. Who could blame her? The grass was growing, the primroses were out— why not hatch a few eggs ? But now we know that this is not really a

5

land where it is 'always afternoon'. As I write there are frozen taps, frozen turnips, even a few frozen tatties, where the pit was carelessly closed after opening.

We had come to think we had nothing more to do than make a start at the ploughing when the days drew out a bit. But now the cold, splendid colours of the sky dazzle us morning and evening. The clink of a pail set down on the frozen cobbles, the rustling of straw in the byre as the cattle turn to look for their supper, the glowing cheeks and eyes of our small girl coming in from school to the warmth and lamp-light—these things mean winter.

We are fortunate indeed, for the milk cow is yielding well and all the cattle still have the gloss of health on them, while the sheep have had a grand tupping season. Fuel stocks are well up, too, and now we can pile on an extra peat and an extra log and sit in to the fire of an evening, secure in the knowledge that the days are steadily lengthening, that come what may we can count on the passing of the winter in weeks now, rather than months. April is not so far off, that way...

February 25th

February has been a bitter month. The wind has come tearing at the house, driving the snow through every chink. Frost has sealed the ground so that no living creature could hope to draw sustenance from it. It is difficult to imagine that it will ever bring forth again. There have been days of east wind, when the mist comes swirling over the high ground, the sleet is blinding and it is difficult to draw breath in the face of it.

The men are glad to spend the day threshing out some oats in the barn. The housewife hurries in from the milking, stokes up the fire and maybe thinks: 'This is the very day to make marmalade!' There is comfort in the smell of the drops of hot orange that ooze over the side of the big pan and sizzle on the stove. Helen comes home in daylight now, but it is a cold, wan daylight. She is glad to sit on a stool at the fire while wet boots and stockings are peeled off and she drinks a cup of hot, sweet tea.

After a night of storm we wake to a quiet, white world. As soon as the housed animals are fed the men go off to the moor to see how the sheep have fared. They find them diligently scraping away with fore-feet and muzzles till they get at a bite of heather underneath the snow. The white on their black noses gives them a comical appearance as they look up at the approach of the dogs.

Helen is kept from school by the huge drifts on the road. She spends a happy day revelling in the snow.

It is most fortunate for us that, so far, the grocer has managed to reach us each week. We have not had to draw on the emergency stocks of food that we lay in each winter. Some Wednesday nights, not sure of the condition of the road by which he comes (our only unfailing daily visitor, the post, comes from the other direction), we gather anxiously at the kitchen window to watch for his approach. A shout of glee goes up when we see the big headlights appear and come slowly down the 'overside' road.

We wait twenty minutes or so to give him time to make calls at two neighbours. Then, putting on our warmest coats and taking torches and a sack apiece, we set off to the road-end to collect our goods.

Groceries, bread, oatmeal, paraffin, everything needed to sustain life is awaiting us. With smiles of relief we bring our bundles into the kitchen, dump them on the table then put everything away. We're secure for another week.

This is winter indeed, yet spring will not be held in leash. After a night of severest frost the midday sun is warmest. There was such a day last week, with deep-blue skies and icicles dripping everywhere. I was tempted out to look round the garden and found buds on the fruit bushes clearly visible.

Next day, on a visit to town, I was rash and hopeful enough to buy packets of cress and parsley seed. I can't wait for Nature to be ready. I shall sow them in boxes in the kitchen, just to see something fresh and green growing again. Two or three days of thaw and the larks would be singing madly.

The men have been taking advantage of the hardness of the ground to cart out dung to the fields on the calm days. It's good to see the small, black heaps that mean so much fertility and growth. Slowly, inevitably, the new season is swinging in.

March 25th

March certainly came in like a lion. An easterly gale piled the snow in drifts again. But March storms soon relent and within the week spring was with us—the real spring of soft blue skies and sunshine warm enough to set the midges dancing. Doors and windows can be opened wide to let the scent of the fields in through the house.

Helen loiters home from school and can't be persuaded, till the very last minute, to come in to supper.

For some time the larks have been pouring their song over the moor and now we upland folk have a great event to celebrate—the return of the plovers. Nothing can lift our spirits as can the sight and sound of them in their mad sky-dance across field and heather.

The hens have had their first taste of spring, too. At last the earth can be scratched and the midden made to yield venturesome insects. The result is eggs by the dozen.

First to produce new life on the croft this year are the pigs. Two sows we have, now the proud mothers of eighteen piglets between them. While the youngsters, fat as butter and pink and white and spotless, lie snug in their deep bed of straw the sows can get out for a prowl in the sunshine and root happily in the softened ground. They are grand mothers and soon grunt to be let in again to their lively brood.

The dung is being carted out in earnest now and fields cleared rapidly of turnips, as thoughts everywhere are turning to the plough. A

Our neighbour at work in the turnip-field

few good days of drying winds and the ground will begin to crumble. Already the garden is cleared and limed and waiting for the spade.

Soon the real work of the year will begin. Meantime, with daylight till past seven, a host of minor but essential jobs can be tackled—fences repaired, roofs painted, drains cleaned.

The cows are turned out early now and seem almost reluctant to come home, as the rough grazing takes on a more appetizing flavour. The sheep are in grand form and can be seen resting contentedly in the midday sun. We watch them trekking off to the dry ground in the evening light and, with the lambing still a few weeks off, we hope and pray no late storms will come to set them back.

We are such a small unit of cultivation, surrounded by the immensity of hill and sky, and so grateful for each sign of beneficence. A daisy has only to bud in the lea of a dyke at this early season and it is as though a jewel had shone up at us. On a still night we take a turn outside before going to bed. We hear the burn, far up the hill, running full with melted snow. Plovers rise, startled and screaming, into the dark. Across the glen we see the fires Duncan has lit in the dry whins. Spring is here. We go in, content and expectant.

April 29th

April is the busiest month on the croft. Drying winds have brought the ground into a fine, workable state. All up and down the strath the ploughs are out. Mostly it is tractors from the 'Board' (the old name clings to the Department of Agriculture) that are hired to do the job, but in some places the horses are still used. Everywhere the horses follow on with the harrows.

Then comes the most satisfying job of all—the sowing of the corn. He who sows a grain of seed has faith, they say. Surely that is what keeps us working away at the land—faith in a tomorrow, in many tomorrows.

Our first lamb was born early this month, on a squally day of snow showers. Its first cries were pitiful, but it is thriving and will soon have many peers to frisk with on the warm evenings. Each day one or two more small, white specks appear on the moor. The flock is gradually increasing.

Helen has the sharpest eyes of us all. It's her job to keep the tally and report the fresh total every night. She is kept busy watching nests, too. Her special favourite is a plover's, on the open ground where the hen bird is sitting on four eggs.

Some domestic hens are sitting, too and soon we hope to be seeing the familiar yellow chicks emerge. We are not buying in day-olds this year, but are making last year's pullets do another season. They have had a good, healthy winter and are in excellent form. We are hatching only a few eggs to provide something for the table later on.

We have said goodbye to the sows and their litters as the present state of the pig trade made it uneconomic to keep them on. One youngster remains, to be fattened through the summer. Calves are appearing on all the crofts. Our own house cow is dry at present and, unfortunately, is calving late this year. But every morning we get two big bottles of milk from a neighbour whose cow has lately calved. This is one of the many acts of kindness which make life so pleasant among good neighbours.

This is the season for the burning of the heather. At night it is a grand sight to see the far hill tops ablaze. The flames destroy parasites harmful to sheep and clear the ground for fresh growth.

Spring comes late in the uplands. On our visits to sea-level we envy the big farms their fields of fresh grass and their budding trees. But though the moor delays we know that it will yield in its own good time. Already we can think of making a start at the peats, when the corn is all sown. As we take our evening walk round the sheep we can see the beginnings of fresh shoots among the heather. As the days lengthen so our working hours increase. There is no clock-watching on the croft. To see animals and fields respond to the season, to feel the sun's warmth on our hands as we work is reward and to spare.

May 27th

May was heralded by a fall of snow! Then came rain, such torrents of it as we had not seen for a long time, and the burn was transformed overnight into a raging river. We feared for the lambs, for the ewes are particularly fond of the lush grass that grows along the burnside, but none, to our knowledge, was drowned.

There are perils in plenty to beset the new-born lamb—hooded crows, hawks, a fox on the prowl, not to mention the stupidity of an odd mother-ewe who may, for some reason known only to herself, refuse to have anything to do with her offspring. One small creature abandoned thus we have in our care in the byre. She is making good progress on a diet of diluted cow's milk and cod liver oil. The rain, though it came with overwhelming suddenness and in overwhelming quantities, was very welcome. The long dry spell had burnt up the pastures, growth was at a standstill and the ewes' milk supply was suffering. Now, with a warm spell following the wet, everything is springing to life with urgency. At last the rowans have burst into leaf, the silver birches are glittering, the grass is growing stronger every day and there is a green flush on the cornfield. The lambs, a fine, sturdy crop, frisk and leap all day long with the sheer joy of being young in such a season.

These May days are almost as busy as those of April, with the tattie-ground and the turnip-break to be harrowed and harrowed again, the garden to be planted, the lambs marked and inoculated. But it's a happy time, when everything seems more than ever worth while. The new growth everywhere, the young life abounding, the real warmth of the sun—these things lift the spirit, so that to work till dusk, and it is a late dusk in these northern parts, is no hardship.

Helen is in her element these days, giving the pet lamb its bottle, crumbling bread for the new-hatched chickens, carrying porridge to the piglet. These small, endearing forms of life that look to her give her a feeling of oneness with the life of the croft and with the great cycle of life itself. What a cry of wonder she lets forth at sight of the first seedlings, sown by herself, in her own small plot, thrusting through the ground! So are miracles brought within the compass of a child.

The cows are out now, night and day, and are only glimpsed, away at the farthest corner of our holding, where the grass grows most lush and tender. Charlie the horse is busy stoking up on pasture, too, in all his leisure time, to keep in trim for the heavy work ahead.

Too soon this May-time will be over. No other month can quite compare with it. All day long the cuckoo calls and at evening the cry of the curlew haunts the heart. Our hills do not flower till autumn, but one walk across the moor reveals the tiny plant life—it dare not grow big, for storms would overwhelm it—pushing upwards. The air reverberates with lark-song and the sound of snipe—'sky-goats' as they are called most fittingly in the Gaelic. All life is singing its busyness to high heaven. None could fail to join in the chorus.

The Shielings

In older times, and even until quite recently in the Islands, in early summer, when the crops of oats, hay and potatoes were established in the low-ground fields and the peats for winter fuel were cut, the cattle, and perhaps a few sheep and goats, were taken up to the high pastures to feed on the sweet hill grass. There, at what were known as the shielings, the women

11

structures with walls of turf and stone, roofs of branches and heather thatch. The remains of these small shelters can still be seen on the hills by the outlying places—Achpopuli and Corryfoyness. One hill is known as the 'hill of the little houses'. The grass round about them still grows bright after the healthy treading and manuring of the cattle beasts.

Life at the shielings was simple but happy. The women made vast quantities of butter and cheese, some of it sent down to the men at the crofts, much of it preserved in kegs buried in the peat, for winter use. They also wove and spun to make winter clothing. The young men herded the cattle, did a little surreptitious poaching and worked in wood, with the aid of a sharp knife fashioning spoons, spirtles, milk-whisks, many useful things.

It was a busy life but a good one, with plenty to eat, dancing on the green sward in the evenings, music and song and sound sleep on the heather beds in the cool summer nights.

Flies and, of course, midges were kept at bay by bunches of myrtle hung in the little 'dairy-house' which adjoined the living place. The use of oil from the myrtle as a midge-deterrent has just been re-discovered today, with tourists in mind!

The men who stayed to keep watch over the growing crops would often take the chance, with their families away, to rethatch the houses. The old thatch, heavily impregnated with peat-reek and making excellent fertilizer, would be ploughed into the ground in spring. The men would also repair implements, some would weave or, by a simple process of tanning, make footwear for the winter. It could be said that the whole rhythm of summer work was a preparation for the rigours of winter life, for both animals and people.

The happiness of the days at the shielings found expression, as all facets of life did, in the spontaneous composing of songs. Sung at winter ceilidhs they would bring back all the feel of the long summer days.

Gazing up at the shieling grounds by Achpopuli we would sometimes envy the women of the last century who summered the cattle up there. Today, there's enough pasture to hand for our beasts, the crops are fenced against predators and our roofs are of slate.

June 30th

This is the season of growth. The days of awakening, filled with incessant birdsong and the heady scent of warmed earth, when to step outside each morning is to enter a world new-minted for delight, these days are over. Now everything is settling down to the sober business of increase.

The birds still sing, but in snatches now, when they can get time off from coping with the demands of their offspring. Everything clamours for sustenance, from fledging plovers to the young shoots of corn and the calves thrusting their blunt noses into the pails of milk.

Little encouragement to grow the crops have had. Bitterly cold north-east winds have chilled and dried the ground. Now, at last, they have veered to the south-west and the rain has come. We had waited to make a second sowing of turnips till there would be sap in the ground. Now the race will be on between seedlings and weeds. The grass, too, has been held back, but soon we shall see the fields rippling in the breeze and hear a rustle through the corn.

The chickens are at the hungry stage, rushing about on gawky legs to snatch at any stray tit-bit on their own, no longer heeding their mothers' agonised warnings of impending danger. Ted, the young collie, has to be restrained hourly from giving chase to these intrepid young-sters when he himself feels he could do with an extra-tasty dinner.

The pet lamb grows more importunate every day. On one occa-sion she came in at the open front door and up the stairs to Helen's bedroom, searching for her bottle. Everything is young and impatient and full of clamour.

With the crops safely in the ground the main job of the day is the cutting of the peats. All around dark scars appear on the hillsides as the men get to work to cut out the solid blocks of fuel. The weather has been favourable for this, at least. As the peats are built into small piles the wind and the sun make short work of drying them. We are fortunate in having on our own ground a deposit of the best black peat, which is nearest to coal in burning quality.

Between days at the peats neighbours gather in the early morning, at each place in turn, to give a hand with the clipping of the sheep. By evening, fresh white specks appear on the hills as the shorn sheep make their way back to their grazings. The lambs have all been dressed and inoculated and now the flock is left in peace till the August dipping.

Our old friends the tinkers are back on their annual visit, one lot encamped on the heather at the march of our holding. They are decent folk, the older generation, though some of the younger are too near the 'spiv' for our liking. They are still adept at their old trade of 'tinning' and have made us a grand steamer for about half the cost of a shop-bought one. The soft goods they hawk around could all be bought cheaper (and cleaner?) in town, but their tinned ware is found on all the crofts. Basins, bowls and pails made by them will last a lifetime.

There are few, if any, other summer visitors to these parts. We are off the track and can only be approached by steep, narrow roads. Yet there

Helen helps with the peats

off the track and can only be approached by steep, narrow roads. Yet there can surely be no lovelier spot on earth than the shore of our own small loch on a midsummer night, when the sun hardly leaves the sky and the hill is reflected in purest lines on the still water. As we walk there, thinking, we could wish to share the peace with the whole world.

The Summer Walkers

The arrival of the tinkers, or 'summer walkers', as they were known, was always accepted as one of the regular events of the season. The little procession of carts, a spare horse or two, dogs, men, women and children was spotted from afar. 'The tinkers are back!' became a greeting, almost as though we were saying 'It's a grand day!' and it seemed almost equivalent, for it meant the long days were here, wet or fine.

Stewarts, Macphees, these were folk whose forebears had been outlawed after Culloden, had taken to the heather and never looked back. They respected the crofters' way of life, kept their dogs under control and would give a hand at some urgent job if they were needed. Their tinware was certainly much valued. In older times they made horn spoons and did some silversmithing. Some of them kept alive the old tradition of story-telling. Luckily, many of the tales have now been recorded so that this priceless heritage can be safely stored for the future.

Our 'walkers' would stay several days at the roadside. The sight and smell of their wood-smoke made us think we had new neighbours. In the evening we would hear the scrape of a fiddle, with no one in miles to throw a penny. Their life was as good as they made it.

July 29th

This has been a very wet and cold July. As I write the rain is lashing at the house, and the wind, although from the south-west, has almost an edge to it. There's one thing we don't need to worry about, at any rate, and that is a shortage of water! Sometimes, at this season, the wells and burns are running very low and we have to carry drinking water from a far spring, take the clothes down to the big burn and wash them in the good old way there, rubbing them on a flat white stone and hanging them on the bushes to bleach in the sun.

Truth to tell, we rather enjoy these laundering expeditions, provided we don't have to resort to them too often. It's grand, on a hot day, to stand in a sun-warmed pool, letting the clear water flow over the rubbed clothes and rinse them clean… Then, when the back begins to ache a little with stooping, the best remedy in the world is to take a spell on the grass verge, breathing in the scent of the heath flowers.

Perhaps a frog may stare for a moment with incredulous goggle eyes at the proceedings before leaping away to cover in some cool, green hole in the bank, or a minute trout may flash in terror through the washing pool.

To recall these days makes one long for a real summer season, and to hope it may not have missed us altogether this year.

Already the evenings are getting shorter and we must light lamps if we are not in bed by ten. The lighting of lamps is soon to be a thing of the past. There has been much stir among us since the announcement was made that we are to come under the hydro-electric scheme. The small white vans of the Board go scurrying from croft to croft. Kindly officials appear, with maps and binoculars, explaining to everyone exactly where the pylons and transformers are to be erected, what the cost of wiring and consumption will be, what equipment will best suit our needs. A year hence, they say, the bright lights will be twinkling with power-driven machines. The tide of civilisation has risen even to our high-pitched doorstep!

The crops could do with some warmth to bring them on, though, on the whole, they have not suffered too badly from the unseasonable weather. The horse comes into his own now, spending many a busy day with the scufflers, keeping the weeds in check and the ground in good order. Turnip-singling is still the main job in most places. Small squads of neighbours gather to work slowly up and down the drills. It's a tiring and monotonous task and everyone is glad when the last field is done. The hay crop is backward. No one in our district has yet made a start with the mower. We hope for sunshine and warm winds when cutting-time comes.

Meanwhile the scent of clover rises, making the world smell, at least, of summer. Over the moor, between the gleaming drifts of bog cotton, great patches of deep-purple bell heather are appearing. While everything moves slowly on its way towards harvest we can take time off, now and then, to 'look at things in bloom'.

August 26th

August has been, so far, almost as wet and cold as July. One day, though, stands out in the memory as fine, with the far hills blue-shadowed and the moor sheeted with heather-bloom—the twelfth. The guns were heard all around that day and several grouse in surprisingly good condition were shot on our own ground. We're still longing for the sun. Growth everywhere is rank and green, with not much body to it. Haymaking has been a nightmare. Along comes a day of drying wind, with a little warmth breaking through, and everyone gets busy with scythe or mower. Then down comes the rain again before we can even get what's cut safely into a coil. It looks as if we'll have to resort to our makeshifts of last year and hang the swathes, like washing, on the fences to dry!

It's heartbreaking work, because we know that, even though we manage to save most of it, one way or another, much of its feeding value will be lost if it is handled too often. It will fill a hungry beast in winter, but will not really nourish it. The hens are doing well in the damp, perhaps because it encourages the growth of insect and grub life which provides them with such a valuable source of protein. At any rate, there is no sign of the torpor which usually afflicts them at this time. Their continued laying prowess has saved many of them from the pot.

The house-cow's calf, although born late in the season, is thriving like a spring beast and is everyone's pet. Its mother's milk has the thick yellow cream of early summer and butter-making is in full swing. So an upside-down season may have its compensations.

One garden crop has yielded exceptionally well—the blackcurrants. I don't remember ever seeing such thick clusters of enormous berries on the bushes and, luckily, this year we managed to cheat the birds of their delight. The result—25 lbs of luscious jam. The taste at tea-time on a winter's night…we can hardly wait! Our thoughts are tuning constantly now to preparations for robbing winter of its sting. In a sense, the work of the whole year is directed to that end. We have a feeling that this year will close down on us early. Already, with scarcely perceptible signs—a clearness in the air on the bright days, a crisp feel about morning and evening, the appearance of berry-clusters, still rusty brown, on the rowans—autumn is making an entrance.

One job of the moment certainly brings winter very near—the carting home of the peats. Charlie the horse is doing noble work here, fetching cartload after cartload from the peat-bank at the far end of the moor. It gives us a great feeling of security to see the hard, black chunks piled into a neat stack near the house. Come what may in the months ahead we can be sure, at least, of having fire in the hearth, warmth in the kitchen. Warmth is life.

The Twelfth

We laid claim to two of the grouse that fell to the shooters on the adjoining estate that day. A brace would make a dinner. There was no need for more. We remembered the rows of dead birds and other game, laid out at the end of a day's sport in older times. With the wholesale slaughter that went on year after year it's a wonder that any wildlife survived in the hills. There is no keepering now. The remains of the old butts still stand, the butts that sheltered the sportsmen as the birds were driven towards their guns.

By the mid-nineteenth century, when the success of the introduction of large flocks of sheep was beginning to wane, owing to fluctuations in the market which afflict all commercial enterprises, landowners were turning their thoughts to the development of sport on their estates. Deer, grouse, salmon, wild game of all kinds could be 'managed' to provide a lucrative income. It was a well-organised affair. Some employment was provided for local people. Gamekeepers were needed, ghillies, rearers of pheasants and so on. One place hereabouts is still known as the keeper's croft. A croft-ing family was removed to make way for him. The result of this development we are seeing now—the vast overpopulation of deer, which has been as *we are seeing now—the vast overpopulation of deer, which has been as damaging to the ground as the overpopulation of sheep.*

The shoot on this particular day was not one of the old style. It was a case of shooting 'over dogs'. This meant a dozen or more people walking through the croft land of our elderly neighbours over the burn, even through the standing corn, sending their cattle cavorting in panic and all for the sake of half a dozen dead grouse. We could only look on in disbelief and dismay, listening to the shouts and the whistles as the party eventually made off to enjoy their alfresco lunch.

September 20th

September, the harvest month, has not, alas, yet brought the harvest weather. As I write, there is snow on the Strathfarrar hills. All month the wind has come battering from the north, the south-east and the west and the rain has come with it in torrents. Yet our little crop of corn has not, miraculously, been laid. It has not ripened, only turned a pale, pale gold. But it is standing, challenging the elements to do their worst.

On our visits to low-ground friends we watch with wondering and envious eyes the heavy, burnished sheaves being swung aloft and fashioned into sturdy stacks. We come home and take another look at our own small crop. Has one day of sunshine helped it on a little while we've been away? We think maybe it has taken on a deeper tinge. We turn away to fill the time with other ploys.

There are sods to be cut as covering for the tattie-pit. The barn is to be cleared and tidied and the byre roof to be painted to protect it from the winter weather. Every other day Charlie the horse takes a long trip to the derelict woodland to fetch a big load of sticks for winter fuel. The time will come, and it may not be so far distant, when snow will hamper all movement on and off the croft. We must prepare while the going is good.

Already, Helen's journeys to and from school are beginning to cause us a little anxiety. She has two burns to cross on the shortcut to the road and last week the water was swamping the footbridges. Along the flat stretch, where the road rises imperceptibly to a thousand feet, before plunging into the next glen, the wind has a real wintry edge to it. Wellingtons, thick socks, gloves and headgear are unearthed from the kist.

We still cling to the hope that there will be an Indian summer in it yet. The good days, when they come, are so very, very good—the sky at its bluest, the sun very hot and very golden, a mauve light about the hills, the rowans standing at peace with their burden of glittering berries, the fields so still as they lie waiting to give up their crop.

There is still new life about the place. Our cross-Shorthorn cow, nicknamed Pet, as this was the only name we could give her when we bought her in two years ago as a sleek, demure and charming heifer, has had her autumn calf. It's good to see it frisking about in fields still rich with grass and clover, oblivious to the cold and wet, caring not a hoot for snow on the Strathfarrar hills.

Snow or sun, our harvest-time will come. Meanwhile, helpers young and old give a hand as needed on the places that are ready.

There is perhaps no job on earth so satisfying as handling sheaves of corn, whether it be tying them with bands of straw as they fall in the wake of the scythe, lifting and stooking them as they emerge from the flying arms of the binder, or forking them on to the cart when they are led at last to the stacks. When we of the heights need help, in our turn, to get the crop in quickly in the shortening days we know it will be forthcoming. We wait still for the sun to do its work, with what patience we can muster.

Caiplich

An area such as Caiplich would probably not have been cultivated had it not been for the 'improvements' carried out by the landowners—as the Highland chief had become, as we have seen—in the thirteenth and nineteenth centuries. The word itself, 'Caiplich', is derived from the Latin Caballus, a horse, and meant grazing ground for horses. As a place-name it is found in many parts of the Highlands. Today, we tend to forget the importance of the horse in the working of a croft. We ourselves had come to acknowledge it fully.

Caiplich is a wide open strath 300 feet up and shelterless. The north side, which forms part of the Lovat estate, was brought into cultivation as long ago as 1732, a century before such things were common. The then Lord Lovat, a far-seeing man, was one of the first landowners to realise the possibility of taming what is now known as 'marginal' land. This land, in a survey made in 1725 by Joseph Amery, had been described as 'Moor ground for about 12 miles long and 3 broad'. Simon, Lord Lovat, signed up three men to 'improve...together with houses, biggings, yards and other easements' for 'the space of seven years', rent free, thereafter to pay the normal rent for improved land.

The south side, where our croft lay, was Grant territory, on what became known as the 'Seafield' estate, and was let out in lots when places had

Our croft, Caiplich

development of sporting activities during the nineteenth century. Our croft was Lot no.4. We later took in Lot no.5 and some extra grazing ground.

The historian Charles Fraser Mackintosh, writing in the 1880s, describes Caiplich as 'a cold, bare, exposed place'. Snow before harvest must have been a common enough occurrence over the years.

October 28th

As I write, there is little we can do but wait in hope for drying winds. All up and down the strath the stooks are standing in the fields, pathetic, sodden little heaps of corn. In some places cutting was only finished a week or so ago. Tattie-lifting is out of the question with the ground a squelchy mess. Only the turnip breaks look well, bright green and flourishing.

For four days and four nights the rain came down. The drains were unable to cope with the continuous deluge and for a while the water was lapping the threshold of the byre. Mercifully, it has not been unduly cold. Only the milk-cow is brought in at night yet. The others roam the grazing ground and flourish on herbage which is still succulent and plentiful.

The hens are snug in their deep-litter house, the pig well bedded in straw. Lucky creatures that do not have to worry as we humans do. While straw. Lucky creatures that do not have to worry as we humans do. While they peck and munch contentedly at their supper we take a turn, during an evening lull in the downpour, round the fields.

Everywhere is the sound of rushing water, from the overflowing ditches round the garden plot, from the rivulets cascading helter-skelter through the heather, from the burn, swollen now to the proportions of a river. On the low-lying pasture gulls float contentedly on new-formed silver lochans. We live in wellingtons and oilskins and the kitchen is draped, night and day, with steaming garments. Then—along comes an afternoon of respite. The wind rises, the clouds disperse, and all the lovely October colours are there again—the russet moor, the gleam of a birch against a bright blue patch of sky, sun lighting up the glistening rocks on the hillside. And the scent of autumn in the hills! Indescribable!

Off we go, in a burst of exhilaration, to the cornfield to turn the stooks, to pick up fallen sheaves, to weigh our chances of gathering the crop. Our thoughts stray with envy to the filled stack-yards of the early places. 'You'll be taking yours in by Christmas,' we almost hear them say down there as they survey their own new-ploughed stubble. And yet, will they have the same sense of achievement we shall have, yes, we shall have, in the end, when ours is in, as it surely will be before another moon?

Meantime, there is an extra baking to be done, for the children are getting busy. In odd corners of the kitchen and the byre we come across strange-looking paper masks, hollowed-out turnips, lengths of horsehair 'tails' and old, forgotten, battered garments.

Soon it will be Hallowe'en and we shall be playing host to the weirdest-looking assortment of guisers ever seen. And they'll be hungry. Let's hope for clear skies and starlight that night as we sit at the fire cracking nuts and munching apples, waiting for the mysterious knocking on the door.

Hallowe'en

Some of the old Hallowe'en ploys are remembered and told about at fireside ceilidhs but are not much indulged in by today's children. A hefty peat or, better still, a lump of snow if there had been an early fall, thrown down a chimney, a cart loosened and pushed down the brae—these were some of the night activities of older times. Though half-anticipated, these activities might have ended in minor disasters. But at least there was nothing of the 'trick or treat' idea which seems current today. You were lucky if you got away with your 'trick' unscathed, or with only a battery of picturesque imprecations flung at you from the doorstep. Most of our guisers sing a song for us and are still young enough to enjoy a handful of goodies.

Sometimes the spooky side of Hallowe'en overlays the fact that it was actually the pagan festival of harvest. When all is gathered in then, perhaps, we do have time to sit and reflect on the meaning of life, of death...perhaps to acknowledge the existence of evil...

If the devil has shown his face this night, this e'en, then tomorrow, the 'hallowed' day, we shall remember the dead. This is the day when, in countries of the old faith, people visit the graves of their forefathers, taking flowers in remembrance. Highland people, whichever form of faith they profess, always have their ancestors in mind and can repeat their names back through the generations. This takes the sting from death, for they are assured of remembrance through the long times to come.

November 28th

November has brought more than its normal foretaste of winter. Our thoughts this while back have been perforce concentrated on the weather, the prelude to every neighbourly chat being, 'What weather! What weather!' The higher hills are thickly covered with snows standing out livid against a dark grey sky. Frost has withered the last of the autumn flowers. Rain has brought the burn down in another spate, gales have ripped the corrugated sheets from the shed roof and overturned a hen-house.

But there have been days—two or three at least—when we have had to rub our eyes to make sure we were not dreaming, days when we could step outside and positively listen to the stillness, when the clear note of a man far up the strath whistling his dog and, close at hand, the sound of the last leaves fluttering from the rowans could be distinctly heard.

Then we have been tempted out on to the hill, to gaze in astonishment at pale blue skies, to feel the sun warm on our hands and to watch the dance of midges in the haze. What an unpredictable thing our climate is!

The corn is in, at any rate, and in surprisingly good order. At one or two places the stooks are still standing, waiting for a drying wind, but from the bigger farms comes the reassuring hum of the threshing mill. The harvest of 1954 will soon become a legend to be recalled at many a ceilidh in days to come! The tatties are up nearly everywhere and now energies are bent on lifting turnips.

They are a good crop. Charlie the horse is kept busy carting them, load by load as they are clipped, to the pit. It's good to see the stocks of winter feed piling up. Very soon the cows will be glad of it, though for the present the grass, which is exceptionally good, is keeping them mostly satisfied. These are busy days among the sheep. The last of the lambs have been sold, fetching grand prices. Now the ewes are looked over and rounded up as the tupping season approaches. Floats are up and down the road daily, bringing sheep for wintering. The dogs are kept hard at it, herding fugitives this way and that. Horse and dog— what grand partners they are! We'd certainly be lost without them. They ask so little—a feed, a warm bed, a friendly stroke when they've done their best.

With the days darkening well before five, our working time is limited now. We're glad of the stock of peat and sticks we managed to lay in to keep a good fire in the evening. Neighbours will plod many a mile through the dark for a fireside exchange of news. Sometimes we can persuade young Geordie to give us a tune on his accordion. Then feet go tapping and eyes glint merrily. The live music is so much better than anything that comes out of the wireless-box.

There are signs that the 'hydro men' are getting busy. As we watch the engineers tramping over the moor and bog with their prospecting apparatus we look forward eagerly to the enlightenment that will be ours next winter. Let's hope we shan't be too busy working at night, with electricity in the barn, to have time to put our feet up at the fire!

Threshing Day

The coming of the mill was looked forward to with pleasure, tinged with a small measure of anxiety. Would the weather hold, would the expected number of helpers turn up, was there enough in the larder to cope with appetites?

Though it was booked for a certain day it might well have been held up at another place by the weather. There was the problem of access to our place, or rather, non-access, no discernible traffic route existing between us and the road. But one should never underestimate the skill of Highland drivers. Cars, lorries, buses, vans, tractors and trailers surmount all difficulties eventually. So it was with the mill. It arrived on the appointed day, at the appointed time, with a cheery grin from the driver and, of course, all our helpers turned up. As well as help at the mill, there was willing help in the kitchen, for the making of soup, the scrubbing of tatties, the baking of piles of scones and oatcakes.

The steady humming of the machinery in the yard, strange sound to our ears, was soon a reassurance that all was well. There was a rhythm to the work—the forking up of sheaves, the feeding of them into the heart of the machine, the bagging of the grain, the raking up of the straw and the eventual building of the stacks—all these separate jobs meshed together as one worker kept time with the next and brought the whole operation to a satisfying conclusion. With the last sheaf stripped we took time to run a handful of golden grain through our fingers. All the months of work, of weather, of worry, were there, in that wonderful reward. One year our oat-seed took first prize at a seed-and-root show, to our disbelief but real delight!

Many snacks of tea and scones later, followed by a gigantic meal of broth, stew and tatties, we saw our helpers off in the fading light and the mill clattered its way cheerily on to the next waiting crop.

Until about fifty years ago the crofters hereabouts took their oat crops to the mill down the road, at Balbeg, to be ground into meal. There, in return for a stipulated portion, probably an eighth of the quantity to be milled, the work was done expeditiously and under cover. In the wood down towards Loch Ness, the remains of a very old type of mill, a Clack Mill, can still be seen in a fast-flowing burn. Many people ground their corn, a little at a time, in querns—two stones, one rotated against the other, by hand. Prehistoric saddle querns—a hollowed stone on which the corn was ground out with a rounded stone held in the hand—have been found in several places.

In some parts of the Highlands, where the laird derived an income from the use of the mill, the querns were destroyed by order, thus obliging people to take their crops to the mill. Some millers were required to provide stabling, ale and accommodation for people coming long distances. In later times barn mills, worked by treadle, were installed. There were also horse-drawn mills, operated outside the barn.

Few ploys can quite compare with the complicated, yet essentially simple operation of a day at the threshing, with neighbours and friends working together, a lot of joking and teasing, a bit of cursing, gleaming smiles of relief when the job's done and there's time to relax over a meal, with stories of other days at the mill, of triumphs and near-disasters, with reminiscences and forebodings, above all with laughter and maybe a song.

December 30th

To have passed the shortest day is a sort of triumph in itself and is, indeed, a reason for rejoicing. In the Scandinavian countries the event is signalled with a Festival of Light, when the youngest girl in the family goes through the house with a lighted candle on her head, bringing radiance into the dark places. I wonder that our ancestors did not adopt some such custom. The return of light is such a blessed thing.

At the moment it seems that the cows are no sooner let out in the morning than it is time to bring them in again for the night, They are lucky, though, for there is still a tasty bite for them outside which relieves the monotony of their staple diet of oat straw and turnips.

To us, who work about the byre in winter, the Christmas story is a very real thing. We can visualise quite clearly a child laid in a bed of straw. We can imagine that his mother may well have been content to see him lying there, the oxen turning their great dark eyes towards him and warming him with their sweet breath. The straw about the floor would shine like gold in the lantern light. The shepherd's gift of a new-born lamb would have been riches indeed. It would all have been very natural and seemly and satisfying to the hearts of simple folk.

We have become almost philosophical about the vagaries of the weather now. It can rain in deluges, gales can blow themselves into a fury, making the whole house quiver—there is nothing we can do about it! So we struggle about with loads of straw and turnips for the cows, clear ditches, break sticks for the fire and spend the worst days threshing out some corn sheaves, in the old-fashioned way, in the barn.

We're lucky that, for the moment, we have the 'black ground'. So far, the winter has brought us only three or four days of snow. The road, then, was quite impassable. Helen had to be kept two days from school when the blizzard was raging. Luckily, by 'van day' things were more or less back to normal. How the vans manage the journey sometimes we cannot imagine, but—it's very seldom we don't find our bagful of necessities when we struggle along to the gate on a Wednesday night. The vanman deserves every penny of his wages. And, of course, we take off our hats to 'the post', who struggles through the worst the weather can do to reach us unfailingly, day in, day out.

Sometimes, as we brace ourselves to turn out, torch in hand, for the evening milking, our thoughts turn longingly to summer days, with daylight almost round the clock and the sweet air coming from the clover. But there are compensations. The sky, on a calm day, at morning and just before dusk, has a radiance of incomparable beauty, and the stillness and serenity of frost make us stop in our tracks in wonder.

Ice crystals along the edges of the burn, the brilliant starshine at night, the voices and laughter of children coming safe down the road from school are all things of winter that make us glad to be alive. Very soon we shall see the days lengthening and know that we are, even if very distantly yet, on the way to another spring.

'The Post'

The arrival of the mail every day is something townspeople take for granted. If it's an early delivery they may never see the man who brings it—the postman. They may hear the flop of the bundle as it hits the floor, the dog may bark, or growl. That's it.

Our 'Post' arrived early afternoon. He had been down to the main road in the morning to collect the mail from the bus, had taken it to the office for sorting before he set out on his rounds. The authorities allowed him only a pedal cycle, but he ran a motorbike at his own expense, for his time was precious.

He had a croft to work and he worked it to perfection. His fields were described by a neighbour as 'like a garden'. Even a motorbike didn't solve all his problems. To reach places like ours he had to leave it at the roadside, walk through the felled woodland, cross the stile and follow the footpath to our house. In rain, gale or blizzard he never failed to reach us. 'Never mind the soap-coupons,' we would shout through the weather. He would just let a cheery smile break out and shout back, 'Ach, I'll be along'. And he would. His croft was very near ours. Many a time he would appear, unbidden, to give us a hand 'before the rain'. He would leave his bike at the roadside, rather than take it down the track to his house at the end of the day. That was common practice when vandals were scarcely known. Once, when a blizzard blew up overnight and continued for several days, his bike was snowed-in and remained hidden under a frozen blanket till the thaw came and it emerged unscathed.

Much of his round was done, perforce, on foot. His journeyings were not unlike those of the 'runners' of the eighteenth century, the men who carried bundles of mail on their backs across trackless country, with the money collected for delivery in their pockets, thus putting themselves at the mercy of thieves on their way back to the receiving office.

In winter our 'Post' would finish his round by torchlight, tired, but never unwell, and satisfied, I think, that his visit, perhaps to someone left living alone in an isolated place, had brought a welcome moment of cheer, a 'news' of the outside world, a greeting from a far-off neighbour, a chance to send a message to another. His function was always much more than that of a plain, unseen deliverer of mail.

1955

This was a year to remember. In older times years were remembered, and named, for their most important feature. 1846, for instance, might have been the year of 'the black potato', when blight caused famine.

1955 was certainly the year of the 'big snows', but I like to remember the summer that followed, when water shortages were forgotten, as clothes— the few that were worn—were washed in the trickle in the burn and the loch was cool and sweet for swimming. There was no need, that year, for a visit to any 'costa' to acquire a sun-tan and skill as a swimmer.

It was a year when you felt very near to the stark nature of things—to the cold that forces the ice into crystals that delight the eye, to the warmth that penetrates the hardest stone. If there is to be climate change I wish that it would come this way, not with hurricanes and lashings of rain.

Then, of course, it was the year of the 'electric'. The coming of power carried on those fragile lines across those bleak acres was certainly a boon. Only as time passed were we to dread, a little, the coming of the bill, in that small buff envelope handed to us, with an understanding smile, by our friend the post. Every time we paid it we would make a silent promise to use less power over the next months. 'Switch off that light' we would call to the children, as they moved from room to room in the evening, revelling in the freedom of light everywhere.

Sometimes, especially when the inevitable power-cuts came, on days of winter storm, when warmth was most needed, we would look back, with a whiff of nostalgia, to the days of the peat-fire, the Tilley-lamps and candles! And we missed the sight of the smoke rising early every morning from our neighbour's chimney, signal that all was well. Mostly we were glad to pay for the hours saved, the convenience.

1955 could well be remembered as the year of 'the light'.

January 26th

The year made a genial beginning. The sun shone, the sky was softly blue, sheep and cows grazed contentedly over the vacant fields... The hens took on a new lease of life and began strutting confidently about, sure that spring was just round the corner.

On the wooded ground down by the big loch thrush and black-bird were singing and there were reports of bees taking wing. We humans made holiday, glad of the calm, bright days to visit friends and neighbours.

Everything was returning to normal. The children were back at school. Thoughts were even racing ahead to preparations for spring work, when—the blizzard struck us!

Straight from the Arctic it seemed to come, a wind with an edge like a razor, a wind that drove the fine snow through every crevice, every chink round door and window, and brought frost that turned everything to stone.

To get from the house to the byre, a distance of some twenty yards, meant pausing a moment on the doorstep to wait for a possible slight lull in the shrieking of what seemed like a hurricane, summoning one's courage, taking a plunge and arriving seconds later, the breath completely knocked out, to confront an astonished milk cow, patiently waiting for her feed.

The journey along to the other steading, where the rest of the cattle are housed, was a major operation, only accomplished by hanging on to the wire fence all the way and hoping for the best!

However, we all survived, man and beast, and when, next day, the wind miraculously dropped and the sun shone from a brilliant sky, we couldn't but wonder at the beauty of the dazzling new world, the fantastic snow wreaths, the shining icicles and frost flowers everywhere.

Milk that was turned to ice cream and eggs that had to be thawed before they would come out of the shells were causes of merriment. Helen had out her sledge and spent a hilarious day with snowmen, snowballs and every kind of joyful ploy the snow could offer.

We went the round of the sheep and found them in amazingly good heart, scraping away at the frozen shoots of herbage.

As the cold grew still more intense the snow hardened to the consistency of concrete and we realised we were completely cut off by road and likely to be so for some days. The food situation was a bit of a worry.

With milk, eggs and potatoes to hand we need never starve, of course, but we were out of bread and had perhaps never before realised how much this quite dull commodity could be missed. We baked a couple of loaves, but somehow they hadn't quite the authentic texture or flavour.

Next day began the trek of neighbour to neighbour, each one giving gladly of her store, a loaf here, a gallon of paraffin there, a jar of jam for a portion of cheese, till at last the good news was brought by the Post, who had struggled valiantly round every house every day, through drifts waist-high, that the snow-plough was on its way.

What a noble sight it was, the small black vehicle glimpsed across the white waste of the moor, the snow-plough making its way slowly, hesitatingly, but surely along the far road!

Another day and the grocer's van was through to us, with bread and paraffin and even butcher-meat and all the other things that have become necessities. There was rejoicing and feasting that night!

But the blizzard had not finished with us. Back it came for another day's raging, lashing the snow in front of it, and the roads were blocked worse than before.

February 23rd

We are snow-bound again, after a blizzard of far greater ferocity than the January one.

Snow had been lying for more than a week, in a strange silence, under black, brooding skies. But the road had been cleared. Tractors were managing to get through.

Then, one night, what we had been dreading came about—the wind rose, shrieking like an evil demon, out of the north-east.

It was the night the supply van was due. We saw it at a point about half a mile away, but we knew it could not win round to us, as there were already drifts piling on the road. We had to watch its headlights sweep round in a big arc across the snow and disappear into the blackness.

By morning we were immured in our dwelling, with every window and door so thickly plastered with snow that it was impossible to see—and difficult to get—out. When we did manage to emerge, muffled in coats and balaclavas and the thickest gloves and footwear we could find, we saw looming the fantastic mounds of snow of all shapes and sizes that hemmed us in. In some places only the tops of the fence-posts were visible. The turnip-pit, only a few yards from the steading, had almost disappeared from sight.

We were completely cut off from our fellows, in a world of whirling, stupefying white fury. Occasionally, during a momentary lull, we could catch a glimpse of a neighbouring homestead, isolated, too, in its own raging world, and we could only hope that its inmates and the animals depending on them were managing, somehow, to keep safe and sound.

All attempts at following the normal pursuits of daily living had to be abandoned. It was a case of riding out the storm. If we could manage to make two trips daily to the steadings to feed the animals and

milk the cow and bring in fuel, that was all we could hope for. Between times we baked and made hot concoctions from whatever was
available in the larder.

Between the house and the near steading there was a drift five feet
deep. Bringing home the milk was quite a job! The trip to the far
steading was a nightmare journey into the teeth of the north-east gale.

The insides of byre and stable were thickly coated with snow driven
in through the crevices. There the patient beasts stood, grateful for
their ration of fodder, turning their heads to gaze at us, as though glad,
too, of our company in their ordeal.

What the sheep must be suffering is a matter of anxious conjecture.
Until the storm abates we cannot even contemplate an investigation.
It is certain there are bound to be losses and that those who survive
will be badly weakened.

It's a mercy we are fit and have enough of the necessities to see us
through for quite a while. We shan't look for the delivery of supplies
of any kind for a good while to come, for every road for hundreds of
square miles must be impassable. We can do without anything in the
nature of luxury, but never have we been so thankful for a sound roof,
four solid walls, a fire in the kitchen and something hot, no matter
what, to put inside us.

March 25th

The first day of the calendar spring was heralded by a third, or 'little'
blizzard. It came from a southerly direction this time. Fortunately,
there was not as much of it as usual, but what there was was as bitterly
chilling as anything experienced during the depths of the winter.

There is something particularly cheerless about a blizzard that blows
up when the days are lengthening and the year is wearing on. One
thinks of the ewes coming near to lambing, their resistance lowered
by weeks of scant feeding on the frozen hillsides. One shudders at the
thought of the arrears of work in the fields—no dung carted, not a
furrow ploughed, and April just round the corner. Yet we know that,
somehow or other, the work will get done. It always does. It has to.
But it would have been nice to have been able to do a little between
times, even to have managed to repair some of the damage caused by
one blizzard before another one came along. But it was not to be.

At any rate we have learned to achieve a greater degree of stoicism,
just to plod along doing what we can and trusting to next week!

Perhaps soon, perhaps even next week, a mild spell will arrive and

Charlie the horse

then, after a little, the grass will come away quicker than ever and everything will catch up with itself again. There are certainly signs of spring about, even now. On the good days there is a fluffiness about the clouds. Across the loch the light comes streaming down the hillside from a high-riding sun. The birds toss gaily on the wind. Whenever the sky is clear the larks respond magnificently, pouring their song over the glistening earth in a riot of joy!

And the plovers are back! It is difficult to express in words what that means to us who have spent this winter on the edge of the moor. We stand on the door-step, spellbound, to listen to their wild, glad cry and to watch them twisting and plunging in their mad sky-dance across the fields.

A pair of sparrows are busy nesting in the gable of the byre. A young cock blackbrid, who has taken up his abode in the byre since the January storm, is overcoming his shyness and warbles his delicious little muted song when he hears the milk spurting into the pail. He is so companionable. I shall miss him when the warm days come and he goes off to seek a mate!

Indeed, we feel a new sort of affection for all the animals which have endured the winter storms along with us. Especially, we look forward to the daily visits of Charlie the horse to the doorstep, where he stands rattling the door-knob till we give him his tasty bite of stale bread and sliced turnip and his 'white drink' of water with the chill off it and a scattering of oatmeal.

Today, the snow is still falling and the path cleared to the steading this morning is once more obliterated. But tomorrow, if the sky is clear, I know the larks will be singing in spite of everything, our sparrows will be busy carrying wisps of straw for the fashioning of their nest, the black heifer will be slower on the move as she comes nearer her first calving. Nothing, not even another blizzard, can hold back the spring forever!

The Stills

The brewing of intoxicating liquor is a craft known world-wide, dating from the earliest times. We have heard of the heather ale produced to great effect by the Picts. The distilling of spirit is a more complicated affair, but one which appealed, as a money-maker, to many people in the Highlands in the eighteenth century, and into the nineteenth.

At that time various laws regarding excise duties were imposed by the government in the south, making the cost of the favoured drink—the water of life, whisky—prohibitive. It was also at this time that the tenants were being asked, or forced, to pay prohibitive rents.

If legally produced whisky was too costly, why not produce some illegally, undercut the market and make some badly-needed money? So, the illicit distilling of whisky became a common practice all over the Highlands. Ingenuity will find a way round many obstacles.

The man whose place adjoined ours at the 'west end' of our holding, and whose garden once took first prize in a competition run by the estate, was a famous 'outwitter' of the law, of laws of many kinds. We were often sorry he had departed this life before we came to live here. He had his still well-hidden up the hill. Others were in caves or camouflaged bothies. His other activities included the trapping of grouse on sheaves of corn left out after harvest. In the days when grouse were plentiful this could be quite a lucrative ploy. Some landlords turned a more or less blind eye to these on-goings, knowing that at least the rent would be paid.

Abriachan was famed for its distilling activities. The water was particularly suited for the drink and there were many inaccessible hiding-places. Many stories are told of the devices used to outwit the Excisemen on their rounds. They would sail up and down Loch Ness looking for tell-tales of smoke rising from the bothies. But by the time they got ashore the smoke was gone and they were met by a hail of stones from the look-out and the distillers. Most of them made a fire of juniper which gives very little smoke.

Some years the officers of the law would lodge in the schoolhouse so as to be quick off their mark and on the trail of any suspect. Bribes were offered to potential informers, but were never taken up.

When arrests were perilously near many tricks were devised to hoodwink the authorities. Bottles would be hidden in the voluminous skirts of a granny sitting dozing at the fire. Casks would be thrown into a hill pool where the peat would preserve them for ever and they could be retrieved years later. Some of the precious liquid did find its way into the town, where it was favoured and could be turned into some welcome cash for the household. Quite a lot was consumed locally, for the enhancement of a wedding, the consolation of a funeral or the simple prevention and cure of winter ills.

April 27th

April has released us into a great surge of new life and activity. The memory of winter storms and darkness and petrifying cold has been wiped clean from our minds. Never, it seems, has the sun shone with so much power, the fresh grass sprung so green. To be able to step outside, lightly clad and shod, and feel the warm air flowing over us, to breathe in the scent of new growth and to let doors and windows stay open all day is little short of miraculous.

Now there is so much to be done that the problem is to know where to begin. Light easterlies have dried the ground and brought it to a grand, crumbly consistency, so that everyone is itching to get busy with plough and harrows. But the dung has to be carted and spread, the last of the turnips have to be cleared, the last of the field stacks to be carried and threshed, the tatties to be riddled for seed. Then there are fires to be lit in the heather and in the encroaching whins and rushes. And there are all the young things to be cared for— the chickens and the calves that are appearing everywhere—not to mention the ever-recurring collie pups!

This is, above all, the season of young things, and we musn't forget our own young one in all the busyness of spring. Time must be found to take Helen, in her holidays, to look for primroses, to see the light shimmering on the deep blue of the loch, to watch the geese flying away north to their breeding-grounds. We could never let these things go unheeded.

On the distaff-side, too, there is many a job to be done—blanket-washing, carpet-beating, and the rest.

In weather such as this one is inclined to wonder, with Richard Jefferies, why houses were invented. They do, indeed, seem mighty cumbersome, with all their trappings, when the sweet sun and air are there, outside to live in! Yet such a thought is hardly fair when we remember how glad we were of the solidity of this particular house a bare eight weeks ago!

The hill ewes have made a start at lambing and so far the tally is quite satisfactory. We marvel at the toughness and resilience of these mothers. It warms the heart to see them lying content in the sun with their offspring snuggled in.

Over and above all the activity of field and household, the wild life that surrounds us is intensely busy with its own affairs. As we sit eating our dinner in the sunshine, among the bleaching linen and the chattels set out to air, the purr of tractors in our ears, we watch a curlew glide unconcernedly overhead, uttering his dream-like, bubbling call. All day, and far into the evening, the moorland air vibrates with the song of larks, the cries of peewit and the drumming of snipe. Midges are dancing. Moles are busy thrusting up the earth. Coltsfoot and daisies, tiny bright suns and stars, shine up at us on every hand. The daffodils are blooming in the garden plot. The hens cluck all day long to announce the laying of yet another egg. There's the greatest rejoicing ever at this wonderful release into life.

Wildlife

Sometimes I wonder—what do we mean by wildlife? Life lived in its own natural way? All life is surely wild, even our own, when we allow it to be. In our clumsiness we have tried to tame some members of what we call the 'animal kingdom', those that may serve our purposes—the horse, the bull, the boar, the cockerel, the ram—with what results we are not entirely sure. Those left untamed are now perilously endangered owing to our greed in despoiling the earth. Plant life, too, is disappearing and changing as we poison and engineer our way into providing easy food.

In the years since our time working in Caiplich so many changes affecting natural life have occurred. I realise how fortunate we were to have experienced the whole natural life of the area—storm, calm, the gleam of birch bark and rowan berry, the glimpses of fox, otter and pine marten and especially the sound of birds. To hear lark-song on a February morning, watch the peewits cavorting, with curlew gliding and calling overhead, to follow a redshank as it flies from post to post along the roadside fence, to hear snipe drumming in the summer dusk, these are, sadly, pleasures of the past.

With little cultivation now and large plantings of conifer the habitats have gone. The black-headed gulls still nest on the island in the loch and tufted duck and mallard are there, but the oyster-catchers no longer nest on the moor and perch, in their brilliance, on the roof of the boat-house. There is no swift flight of sandpipers skimming the water. So many sounds and sights of summer are lost.

Swallows still swoop, swifts scream and dragonflies dazzle. Along the loch shore there is the scent of bog-myrtle and meadowsweet. We're thankful for the inbuilt resilience of all natural things. As one great Red Indian chief said, 'sadness is soon swept away by nature's forgiving arm.'

This same Chief, in his abhorrence of the 'cities' he saw rising in his land, also said: 'There is no quiet place in the White Man's cities. No place to hear the unfurling of leaves in spring or the rustle of insect's wings… And what is there to life if a man cannot hear the lonely cry of the whippoorwill or the arguments of the frogs round a pond at night?'

And: 'What is man without the beasts? If all the beasts were gone, men would die from a great loneliness of spirit.'

And: 'Where is the thicket? Gone.
Where is the eagle? Gone.
And what is it to say goodbye
To the swift pony and the hunt?
The end of living and the beginning of survival.'

These people of the old America were surely environmentalists in the deepest meaning of the word.

May 25th

May can be a heart-breaking month. The cuckoo calls and under his hypnotic spell we dream of soft blue skies and of warmth and growth and blossoming. Yet the reality we wake to this year is harsh indeed. Bitingly cold winds, snow, sleet, rain—every variety of unseasonable weather has come our way. But the hills can't be perpetually white. Surely this must be the last of our monthly blizzards! It seems as if no life could ever spring again from the cold, sodden ground, yet, in spite of everything, the cornfields are showing green.

There is much work to be done—tatties to plant, turnip-ground to prepare for seed, and the garden, that often neglected but important plot, to be sown and planted. This is a particularly busy and anxious time for the shepherd and his dog. The lambs, small bundles of misery, their fleeces sodden and bedraggled, huddle against their mothers.

A harsh May is hard on all young things. Do the new-hatched chicks wonder why they ever bothered to come out of their shells? The calves stand, heads down against the storm, waiting patiently to be let into a warm, dry byre. As for the hens, they have become so used, by now, to inclement weather that they are more or less adapting themselves to it. The only wonder is that they are not developing webbed feet!

There is great activity in our district on the 'Hydro Board' front. Most houses are ready wired for electricity, the positions of the poles are plotted and small white flags flutter at strategic points across the heather to mark the sites of various erections to come under the scheme.

The contractors mean to make the most of the summer days and to have the supply installed by autumn. So, next winter, whatever the weather may have in store, we should be warmer than last.

Our thoughts these days are still turning to ways of keeping warm. In the bright mornings and long clear evenings it would normally be so good to be outside. But these mornings we huddle under the bed-clothes till the last minute and are glad to get in at night to a fire in the grate. We pity the lambs lying out on the bleak hill.

Yet life is on the move. The rowans have burst into leaf. The grass is coming away and giving the cattle enough to keep them cudding happily. All is ready and eager to bloom if only the sun's heat would draw the stiffness from the bones of things… Now and again, as evening falls, we get our brief glimpse of Maytime, when the wind has tired of blowing, the sky has cleared and there is almost a softness in the air. Then the bleating of the lambs rises from the farthest places of the moor and, in the stillness, the call of the cuckoo comes, no longer brash and derisively announcing snow, but mellow and tender and echoing the memory of every vanished Maytime.

June 29th

June has, agriculturally speaking, been a disappointing month. People concerned with trying to make things grow seem never to be satisfied with the weather. There it is!

There have been days of glorious sunshine, with skies as blue as only June can make them and, night after night, the sun has gone down at last behind the hill in such red and gold splendour that we linger at the window, loth to go to bed. On such days we're tempted to wish that we were holiday-makers, with hours to spend walking the hills or lying in a sheltered hollow among the buttercups down by the burn. But we have to think soberly of seedling and young root and tuber seeking desperately for sap in the parched ground.

For weeks now the wind has come from the east and north, carrying off every drop of moisture from the earth. A cold drought is a menace. There has been little real growth. Clouds of dust rise behind horse or tractor as it goes about its work. Still, all the seed is sown, the last of the lime spread and the young corn is showing valiantly green. There is a ripple on the new grass.

We can only wait in hope that the wind will veer to the beloved west and that moisture will follow in its wake. Occasionally we get a whiff of it, that intoxicating scent of the west, to which all our being is attuned, and our step quickens as we breathe it in.

Meantime we are glad that the dryness of the ground lets us get ahead with other jobs. It's a grand time for peat-cutting.

Days at the peats are reckoned almost a holiday. Some crofts have peat-banks quite a distance from their holding and the whole family will set off early with as many neighbours as are available. A basket of food and a kettle are stowed away, along with the peat-spades at the bottom of the cart or tractor-trailer.

All day the work goes on, the cutting and stacking of the neat brown sections of peat, and it goes with a swing when so many share in it. Towards evening the smoke will rise from a little fire of heather roots and old peat, while the kettle boils and tired limbs relax in the sheer enjoyment of work well done.

It is possible now, with the ground hard-baked, to take horse and sledge, or tractor and trailer, to places usually quite inaccessible and to fetch good loads of wood for winter burning. Many long days are put in at this work.

There are also busy days to be spent clipping the sheep. The poor beasts look grotesque in their new nakedness and they show up startlingly white against the still colourless hillside. But they must be glad to be rid of their heavy fleeces in the beating sun.

The ewes would be grateful for some good, soaking rain to make the grass more succulent, and it would help the lambs' milk supply, for the long spell of drought dries up the udder. The young cattle beasts are seeking everywhere for a long, cool drink. The burn is reduced to a succession of still, shallow pools, quite unlike its normal bubbling, cheerful self.

Domestic water supplies are dwindling, too, as the springs become mere trickles. But we have not yet had to take our washing to the burn.

The level of the loch is so much reduced that quite a stretch of sand is now revealed as its edge, much to the delight of Helen who can build castles on this miniature beach and splash and paddle to her heart's content in the shallows. We all realise more clearly than ever our utter dependence on water.

It has indeed, been a drouthy month, but the moor is starred with its own tiny flowers—yellow and mauve, blue and white. Their small roots don't demand much in the way of moisture. The cotton grass is waving its plumes in the bog.

The air is alive with the cries of agitated parent birds—plover and snipe, lark and grouse—as they shepherd their fledglings and search desperately for food to stuff into gaping beaks.

The year is moving on. We have passed the longest day. Strange to think we shall soon no longer be going to bed in daylight. Perhaps, too, we shall no longer be dreaming we hear the rain cascading everywhere in gleaming spouts and splashes and rivulets. We hope that will soon be the reality!

The Peats

The cutting and stacking of peats was certainly laborious. But it went with a rhythm, people working in pairs, one cutting and lifting, passing the block to the partner who handles it for stacking into a small pile of four or five for the initial drying. To be in the high air, on a day of sun and wind, in good company, lent a kind of lift to the job. I don't know of a song to accompany this particular work. There were so many—for milking, for churning, for spinning, for rowing a boat. Perhaps at the peats people used any breath they had to spare in joking or gossiping.

The children enjoyed the day, helping to stack, indulging in the odd bout of peat-slinging. Many a school log-book would record absences as 'working at the peats'.

Later in the summer, the small stacks would be gathered, carted down to a suitable place near the house and built into a large stack. Great care was taken in the building of the final stack, the beautiful symmetry and shaping allowed the rain to run off. It was suggested lately that some of the specially well-built ones that are to be found still in the outer isles would qualify as works of art and could be shown at any art gallery in the world!

Many peats were needed to warm even a small house through the winter, when no other fuel was available, not even much wood, except driftwood. The stacks would dwarf the little houses.

Occasionally interesting things would be uncovered in the process of digging. Peat is a great preserver. The one thing everyone hoped to find was a keg of whisky thrown into the bog in desperation when the excisemen were on their rounds!

The peat fire was the centre of life. In the evening it would be 'smoored', that is covered over with ash, then, in the morning, it would be blown into flame again. There is a song for that, or rather, a prayer:

'I will smoor the hearth
As Mary would smoor:
The encompanisment of Bride and of Mary
On the fire and on the floor,
And on the household all.'

This is one of the many songs and blessings collected in the islands by Alexander Carmichael last century.

There have been houses where the fire was not extinguished in 200 years. Fire, one of the essential elements, had to be venerated, as were earth, air and water. Today, electric heat is fine and handy, but there's little magic in it, no memory of summer days, of neighbourly banter, of music on the 'mouthie'. And now we're told to go easy on the peat. It is not inexhaustible. And it takes hundreds of years to 'grow'. Commercial exploitation is what would kill it.

August 3rd

July came to its end and we still had no appreciable fall of rain. As day after day went by and we watched the pastures growing scorched, the dry beds of the water-ways showing cracked, parched earth between the stones, we shook our heads and wondered how it would all end.

Would there be a sudden cloud-burst which would flatten the growing corn and put a stop to thoughts of hay-making, or would it be that the rain would come gently, softly, out of the west, as we would like it to come?

It's wonderful what progress the root crops have managed to make, in spite of the powdery state of the ground. Many a long, hot hour has to be put in now at the singling of them. And the tatties are beginning to flower.

It's just a pity that the grass has not made enough progress to allow cutting to be general. It would have been such perfect weather for making hay. We look enviously at the low-ground fields with their neat coils just waiting to be stacked.

We're lucky that our domestic water supply is miraculously keeping up. We hear tales of many large farms going dry and having to cart water daily from the nearest river. This must be a sore burden at such a busy time of year, especially when the heat makes any strenuous labour doubly irksome.

These are indeed the dog days! Fine from the photographer's point of view, for any animal, even the most wary and shy, is quite content to lie panting in the heat and allow its picture to be taken without protest.

Fine, too, for the children holidaying from school. Never have they been as sunburned as now. It's good to think of all the vitamins they must be storing up. They'll need them if next winter is anything like last.

In the fields the cows loll about ankle-deep in sweet white clover, their glossy flanks bulging. We remember the bags of bones we turned

Bell Heather

out of the byre only a month or two ago and wonder—can these really be the same beasts?

Meanwhile, in the deserted steading, a young family of house-martins is preparing to leave its nest under the rafters. We refuse to think, yet, of the day when they and their parents will part from us for good.

The hens are laying on staunchly, not even going broody, though they must be sorely tempted when the thermometer registers 82 degrees!

The loch grows shallower and shallower. Bits of rock that we cannot remember ever having seen before stick up above the smooth surface and the water along the sandy edge is as warm as a summer bath.

The moor is strangely silent in its shimmer of heat. The birds are too much engrossed in rearing their families to have time to indulge in singing. The lambs, grown sturdy and sedate, no longer frisk or bleat!

But the bell heather is in bloom. Great patches of it glow along the roadside and over the moor and, in the cool of morning and evening, as we look at the glorious colour of it and breathe in the scent of the clover fields, we thrust all thought of the drought and its worries from our minds and revel simply in the flowering of high summer.

Cattle

Those cattle beasts of ours were the source of our greatest worry and our greatest joy. The worry was in the sometimes inadequate provision of winter fodder, this being in the hands of the weather gods, the joy was in seeing them shine with health in the summer air.

Until the time of the establishment of the crofts, with their limited amount of ground, and the coming of the 'big sheep', cattle had always been the mainstay of the Highland people. They had kept a few sheep, mainly for their wool and for milk and a few goats, but the cattle were almost kinsfolk, sharing the house with them in winter. At the door, in the evening, the cows would go in one way, the people the other. Most of the year's work was to ensure an adequate supply of winter feed, once the family's needs were met. There was always a boy or two at the herding. In summer the cattle were taken up to the high pastures to graze the sweet grass.

For the Celtic people wealth and status were always reckoned by the number of cattle owned. A bride's dowry often consisted of cattle.

The bull, of course, with his tremendous strength and power, and his horned head, was virtually deified. The great Irish legend, Tain Bo Cualnge, the cattle-raid of Cooley, tells of the huge battle between the provinces of Connacht and Ulster to gain possession of the famous brown bull.

The cow, with her bountiful supplies of milk, was a symbol of fertility. Still, in India, she is the most sacred animal, as she was to the Celts. The two most important festivals of the year—Beltane and Samhain, the first of May and the first of November—were connected to the movement of cattle. In early summer they were driven through the sacred fires as a purification ritual on their way to the pastures, in autumn they were installed in their winter quarters.

In the Highlands, until late eighteenth-century times, cattle-raiding was a common pursuit and was not looked on as a criminal offence, but rather as a way of life, carried on on a heroic scale by chiefs and clansmen alike.

When markets were established in the south, to satisfy the demand for meat by an increasing population, many highlanders would drive their cattle to these centres, walking miles every day, sleeping rough, wrapped in their plaids and subsisting on raw oatmeal. Sometimes, on the way home, they would be waylaid by thieves eager to relieve them of their money. The routes they took through the wild country, the drove roads, were the first tracks of any kind to be made in many parts of the Highlands. Some of them can still be walked today. One of the early exports from the Highlands was that of hides and skins. We certainly became well acquainted with our cattle beasts—cows and young heifers and stirks. They were soon given names—Hope and Pet and Mairi Ruadh, Hamish and Bob, for a start. We got to know their ways, which of them would linger on a cold night and would need a good prod with a willow wand when you wanted them all housed quickly, which would grab a slice of turnip before you had time to down the pail, which would turn to give you almost a kindly look as you fastened its halter. We remembered hearing how, in hungry times, a beast would have to be bled and the blood mixed with oatmeal to make what we call black pudding today. We were glad we hadn't to do that.

The 'house-cow', the one who supplied the family's quota of milk, milk which in summer also gave butter and cheese, was clearly the one most closely associated with her human guardians. Many croons were made for singing to the cow. One, collected by Alexander Carmichael in Barra, was:

> 'Give the milk, my Treasure!
> [repeated three times]
> Give the milk
> And thou'lt get a reward
> Bannock of quern
> Sap of ale-wort,
> Wine of chalice
> Honey and the wealth of milk, my Treasure!'

It was found that the cow preferred one special song to another, giving milk generously to her favoured one. Mine, I found, seemed to like 'Lili Marlene', not a very poetic song, but one which did the trick!

Today, when the depredations made by the vast overstocking by sheep has become apparent, there is a movement to bring back the cattle. They are much more 'environmentally friendly', to use a current idiom. They tread down the rank weeds and do not crop the herbage too close. Housed in winter, they provide a readily accessible source of manure. Some hardier breeds can be out-wintered, with open sheds for shelter in storms.

August 31st

By mid-August the harvesting of oats was under way. This is one of the earliest harvests on record. We think back to last year and remember how the end of October saw sodden stooks in the fields and we marvel again at the diversity of our climate.

It's not a good crop, light in the ear and, for the most part, short in the straw. On the smaller places much of the cutting is being done by hand, but it is being gathered in ideal conditions.

In the golden sunshine, with the light, warm breeze sending a ripple over the little yellow fields, days at the harvest pass in a sort of timeless dream. Cutting, binding, stooking—so the immemorial rhythm goes.

At the back of our minds is the knowledge that winter feed will be scarce, with the hay lacking bulk, the straw scanty and the turnips dwarfed for lack of moisture. But the present is so golden, so benign, that we are lulled, despite our forebodings, into a pleasant state of content.

For the children each day is paradise enough. Barefooted, burnt brown from top to toe, they scamper about their endless happy ploys, refusing to believe that next week will see them shut up again in the schoolroom.

Helen has had so many dips in the loch that the water has become her natural element. If only the loch were on our very doorstep and some of it in the house!

The water shortage has become so acute that the cattle have to be shifted to marshy ground, where they can get some semblance of a drink and where the grazing, though rough, is more succulent than in the parched fields.

In many places it has been impossible to find enough water to dip the sheep. They have had to be sprayed instead.

Morning and evening see the trail of housewives, with pails, to some distant well remembered by the old folk. We are not geared to conditions of prolonged drought. Domestic chores become doubly laborious.

There have been serious outbreaks of fire over moor and peat-ground. The bitter smell of the smoke is wafted for miles and at night the sky is lit with a fantastic glow. Only a heavy downpour could possibly extinguish these fires. They could go on smouldering in the peat layer for a long time.

Milk yields are down and the young cattle, though thriving reasonably well, are missing the succulence of green growth. In the empty hay-fields there is practically no sign of aftermath.

The peat-stacks are built and the wood piles have grown big at the gable of the barn. The berries are glowing red on the rowans and the robins have started to sing. On the low ground the birches and brackens are yellow and wilting in the heat. But the swallows have not left us yet.

Corn in the stook, the yellow leaf, the robin singing in the rowan— autumn signals, tenderly, her approach. We are loth to recognise it. Summer has been too genial.

The heather is magnificent. Seldom have the hills been spread with such a blaze of splendid colour. The sky arching over them is the most brilliant blue. Despite all the problems it has brought us, this is a summer we shall remember. On many a freezing winter's night we shall close our eyes and think of the colour and the blessed warmth of it, smell the honey-sweet scent of the heather bloom and hear again the drone of the bees in the clover.

September 28th

September has brought at least two unusual things our way—weather that no one could grumble at and also, believe it or not, a spell of leisure!

As a rule, it is a month of heartbreak, one spent in snatching every odd day, between gale and downpour, to cut the corn and to stook it and stook it again. Stack-building is hardly ever even contemplated until the stubble is crackling with frost and the stooks have had at least one covering of sleety snow.

But this year, it seemed, the corn was no sooner in the stook than it was in the stack. In the long, warm days the sheaves were swung aloft with a will, a sort of incredulous joy animating every harvest worker, and, as if by magic, the golden stacks sprang up all around.

In yield it may not be a first-class crop, but at least not an ounce of it has been wasted by the weather.

Indeed, this famous weather really has behaved magnificently, for no sooner was stacking completed than down poured the much-needed rain. Now, while we wait for the moisture to swell the tatties and turnips, we have time to revel in the freshness ourselves. It is actually a pleasure to squelch about in one's old familiar gum-boots again, to hear the water gurgling and splashing in the gutters and to watch the burn slowly rising to something more than a trickle. And to smell moist earth again...! Already the grass is coming back to life and there is a flush of green among the stubble.

The cattle are frisky, the sheep look startlingly white as though they'd had a fresh shampoo.

We have had time to gather our little harvest of rowan berries, before the winter migrants arrive to demolish them. The rowan is such a useful and decorative tree. Its original purpose, of course, is to keep evil spirits away from the croft. That done, it proceeds to delight us with its delicate foliage and its creamy blossom in early summer and with the cheerful fire of its berries in autumn. These berries we make into jelly and wine and some clusters we bury in a tin in the ground and dig up at Christmas time, in all their glowing freshness, to decorate the house. One of our oldest and finest specimens of rowan was, alas, blown down in the worst of last winter's gales, but its dead limbs still did us good service by making a wonderful fire in the hearth.

This winter we shall be less dependent than hitherto on wood and peat to keep us warm, for the electricity wires have reached our doorstep. It's a little alarming to see the great, gaunt poles striding across the moor and around the contours of the arable ground. They look fantastically geometric in a landscape of soft curves and wild, sweeping lines. Probably we shall become so accustomed to them soon that they'll never be noticed.

The swallows and house-martins have accepted them already and find the wires, which are not live, ideal as rallying-points for the southward trek.

It is strange that we, who pass in the bus along a good stretch of Loch Ness once every week or so, should never yet have seen the 'Monster'. One evening, not long ago, we very nearly did!

We chanced to meet two young neighbours coming up from the lochside on their bikes. 'Guess what we've seen', they said. Jokingly, we answered 'The Monster...' 'Yes', came the startling chorus, and the wonder of it was plain in their eyes and their voices. 'A head, two humps and a threshing tail' was their description. They had watched the creature disporting itself for fully an hour quite near the bank. We wished we had been there with our camera to disprove the cynics! We shall probably never again come as near to seeing it for ourselves. At any rate, we had, by proxy, a rare tail-piece to a truly phenomenal season!

The Rowan

One neighbour of ours, living latterly alone in a remote place, would reso-lutely refuse to burn rowan wood in her house, no matter how low her fuel-stock had grown. She would make a fire of it outside, to boil food for her hens, but never in the house.

The rowan is associated, in Highland lore, with the goddess Brighid, who became known as St Bride during Christian times and was regarded as the foster mother of Christ. It was valued as protection against evil or harm. An extremely hardy tree, it could flourish at great heights and grow even in rock crevices, where a passing bird might have dropped a seed. Every house had a rowan growing near and a branch would be placed over the entrance to the byre and stable to safeguard the animals.

A plank of rowan wood would be built into the prow of a ship to ensure safe voyaging. Small carved objects and hand tools were often made of rowan. It is said that the bards would use mats made of woven rowan to sit on in their quest for inspiration. The berries had an oracular use for the seeker after an answer to questioning. They had a practical use, too. Con-taining organic acids, tannin, sugars and vitamin C, they were used to treat kidney disorders. Today, we still use them, of course, to make that jelly to accompany game and a wine which is said to contain the secret of eternal youth. Our neighbour who refused to burn rowan on her house-fire was among the last of those who kept to the inherited beliefs and customs and we were glad to have known her. She it was who was reluctant to pass by the loch at dusk in case something... a kelpie? might be lurking there. And she 'knew' when another neighbour, who lived alone, was about to die. She was the most practical of people, looking after her cattle and sheep single-handed when she was left a widow.

There was still a belief, until the last generation, in the 'little folk', who need not be feared, but must be placated by small offerings of milk or meal. Perhaps belief in 'another world', of any kind, was a help in the under-standing of the world one could see and touch daily—the world of shattered tree, of immovable rock, of the towering wave, the remoteness of moon and star. It's somehow a more genial world, the world that includes an element of uncertainty and wonder, a world more akin to our own inner world, with its doubts and uncertainties.

One evening, this same neighbour came in to ask if she could use our phone as she thought there were some strange wee folk lingering about near the phone box which was in a lonely place up the road. 'Some of the kids from up-by', we suggested. 'Well, I'm not sure...' 'Come in', we said. 'There's a cup of tea just ready...'

There may well have been, in former times, groups of smaller people, perhaps only about three feet tall, like those we call dwarfs today, who kept themselves to themselves, were not very adept at hunting and went about stealing, perhaps had to steal, to keep alive.

Belief in the existence of such creatures was frowned upon by later religious leaders. Students of folklore asking older people what they remembered of stories of the 'little folk' were most often met by embarrassed denials of any such memories.

BUAIN A' FHROINICH

Translation:
I am weary and alone, pulling the bracken on the moor; I
am weary and alone, always pulling the bracken.
Beside the knoll, on top of the knoll,
Beside the pretty knoll; beside the knoll,
On top of the knoll; every day alone.

A man of Abriachan who became a much respected minister of religion told us how, when herding the cattle as a young boy, he came on a group of small people going happily about their business in a hollow on the moor. Returning home, he told his mother what he had seen and was promptly given a thorough skelping!

The mythical was always part of Highland life. Fairy lovers appeared and disappeared, bringing happiness or grief. Many fairy songs were composed. One, still often sung today, is 'Buain a' Fhroinich'—'Pulling Bracken' (see previous page). It's the story of a girl who had a fairy lover who used to help her with pulling bracken and stacking peats on the hill. Her brothers discovered her secret and hid her in a far-off place. The song is the lament of her fairy lover, left alone and weary on the hillside.

October 26th

We're adjusting ourselves rapidly to winter. One day last week we woke to old, familiar sights and sounds—snow whirling out of a black sky, the kitchen windows plastered with frozen flakes and the north wind moaning around house and steading. It seemed strange to be plodding through the slush, carrying hot mash to the hens, when only ten days earlier we had walked over the hill and found plants that hadn't managed to flower at the normal time because of the drought coming belatedly into their own.

Now, with the leaves still on the rowans and the grass greener than it has been all summer, snow and frost are rapidly snuffing out growth once again.

The water supply has still not recovered its normal autumn abundance, yet the tap on the rainwater butt is frozen! We seem to have skipped a season and have, at least temporarily, lost our sense of time.

Thoughts and energies are concentrated on the problem of keeping warm. Already the great, sturdy hydro-electric pole outside the kitchen window seems like some benevolent, half-human creature, with its promise of heat and light to come. Any day now, they tell us, we shall be connected—and it can't be soon enough!

Two neighbours across the strath were 'switched on' several weeks ago. Every evening we gaze enviously across at the glow of their windows and watch the lights winking, like red-gold eyes.

To have a light, not only in the living-room, but in the lobby and in the porch, to be able to slip upstairs to one bedroom and into the other, flicking lights on and off as we go, seems to us little short of a miracle.

Needless to say the talk around every fireside nowadays is of the merits of this or that type of electric kettle or cooker or heater.

Meanwhile, tattie-lifting has hardly begun. The crop is better than expected and we only hope it can be gathered before frost and snow do any damage. Up to the beginning of the cold spell work was well advanced, dung carted out and preparations made for autumn ploughing.

There's great activity on the road these days, with floats coming and going, taking calves, stirks and lambs to market and bringing sheep to their winter quarters.

The memory of last winter's drifts is still fresh in our minds. We are beginning, like squirrels, to lay in stocks of food. The wild harvest of the district has been abundant. We have hazelnuts stored up for Hallowe'en, as well as pounds of bramble jelly. On the larder floor stand 'ten red bottles' of rowanberry wine!

We do seem to have been plunged straight from the long, golden dream of summer into the black-and-white, sharply etched reality of winter.

The other day, heads down to the wind and shoulders powdered with snow, we passed along the shore of the loch, where only a few weeks ago half-naked children were shouting and splashing. The water was lapping among the shivering reeds. Two swans swam coldly past. Only the tufted ducks seemed to be enjoying their natural element.

We have had our moments of autumn wonder, to be stored greedily away like any other harvest—a flight of wild geese honking and creaking their way, one evening, out of the black north sky and heading for the mauve-pink light to the south; morning mist lying in a silver hush along Loch Ness; long sunbeams floodlighting the spiders' webs among the grasses.

Now, willy-nilly, we must direct our thoughts to indoor things. There is the feeding and bedding of the animals. We must look out our thickest socks and gloves and scarves. Peats must be piled on the fire to enable us to do an extra baking for the guizers. They'll soon be here, with numbed fingers and enormous appetites, on our frozen doorstep.

Wild Harvests

We could have learnt much about the use of wild foods from the Highland people of a generation ago. A neighbour still living, now a nonagenerian, tells us that nettles always went into the broth and an infusion (called tea) was often made of the dried leaves of willowherb. This same man knew of people rubbing rheumaticky knees with nettles. Did the sting counteract the pain? Was this a 'sympathetic' cure? It seemed to help, in any case.

Thyme made a healthy infusion and the heather produced an ale which, according to legend, gave the Picts their superior strength in battle. The Romans tried, in vain, to sneak the secret of the brew.

Children would suck the liquor from the primrose stem when sweets were scarce. Wild mint and wild garlic are there for the picking, in the hollow by the burn, ready to flavour any dish.

Processes tried out and experimented with over the generations resulted in the production of many nourishing foodstuffs. For our ancestors it was a question of necessity. Flour could be made from the roots of silverweed, when other sources failed. For us it's mostly a question of taking a look at alternatives. Why buy—if you can find it at the chemist's—that rosehip syrup that was so prized during the last war as a source of vitamin C—why try to buy it when you can make it at home cost-free? I like to think that our ancestors, the hunter-gatherers, would have just chewed on the rosehips and would have found some of the wonderful summer fruits that we enjoy —the wild raspberries, the tiny woodland strawberries. Their tastes were probably different from ours and would have supported the flavour even of the berries of hawthorn, rowan and sloe. They are all there for us today, to be processed by the methods of today, if they cannot be eaten raw.

We are fortunate indeed that at the present time little spraying of chemicals is being done in the area, though we worry that some applied to the plantations of conifer on the far shore of the loch is seeping into the water and causing the growth of algae, which smother the fish.

The food plants are there, flowering and fruiting, year after year, for our health and benefit.

November 28th

For the last four weeks we have been enjoying a spell of magnificent weather. 'Enjoying' is the word, for now, with the back of the season's work broken and with good prices secured for the lamb and calf crops, everyone can take a stroll round the stubble-fields with a mind at peace.

Last month's brief onslaught of winter was evidently a false alarm, but it served its purpose. It made us see to the weak spots in our defences.

Now there is time to spare for the Cinderella jobs that, somehow, always seem to be neglected—the clearing of drains, the patching of steading roofs, the mending of fences, the tidying-up of the odd corners about the place.

A good autumn is always a great help. It means we can go easy on firing, save the precious stocks of peat and wood for the time when they'll be really needed. It means, too, we can go a little easy on the beasts' winter feed, which has to be hoarded like gold for the bleak days of early spring. The hens get a chance to grow new feathers before the cold gets a grip and the ewes come in good shape to the tupping.

There are sheep about in their hundreds now, for almost every croft has its 'winterings'. The crofter and his dog have a few anxious weeks of shepherding till they get them settled peacefully into their new quarters.

The only drawback to this spell of pleasant weather is that the springs, so badly depleted by the exceptionally dry summer, are not getting their normal replenishing. That may come yet, in embarrassing measure!

Meanwhile, we can look with almost complacent eyes at the well-filled tattie-pit and the mounds of turnips that grow steadily bigger at the field-side. We can congratulate ourselves on being as well prepared as we can ever hope to be to meet winter when it really comes.

This autumn is certainly doing its best to beguile us in every way. The birches and bracken have turned the mid-day hillside into a dazzle of brilliant gold. At tea-time the half-moon rides above the pines as on some evening remembered from spring.

True, the days are shortening rapidly. Helen comes home from school as the sun is slipping from the pale green sky behind the hill. But this is a darkening we can't resent. It's still a joy to be outside when the first stars glint, for the air has a benison left over from summer.

Even the birds seem to have forgotten it's now officially winter. Though the chaffinches are in flocks they are still wary of us humans and rise in a flash to fill the bare branches of the rowan when the barn door clatters open. Later on, we shall enjoy the tameness of them as they come jauntily begging their food.

The other evening I almost refused to believe the amazing story my ears were clamouring to convey—that a peewit was calling, in the darkness, over the moor, as on some calm April night! Surely, I thought, a bird could not be duped to that extent! But I believe it was.

Our only enemy about the place is a stoat who periodically squeezes his way into the hen-house and has accounted for the gruesome deaths of two hens. We can understand his motives for, like all God's creatures, he must eat to survive and, with not a rabbit in miles, he must often be crazed with hunger. We wish he could adapt himself to circumstances by turning vegetarian.

Eggs have been disappearing mysteriously, too, and we suspect the same wily criminal is responsible for this. Perhaps we shall trap him yet, in his winter garb. A dashing ermine tippet?

December 28th

It's Christmas-card weather again! A week or two ago the mildness came to an end. The soft air took on a sudden edge of chill. Snow whirled out of the north-east.

Then the wind veered to the south and blew the snow horizontally off the hill, so that the children had to be kept one day from school. Snowmen appeared, slides were made, snowballs whizzed!

Then came the thaw and a little later a light fall of powdery stuff, just enough to remind us that we are, after all, in December, but not enough to cause any serious inconvenience. These are grand, invigorating days. We wake to find the windows covered with the most fantastic frost-flowers. As Helen sets off to school the sun is turning the tops of the far hills an exciting shade of pink. The full ball of it bursts over the south-eastern horizon and in a few minutes everything is sparkling and crackling with light.

The icicles glitter. The little conifers in the new plantation shine against the blue sky like a thousand Christmas trees. It's as if the whole of our world had put up its Christmas decorations.

Much too soon, of course, the sun sinks in the afternoon, but the snow is then flooded with pink light again and the darkening sky takes on every conceivable shade of red, yellow, mauve and green.

Winter certainly does have its compensations and the great thing is that we have time to enjoy them, especially now that the whole of our community have just celebrated their own particular festival of light. We are 'all lit up' with electricity in time for Christmas and New Year!

There's no more fumbling morning and evening with torches and matches, methylated spirit and paraffin and candles. To slip from bed in the dark and, with the flick of a switch, to fill the room with light and warmth seems like a miracle. To come in at dusk and repeat the performance still makes us wonder 'can this be true?'

Nearly every house has invested in a light outside the door. Before leaving, on a pitch-black Wednesday night, to collect the messages from the gate at the roadside, we switch on this light and it shines out like a beacon to guide our fumbling footsteps as we stagger home with our loads along the twisting track through the heather.

So many chores are accomplished so quickly now, it will take us a little while to adjust ourselves to the new tempo. Who ever heard of a kettle that boiled before you even had time to put tea in the pot and set out the cups?

Byre, stable and barn also share in this glory of illumination. The cows come ambling home from their afternoon outing for a leg-stretch and a drink, to find their quarters shining a welcome.

No longer do we have to make do with a swinging lantern to coax the hens into laying winter eggs. The lights fairly blaze at them, with enticing, spring-like golden beams. Early chickens can now be brooded with health-giving infra-red rays. On the bigger places the barns hum with electrical devices for threshing and bruising the corn.

It is certainly amazing what comfort and joy is wafted along the slender wires. All praise to the cheery band of men, of all types and nationalities, who toiled away, through the blazing summer days, careered through bog and heather in jolting jeeps and lorries, blasted rock, dug holes, hauled on winches, climbed cat-like, with spurred boots, up the poles. They have given us the brightest Christmas ever.

First-footing will be a much simpler matter than usual. Every house will have its pilot-light to guide the revellers on their, perhaps, none too steady legs. It looks as though night will really be turned into day as we welcome this coming New Year.

1956

January 25th

We're having a January version of April weather. We start the day under a sky of soft, almost spring-like blue, with the yellow sunlight glinting on the small puffs of cloud. Then, as though at a given signal, a bank of blackness builds up behind the gleaming hills to the north-west and, within minutes, everything is blotted out by the whirl and howl of swiftly driven snow.

We quickly abandon whatever outdoor job we are engaged in, run to the shelter of barn, byre or kitchen and get on with some ploy under cover. In twenty minutes or so the sky clears, the wind drops and the sun glints on the smooth, white surfaces again.

In spite of these sudden outbursts of fury there is, on the whole, a stillness about life at the moment. The animals are, for the most part, housed. In the afternoons, when the winter world is at its warmest, the cows go out to amble slowly along to the nearest water-hole for a drink. They are glad enough to get back to the comfort of their strawed stalls.

Charlie the horse has an occasional job to do, pulling a load of fodder or fuel on the sledge. Mostly he likes to stand, for hours on end, dozing in his stable. The hens are, perhaps, the best off of all, for they can get on with the job and fulfil their function in life without ever having to leave the warmth of their dry litter.

The humans are thankful for an excuse, when the squall is a particularly vicious one, for a heat-up in the house. The teapot certainly works overtime, helping to thaw out chilled insides.

All in all, this is a time for taking stock, for reviewing last year's failures and successes and for making plans for next season. Shortage of winter fodder is a worry not yet in its acute stage. Like a nagging tooth we know it is with us, for last year's dry summer resulted in a poor bulking of straw and hay and prices for these are extremely high, but, for the moment, we haven't reached a crisis. There's no use meeting trouble half-way. Who knows, this may turn out to be one of the earliest springs on record and we may dodge the hungry gap yet. The weather has set up so many extraordinary records lately that we are learning to be surprised at nothing.

All our work at this time has a homely, domesticated feel about it, concentrated as it is about the yard and steading. Taking feed and water to the animals, keeping them comfortable and clean, we enter into a new, friendly understanding with them, as we realise how closely interdependent we and they are.

One thing we have been meaning to do for years we have managed to accomplish at last—the planting of conifers round our garden plot. They stand sentinel now, right round the house, tiny tongues of green flame against the snow. In imagination, we see them, grown big and sturdy, sheltering us from gale and blizzard, making a happy hunting-ground for the small birds we like to watch, keeping the house dry and snug.

We hope fervently they will flourish. There is something very significant about planting a tree—a tree, that is, that is not destined to be felled as timber in a stated number of years, but to give, indefinitely, shelter and delight. It is like casting a small blessing on the future.

The days are lengthening perceptibly. It is well after five, now, before we need stamp the snow from our boots and come in for the night.

The New Year ceilidhs are over. The bottles are empty, the raisin-cake is done. But it's very pleasant to sit toasting our toes, listening to the wind in the chimney, making plans. We do still prefer a good blaze of sticks and peat in the evenings. The 'electric' is a wonderful boon for any quick heat-up, but for the evening... well, there are no pictures in an electric fire!

This is a time for contemplation, a time loaded with expectancy. Tonight there's a bit of a blizzard, but tomorrow morning the sparrows will be chirping on the steading roof, silhouetted against a brilliant sky, the icicles will drip and we'll feel in our bones the slow heaving of the earth towards the sun.

The Ceilidhs

The ceilidh has always been an essential feature of winter life in the highlands. Today, the word has mostly come to mean a somewhat formalised meeting, probably in the local hall, with a programme of song, maybe a story, and music, sometimes followed by a dance.

In older times, and still today in the more isolated places, it meant a gathering in someone's house, of a very informal character. The dictionary meaning of the word is a 'gossiping' or 'visiting'. A house which was particularly welcoming to such gatherings was known as a 'ceilidh' house. Every house had its share of such gatherings.

To go 'ceilidhing', as it was originally a verb, meant to join a group of neighbours, some from quite far-off places, to exchange news and views on every kind of subject, from the weather, that all-important factor in everyone's life, to the on-goings in the Scottish Office or even at Westminster, which also affected our lives, but which seemed infinitely remote.

Then the fear an tigh, the man of the house, would perhaps tell a story and out would come a fiddle or an accordion and worries could be forgotten, at least for a while.

In older times the women would be busy working with wool—carding or spinning—and the men might be making heather ropes or utensils of wood while they listened to the music or the telling of tales or of family history. No youngster would think of interrupting, though the tales might have been told many times. This was their history lesson, better than the one they might get in school. From the time of the bards the gift for composing poems and songs had been highly regarded. The Druids had been the forerunners of the bards, their compositions transmitted orally, as writing was considered bad for the memory. To become a bard, some 2000 years ago, meant a rigorous training over several years, spending time lying in a darkened room, composing and memorising. St Columba is said to have had bardic training and to have composed 25 'lays'. Later, the Highland chiefs had a bard as part of their retinue. In the nature of a poet laureate, he was to write praise-poems in honour of his patron and exhortations to the clan in time of war.

Some bards wandered around the country and were entertained by various chiefs in return for some story-telling and songs to while away the winter evenings. As well as the almost 'official' compositions of the bards, much lyrical poetry was written, in praise of nature.

All of this—poems, songs, stories—formed part of a vast oral repertoire, committed to memory and passed on from generation to generation. Sadly, much of it has been lost, but some still lingers in the minds and memories of the last of the wanderers—the tinkers.

The ceilidhs, the coming together for discussion, the recital of stories and genealogy, the singing of songs in their own language, all this was what gave people a sense of their identity and was to help them greatly in their struggles with the alien authorities that were trying to change their way of life.

February 26th

February has been, for the most part, a still, white month.

At the beginning there were one or two rare, memorable days.

There was the day when the little, soft wind came out of the west and the warm air set the midges dancing and the hens scratching furiously at the midden and we found ourselves taking a look round the garden and even turning over the patch that had been rough dug in the autumn.

There were worms and beetles and slugs about and the hens went crazy with excitement. That was the day Helen found a daisy in flower and put it in a pot to decorate the kitchen window-sill.

There was also the morning when six larks appeared suddenly in the sky above the roof-top. We stopped in our tracks and called all the household out to watch them as they tossed and tumbled in the blue air and flew higher and higher, spilling out their wild overflow of music. We haven't seen or heard them again, but at least they've paid us a visit. They'll be back.

The rest of the month has gone by in a sort of dream-like stillness. There have been no blizzards, no fantastic drifts, no shrieking north-east winds.

The snow has come noiselessly, floating down out of a still, grey sky. It hangs like blossom on the bare branches of the rowans. It is draped like lace on the stobs and gate-post. Occasionally, when the sun is up and out, it slides off the roof and lands with a soft thud on the ground below.

Quietness has been the keynote of our month. There's only the sound of muffled footsteps as we plod around the jobs about the

Coping with the snow—a neighbour's horse-drawn sledge

steading, the sharp ring of the axe as we work endlessly away at the woodpile.

We can sense that, under the smooth white covering, at the snug roots of things, life is on the move. Where a patch of snow has melted, in the lee of the house, we can glimpse a green shoot here and there.

The mornings are lightening, the evenings stretching out. The scholars are no longer let out of school half an hour earlier than usual, as they are in the dark days. But they still have time for a snow-fight, or a few hectic runs on the sledge, before they come in bright-eyed and glowing, for supper.

It's a hungry time of year for the wildlife that swarms, mostly unseen, around us. The other morning, as I set off to see Helen to the road to school, I saw that the dog was lifting her muzzle to sniff the air, in an excited way. Then I noticed, in the fresh-fallen snow, the single line of delicate pad-prints ahead of us. We followed them to the gate and saw the spot where the fox had crouched, jumped, and landed on the other side.

Away down the road the track led and was mixed with a jumble of others—of dogs and men and sheep. On the way back I followed the track in reverse and I could read, as though in a book, the story of what must have happened in the early hours of the morning. A hare's tracks joined the fox's, there were the marks of a scuffle, another double track, another scuffle, and then the fox's track alone. Reynard must have had a good breakfast that morning!

Luckily, our hens are well protected in the solid shelter of the barn. They 'sing' contentedly in greeting when we take them their morning mash and they are laying eggs in almost spring-like quantities.

Now, a few flakes of snow are drifting down, softly, like feathers, from a blanketed sky. A pack of grouse go gliding on silent, dark wings across the white moor. On the hill, I can see the sheep patiently scraping away at the heather.

There will be no bus to market tomorrow. But the vans have been getting through, so far, with a struggle. Luckily, we have no business to do in the market-place just now. We are quite content to be hibernating quietly in this still, white, world.

A Winter Meeting

There are many stories to be read in a fresh fall of snow. A surprising number of creatures are on the move, hunger driving them to take exceptional risks. The tiny imprints of a field mouse, seeming to lead nowhere, make one wonder—did he survive? What predator could have snatched him, leaving no trace? There are unsolved mysteries.

One which intrigued me was the meeting of two well-known trails on the loch shore. It was morning. The otter had clearly come up for a forage at his favourite place—the mouth of the hill-burn which feeds the loch, where he hoped the water might still be on the move.

The fox, who was as hungry as himself, had been on the prowl, skulking among the frozen rushes, peering into the possibility of finding an unwary duck. And—he'd come on the otter. A cold and squelchy meal? But... the fellow was as big as himself, and his jaws were threatening. Did they look at each other for a split second?

The otter made off across the snow-covered ice. It was part of his winter domain and he was familiar with all its ways. The fox followed. Their two trails were etched clearly and hardening in the persistent frost. I followed them as far as my eyes allowed. I didn't venture far on to the ice for I was alone. Did the otter make for one of the holes where spring water softened the ice and where the fox could not follow? Did the fox reach the other shore to look elsewhere for his breakfast? I shall never know.

March 29th

Spring has come at us in one mighty bound. All that was needed was for a good drying wind to blow for a little while. And blow it did, for several days, till we saw the ground turn from an intractable, sodden, black mass to a rich, almost crumbly substance.

So friendly and inviting did it look that one wanted to pick it up and let it trickle through the fingers. There was even dust to be seen rising in clouds behind traffic on the road.

It was a case of out with the dung-cart while the going was good, all hands mustered to get the muck spread. Then horses or tractor could set to with a will to the ploughing.

Each evening now, as we look down the strath from the kitchen window, we can see a few more acres of freshly turned ground, gleaming black against the dun and green of the pastures.

The grass is beginning to freshen. Below the long tangle of old growth there is a flash, here and there, of emerald.

The croft wife, too, like her man, is eager to take advantage of the rare drying days. Blankets and covers of all hues and descriptions flap merrily in the breeze.

The hens have reached an ecstatic peak of laying. The family can revel in dishes of a Mrs Beeton-like extravagance. 'Take six eggs', we chant happily, without a twinge of conscience, as we mix a cake for Sunday, when normally we would make do with two.

The dryness of the ground is such that the Forestry Commission has issued a fire warning. The other day a fresh supply of fire brooms was deposited at our gate and one evening the Fire Brigade arrived.

But the authorities were being, perhaps, a little over-anxious. It was only the good sheepmen of the district taking thought for their high grazings and burning the old heather. Everything was under control.

Almost every night we see these fires blazing away. Sometimes, in the gloom, they seem to reach terrifying proportions and it looks as though everything in their path will be destroyed. But we know they are being carefully watched. In the morning, only a few, surprisingly small, charred patches appear on the hillside.

Our nesting birds are back with us now. All day long, and far into the darkening, the peewits flash about the fields. Curlew are gliding over the moor again. Snipe dart here and there and the air vibrates with the singing of the larks. The pair of sparrows that have been sharing the hens' mash all winter are beginning to preen themselves with delight in the sunshine, making the most of their few carefree courtship days before the duties of parenthood come along to sober them.

Soon the first lambs will be appearing. The men of the district have been preparing for this by going after the fox. Rabbits being practically non-existent since the advent of the myxamatosis, he is likely to be a bigger menace to the lambs this year than ever before. Several shoots have been organised, but so far there has been little result.

The hill sheep, roaming as they do into lonely, inaccessible places, are certainly in need of protection. There have been reports of buzzards and other large birds destroying sheep that have got on their backs, unable to rise.

It's been a good winter on the whole. No sheep hereabouts have been lost in snowdrifts. The cattle have come through with a shine.

Extra keep, as was expected, is costing a fantastic amount—£15 for a ton of straw! At least it is procurable and doesn't have to be humphed, as it was last winter, in bundles on our backs through the drifts.

The other Sunday, casting all cares aside, we put some sandwiches in our pockets, took our sticks, whistled the dog and set off over the hill for a walk into the next parish. The flanks of the Strathfarrar hills were very blue under their topping of snow. The larks were singing madly. The wind was blowing softly out of the south-west.

We sat in the hollow at an unfamiliar burn to eat our sandwiches. We threw small pebbles, idly, into the water. We stroked the pussywillow catkins and felt the sun warm on our faces and hands. We came home light of foot and heart. We had had our own small, unofficial festival of spring.

An Early Settlement Comes to Light

That year, after an extra heavy burning of the heather on the common grazing hill over the road, we noticed the emergence of several circles of stone. In the long rays of the sinking sun they showed up quite distinctly.

This was the hill on which, according to our title deeds, we had the right to: 'graze sheep, cut peats and bleach linen'. As we had enough grazing on our outrun and good black peat there, too, we had not so far made use of the hill, which was unfenced and needed a lot of shepherding. 'Bleaching linen' we took to refer to the time when flax was grown.

The name of the hill—Croc ha Eachdraighe, meaning the 'hill of history', had always intrigued us. Had a battle taken place there or... had people realised that this was the site of a very early settlement?... There were the stone founds of what must have been eleven circular dwellings. One larger oval structure, near the top of the slope, had possibly been the home of a headman and his family, we reckoned. We noticed that the ground had been terraced, to make level stances, and we found the remains of small dividing walls.

Enlisting the help of experts, we walked the hill many times, till finally it was brought to the notice of the authorities and it has since been scheduled as an Ancient Monument. As it is readily accessible, on a slope alongside the road, we hope it may be available to people interested in archaeology.

'A small iron-age farming settlement' is its designation. Many times we have visualised those remote ancestors, filling their days with tasks similar to ours—tending small fields of bere (a primitive form of barley), herding their few cattle and sheep, gathering wild plants and berries, suffering the same wild storms, hearing the larks and the curlew. The sense of solidarity is very real.

April 25th

April is, perhaps, the busiest month of the year. There is so much to do all at once that, even with the lengthening evenings, there are too few hours to the day. But it's good to feel this surge of activity after all the long, still months of winter.

The weather has been helpful, on the whole, though we could now do with some of that warm dampness that comes out of the west. Still,

That wicked young cross-highlander—Red Mary

the easterly winds certainly dried out the ground and let the plough get busy everywhere.

People hereabouts feel that the abandonment of the Government tractor service is a great miss. Private contractors are none too plentiful and some grudge coming to the small, outby places in the heights. Yet, somehow or other, the work is being done and every day sees another field lying ready to receive its sowing.

The last of the wintering sheep have been sent, with sighs of relief from their guardians, back to their summer quarters. Now all attention is concentrated on the breeding flocks. The shepherd never knows at what hour of the day or night a ewe might need his help. He has to go his long round early and late.

He has his reward. The hillside is dotted with fresh, white spots as the lambs make their appearance in ones and twos. There can be few sights more satisfying to a hill-man than that of a sturdy, black-faced lamb snuggled into its mother's flank on an April day.

What moisture we have had lately has been most welcome, even though some of it fell as sleet or snow, for the ewes' milk supply is entirely dependent on the succulence of the bite she can get. Towards the end of last month the drought was such that supplies of water, even for domestic purposes, were getting extremely low. There's enough moisture now to gladden both man and beast.

Calves are tottering about on unsteady legs. Even the most sedate of the cows tacitly admit they are glad to see less and less of the byre. As for Red Mary, Mairi Ruadh, that wicked young cross-highlander, she kicks up her heels and fairly revels in the freedom of the fields!

Almost every day sees the arrival of a new bird visitor to these parts. The starlings are here, in cheerful bands, to waken us in the mornings, chattering on the chimney-head, and strutting along the rhone outside the bedroom window.

A wagtail darts across the grass by the back door. A pair of oyster-catchers rise from the rushes by the burn and make their way to the loch, calling cheerfully and excitedly to each other as they go.

Our world really seems to come into its own when all the busy, happy bird throng is about. Ben Wyvis may be still topped with snow, the east wind may have an edge like a saw-toothed knife, but the birds are a sure barometer. As long as they're about us we know the warm days must be coming.

On the wooded slope down to Loch Ness-side the primroses are breaking into flower and, here and there, a violet. Helen and I went down the other day. The rain was pouring down. We slithered and squelched up and down the bank. But we found the flowering and so fulfilled an old Easter holiday rite.

Now the children are back in the schoolroom, already longing for the barefoot, carefree days of summer. Each day Helen rushes home to watch the antics of the twin lambs whose mother haunts the garden and tries, by every cunning device, to snatch a bite of the hens' feed!

The child's laughter, the bleating of the lambs and the piping and calling of numberless birds make the music of spring.

These are the busy days, but they are crammed with interest as well as work, for things are being born again. That's the thrill and the reward.

May 30th

May has been a disappointing month. The wind just simply would not lie down and leave us in peace. From whichever direction it came, it battered and nagged at us persistently.

We longed for the soft, mild dampness that would encourage growth, but the winds carried off every drop of moisture before it got a chance to soak in. Luckily, our soil is of the tough variety and it does, at least, stay put, however dry it gets. From low-ground places, not very far away, we hear reports of whole fields, some sown with corn, having been swept sky high by the force of the wind. We can congratulate ourselves on having escaped that calamity.

It has been as cold as March. The children go off to school bundled in winter coats. People who came through the winter without a day's illness are now complaining of chills and coughs that won't be thrown off. Water is becoming scarce again. Already there is a wide margin of sand at the loch shore and rocks are showing above the surface. We've started to train our household in water economy, in anticipation of a real drought later on.

It's amazing what can be saved in small ways. The contents of the hot water bottle (these nightly comforts are still necessary when Ben Wyvis has a fresh covering of snow) is still warm enough in the morning to wash out the tea-towels or wipe over the kitchen floor. The tatties can quite well be scrubbed with rainwater from the butt outside the door. It's just a question of adapting oneself to a new routine.

In spite of the long, chilly drought, nature is getting on with the job. There is a fresh green braird on the cornfields and a ripple through the young grass. Pastures are brightening, too. The cows are getting a satisfying bite at last. Lambing has gone well. The ewes are able to settle at peace now that they don't have to search so frantically for a green mouthful.

On most places the tatties are safely in. Once the turnip-ground is prepared we can make a start at cutting peats. That's the one job for which the present weather is ideal. With the ground firm and dry the spade goes through the peat like a knife through butter, bringing it out in solid chunks that dry in no time at all.

We still mean to secure our peats. Electricity or no, it will take a long time to wean us from our idea of what a winter fire should look, and smell, like.

Our birds are quietened now, except for an occasional outburst from an irrepressible lark, or the frantic screechings of a hen plover, as she distracts an intruder from her brood of nestlings. Even the cuckoo seems subdued this year, perhaps because his call is carried away on the back of the wind.

The new generation of sparrows chirp happily enough, from morning to night, in their cranny in the steading wall. The house-martens glide silently, all day long, in and out of the broken window in the byre roof, carrying beakfuls of mud for the building of their nest. We can't repair the window till they've gone. The moor is studded, now, with its own exquisite small flower gems that no drought can quench or winds batter, so perfectly adjusted are they to their environment.

The wind, today, is still blustery, but it's got round a little to the south of west and there's a faint semblance of a caress about its blowing. We hope it will soon lie quiet and let a shower through to give growth the blessing it so badly needs.

Wild Flowers

We are thankful, today, that our predecessors on the crofts here were reluctant to use the 'artificials', even when advised by experts to do so. Lime, yes, that was applied, as it had been for many years. It was available naturally in the area and its benefits could be clearly seen. There is an old lime kiln not far away. The 'Good Sir James' of the old estate had insisted on its use. Cattle and horse dung had kept the fields in good heart. Along the field sides and the broad roadside, wild flowers could flourish in the poor soil that suited them. Primroses and tiny white anemones in spring: in summer lady's smock for the butterflies, vetch, bedstraw, foxglove, speedwell, harebell, willowherb for the bees, ragged robin, orchids and meadowsweet

Primroses

by the loch: in autumn scabious and golden rod… the list is endless.

One year, a small girl summer visitor from the south, getting out of the family car and spotting a patch of harebells by the roadside exclaimed in amazement, 'Oh, do they grow here? My granny told me about wild flowers…' To her, wild flowers were only hearsay.

A childhood without wild flowers…? Only rapid journeys strapped into a fast-moving car on the way to a theme park somewhere…? I turned from the thought in dismay. Sadly there was no time for the child to see more. The car moved off. We exchanged waves.

Would that glimpse be enough to lighten up her later life? Would she join with other young people to try to halt the destruction of their inheritance? Without the company of wild flowers, trees, birds, animals, the human heart grows cold. The mind stagnates without the space of unencumbered earth and sky, the depth of loch, the flow of river. Economic progress may be a chimera. There are other calculations to be made.

June 27th

The midsummer month of June has not brought midsummer weather. There was the odd day on which the sun blazed from a cobalt sky, the cattle lay gasping in the lee of stone buildings and the lambs looked absurdly overdressed in their thick, fleecy coats.

For the most part, however, we've been glad of a fire on the hearth and the long, light evenings have not enticed us out for a pleasure stroll round the fields before bed. It seems scarcely possible that, from now on, the days will be shortening—and summer not yet come!

One day of thundery rain—and a storm that made some of us novices a bit squeamish about using our electric gadgets—saved the water situation, at least temporarily, and gave the struggling crops a new lease of life. The young grass has taken on its russet tinge and the corn is a brilliant emerald.

The last of the root crops are in and now everyone is forging ahead at the peat-cutting. Fresh, dark brown gashes are appearing on the hillsides as this precious and seemingly inexhaustible harvest of fuel is gathered in once again. The peat has an amazing power of preservation. We are always hoping we shall one day come across an interesting relic of bygone days when we dig into it. All we've found so far are some birch branches, the bark still gleaming silver in the light. This in itself is amazing enough when we realise that there has not been a living tree in these boglands for hundreds of years.

We've had more than the usual reasons this year for wanting at least one week in June to be graced with genial weather, for sunlight and blue sky can do so much to make a success of the Royal Highland Show. The best that could be forecast as the opening day drew near was 'bright intervals', but when these did come the site at the Longman in Inverness certainly looked enchanting.

The dark, wooded slopes of the Black Isle to the north and the rounded hills to the south made a perfect backcloth for the bright stands and the colourful displays of farm machinery. The flags streamed and crackled in the breeze and the showers, though heavy at times, were soon over. We were glad that the beasts on show didn't have to suffer from a sweltering heat.

There is something a little unreal for crofting people about a show of the magnificence of the 'Highland'. The cattle beasts are almost monstrous in their exaggerated perfection...

We stand and gaze at a champion black heifer and wonder what on earth she is fed on to acquire such gleaming sleekness. We recall to mind, a little wistfully, our own beasts that we thought so sturdy, in the little fields at home.

And the Highland ponies—is it really possible that they can be bred to such proud magnificence and still endure a winter on a bit of indifferent hay? As for the farm machinery, we can only stand and gape at it and we have to give ourselves an occasional pinch to make sure we have not strayed into an automatic world of the 1980s!

We pass on to the handicraft section. That cromach with the horn handle is something we can understand, for we have a neighbour who's clever at making them. And the handwoven cloth—we've seen that being made on a trip we took to the West. We do know a little of what's gone into the making of these things. We stroll into a display of dairying equipment. This should appeal to us, but... could we ever learn to work with those wonderful separators and churns ? I suppose we could, with practice.

We come to an exhibition called 'Electricity on the Croft'. This looks like homely ground. The outside of the stand looks familiar enough—the small stone house with its little flower patch by the door. Inside we find another dream world, streamlined, efficient and labour-saving to the nth. degree. We heave a small sigh and resolve, somehow or other, to put a little by for that cooker, that water-heater, that washing-machine—that electric blanket, at least.

The 'Highland' is certainly an eye-opener. It's grand to rub shoulders with farming folk from all over the country and far beyond, to hear the same old topics being discussed, in snatches of talk in startlingly unfamiliar accents—the drawl of Aberdeenshire, the clipped mono-syllables of North America, the cheery twang of Australia and New Zealand.

Ultimately, we're all faced with the same problems. It's only a matter of perspective. But it makes you think.

July 25th

According to the calendar the year is already on the wane. Even our long, northern evenings are beginning to grow perceptibly darker. For us, in the uplands, however, we have only just reached that peak of high summer,when the scent of clover is everywhere, the ground is warm to the touch and the hills begin to glow with the first deep blooms of the bell heather.

It's a time when all things, from calves to turnip seedlings, are in-terminably thirsty. So far, luckily, we have no real drought to complain of. The rain has come in good, reasonable amounts, the springs are still flowing clear and everything has a sparkle to it.

Of course, the weather has been up to one or two odd tricks. It has to live up to its reputation. There were days when the sun would shine from a brilliant sky all day, then, as though at a given signal, towards six o'clock in the evening, the wind would send the mist swirl-ing down over the hill to the east and within minutes the whole strath would be enveloped in thick grey fog which wouldn't be dispelled till the sun was well up next morning. But it's been good growing weather on the whole.

Turnip-singling is nearing completion now, and no one is sorry. A day or two at the hoe is pleasant enough. There's something very satisfying about working to the rhythm of a squad of good neigh-bours, with plenty of lively chatter and banter to keep everyone's heart high. And it's grand to see the drills coming up clean and even. But it does get wearisome after a while. You begin to see turnip seed-lings sprouting in your dreams.

The cattle lie cudding in the lush pasture beyond the fence, eyes half closed, blissfully unaware of all the labour involved in providing them with a succulent bite for the winter days ahead.

The sheep are roaming the high tops of the hills now, glad to es-cape the heat and the flies of the lower slopes. Startlingly white they look, in their new-shorn state, and the lambs seem almost as big as their mothers.

The few bottle-fed youngsters have reached that cheeky, aggressive stage, when they charge into the kitchen and sometimes right through the house and even up the stairs, blatantly demanding sustenance from their foster-mothers.

Now that the jam-making season is upon us the electric cookers are working overtime, keeping the pans of fruit on the boil. We are lucky enough to have a fruit garden in the district. At the cost of a pleasant three-mile walk we can have the fruit in the pan on the evening of the day it is picked. The children are loth to go to bed when the kitchen is filled with the sweet fumes of the bubbling strawberries. The promise of a 'strawberry piece' for breakfast will usually do the trick. There are still the raspberries to look forward to and the black-currants from our own garden plot.

July is a happy month, with everything growing and thriving and the children racing about and revelling in their birthright of sunshine. The holiday spirit gets into the adults, too. Everyone manages to wangle a day off to go to one or other of the local festivities—hoeing-match, sheepdog trial or Highland Games. These small gatherings are great fun, when each of the competitors, two-legged or four-footed, is known to everyone and his or her prowess compared to the forebears' and talked over endlessly in the crowded beer tent.

The last days of July make a pleasant breathing space before the worries of the hay harvest come along. We're sorry to see them slip away.

August 20th

High summer is the supreme moment of the year. There's work enough, goodness knows, to keep the back bent and muscles on the stretch from morning to night. The last of the turnips are hardly singled before it's time to make a hopeful start at the hay. Meanwhile, the dockens and thistles are rioting round the place and shouting to be lopped.

Into the pattern of fieldwork must be fitted those expeditions to the moor to cut peats. This, of course, is a job in which all can share. Even the children can help with the stacking and if a few peats are used as missiles they'll burn just as well later on.

In spite of the widespread use of electrical appliances I think it will be long before the flame of the peat-fire dies. Convenience is not everything. There's an old magic in fire.

All this summer work is happily accomplished when the smell of clover rises on the morning air, when you can lie stretched, during the dinner-break, in the shade of the rowans, listening to the drone of bees and when, in the late evening, you can walk round the fields and almost see and hear things growing. The tatties are ready to flower, the turnips are beginning to swell, the grass is standing tall and still, ready for the mower, and the corn is green, bright green.

The flanks of the cattle shine, now, as though they'd been polished. They move slowly about pastures that are lush at last, or lie cudding contentedly on the scented moor.

The sheep are at peace, too, for the hill is green and, shorn of their heavy fleeces and with the lambs making fewer demands on them, they can enjoy their short season of ease.

There is not a note of birdsong to be heard now, for the task of rearing the young is all-absorbing. Such toll is taken of eggs and nestlings when eggs have to be laid on the bare ground that it is a wonder to see a string of four or five fledglings following an anxious parent. To watch a young peewit freeze against a lichened dry-stone dyke, its perfect camouflage rendering it well-nigh invisible, makes one marvel at the intricacy of the pattern of survival. Occasionally the harsh alarm of a grouse bursts, like a report, into the still noon air. In the evening a curlew's call sounds eerie and remote.

In the uplands, at summer's height, it is always as though a finger of magic had touched us. All the weariness and anxiety of winter and spring are forgotten, the coming trials of harvest-time are ignored, as we hold our breath and watch this serene miracle of growth. It's a time of reward and promise.

A Highland Bus

Ours is a community of crofters, smallholders, and farmers, scattered along the strath and up the small glens running into the hills west of the Beauly Firth. Inverness is our market town.

We are, it might be claimed, individualists, living lives cut roughly to the pattern of our neighbours, since we all win our bread in much the same way. Yet, for the most part we are self-reliant, even a bit stiff-necked, retaining our own personal viewpoints on the problems of life and of living.

But on one thing we agree absolutely—our complete and utter dependence on our local bus.

She is our twice-weekly meeting-place, our social club, our friend in every kind of need. And, of course, looming even larger in our lives than the bus is her driver, Donny. They combine to provide an example of private enterprise at its very best.

Unlike her sleek, soulless sisters of the main road network, with their uniformed drivers running to the stop-watch precision of a hard and fast timetable, our bus takes her character, her value of time and other things from her master.

Big, burly, genial, with a heart of gold and an uncanny understanding of human nature, Donny is very much the master of his bus and slave to no one but his passenger friends.

True, he runs her to time. Sharp on the dot of 9.30 every Tuesday and every Friday he sets off on his run to town, and equally sharp on the dot of 4 he has us home.

He must, for has he not the bairns to put home from school after that?

Between times, as often as not, he will go half a mile off his road to put Granny Mackenzie up to her door if her rheumatics are bad or it looks like snow. Then with a burst of speed he makes up the time on the straight road further on.

Should Mrs Fraser not be standing at her gate as he passes in the morning he will stop and hoot till she comes running out, beaming and full of apologies at the delay. You see the cow was newly-calved and she had to see the calfie settled.

At Mrs Macpherson's gate a small child will come running at the hoot, clamber into the bus, and shyly hand over a purse and a line.

'Mum's not well the day. She says would you please get her two loaves and a bit meat and put them at the door the night.'

With a smile and a wave and a sweetie tossed through the window for the bairn, we are off again.

Further on we make another stop and out gets Donny to help blind Jock on and settle him in his seat. We pick up a wireless battery that needs charging, a bicycle wheel to be fitted with tube and tyre, letters for the post.

And between each stop the quips and jokes come crackling out of Donny like machine-gun fire, so that by the time we reach town everyone is in such good humour that we are loth to leave the friendly bus.

Baskets laden, we sink into our comfortable seats again at three o'clock, compare notes on our day, and wait to be wafted safely home again.

On the return journey each passenger is handed off with her baggage and sent on her way rejoicing. If she's overspent herself and hasn't enough for her fare—what matter?

'Aach, I'll get it on Friday,' says Donny, with a hoot of kindly laughter to cover her confusion and away he roars to deliver Mrs Macpherson's messages.

Every summer when school is done for the year, Donny takes all his scholar passengers, at his own expense, complete with tea-urn and gramophone, for a whole glorious day at the seaside.

*No wonder we all have an affectionate regard for our Highland bus—
and her Donny!*

September 26th

We're revelling in real summer weather at last. True, it's an Indian
summer and we have to try to shut our eyes to the beauty of the
golden leaves on the birches and the enormous clusters of berries that
glitter on the rowans. Better an Indian summer than no summer at all.

A couple of days of warm sunshine and a soft breeze and we're
ready to forget the days of ceaseless, driving rain, to forget even the
day of the cloudburst, when the field below the house turned into a
lake before our eyes, when the water came swirling under the doors,
when the rhones couldn't take it all, and it had to be kept at bay with
the yard broom.

Great chunks of the road were carried away that day. The teacher
had to shepherd the children up the hill till they were met by a neighbour who saw them safely home.

Now the last of the hay can be stacked. A lot of its feeding quality
must have been lost in the continual drenching it got, but at least it
will give a hungry beast something to chew in the winter. And the
fresh green aftermath is a joy to see.

As for the corn harvest, it's still a good two or three weeks away.
There is only a tinge of yellow in the crop now. But one advantage of
having a late season is that the summer storms do the crop little damage.
Only a patch here and there has been laid, whereas, on the low ground
we see whole fields where the crop is lying in tangled, twisted heaps.

Last week we had a displenish sale in our midst. An elderly neighbour, seemingly hale and hearty, died suddenly. We had hardly
recovered from the shock of his going, when we were bidden to attend
the dispersal of his wordly goods. Normally, sales are quite a social
event, eagerly seized upon as a chance for scattered friends to meet.
But, somehow, this was different.

We greeted each other soberly. It seemed scarcely possible that we
were not to see Willie again about his fields, at the market, striding
down the road to the bus, in his green tweed suit, drawing on his pipe,
a twinkle of greeting in his dark eyes as he passed the time of day.

The sound of his voice, with the Gaelic lilt and the gruff independ-
ence of his views always did your heart good. He was a man. He was
full of character and kindliness. And he represented a way of life.

It was inexpressibly sad to see his possessions laid out, ticketed and docketed, for inspection, while the pale yellow sun shone on his little field of oats behind the steading.

There were four magnificent black cows that had been his quiet pride. As each was driven from the byre, her sturdy calf trotting at her heels, she stood eyeing the circle of bidders with mistrust. They were bought by a dealer. There were the two or three score sheep, huddled in their pen. There was the tractor and the threshing mill, only lately installed, that represented a long lifetime of saving. The old horse-drawn implements went for a few shillings to a scrap-merchant.

When the sale was over we took tea in Willie's tiny, homely house. A brand new electric cooker stood in the passageway, but the kitchen fire was bright with old-fashioned flames.

What must have been in the hearts and minds of his sisters as they dispensed tea and spoke quietly to their visitors, we can only guess. They have the reticent, kindly manners of all hill-folk. But Willie will not be forgotten. Of that they can rest assured.

October 24th

There's a stillness in the air now, with a hint of autumn in the stillness. From the rowans, where the berries are reddening and a leaf, here and there, is turning yellow, comes the small, sweet sound of the robin's song. At once, one thinks of frosty mornings and a leap of flames in the hearth. We're glad of the stillness for it has been such a wild sort of summer, with gales and more rain than we knew what to do with.

We came off better than the low-ground places, where the rain flattened a lot of the corn and the water is still bogging the fields.

With us the corn was not heavy enough to be laid flat and the water always runs off eventually. But seldom have the burns been in such spate as they were a month ago.

Footbridges were washed clean away. The hill road was running like a river. Only the geese enjoyed themselves, sitting delightedly under the overflow pipe from the butt at the back door, heads tucked under their wings, while the water trickled ceaselessly over their backs.

Those folk who cut their hay early are still forking over the last few swathes, or making them into small ricks, not risking the building of stacks until the hay has another drying. Those who waited are getting busy at last and the clank of the mower and the swish of the scythe come clearly through the still air.

As for the corn harvest, it is still a long way off. The fields are hardly yellowing yet. It will take some weeks of sunshine to ripen the grain. It has certainly been a grand season for the pastures. Whereas last year they were yellowish and bare, this year they have been lush and green and the cattle have put on enormous layers of flesh.

The children are back in school and that's another reason for the stillness in the air. They have a good tan on their skins, in spite of the lack of sunshine. They always get what sunshine there is and the wind and the rain give them a healthy, burnished look.

They've had poor holidays compared to those of last summer, no water sports at all, not because of any lack of water, but because of the coldness of it and the fact that the loch has been so high all summer that the little sandy beach has been completely submerged.

There is one more stillness to record—the stillness of the grouse moors. Only once have we heard a gun popping since the start of the shooting season. It seems as though the few grouse which escaped the perils of fire and flood are being left in peace now.

Our other bird neighbours are quiet now, too. The peewits are flocking again, the house-martins in the byre nest are safely fledged and have flown. These are busy days for the croft horse. When he's not hard at it, carting hay to the stackyard, he's off to the moor to bring home a load of peats, or away down the road to fetch sticks from the old woodland. We must be sure of firing for the months ahead.

When the robin's song is in our ears, the children are off to school every morning and there's a gleam of yellow in the bracken on the hill, we simply have, alas, to turn our thoughts once more to winter.

Croft Gardens

The garden, along with the care of the milk-cow and the hens and, of course, help at the peats and the harvests, was always considered the province of the woman. So it was with us, though I was lucky to get help with the initial clearing of the ground, the fencing and the digging. Our garden was just the corner of a field taken in from the heather a hundred years ago. A dry-stone dyke on one side gave shelter from the prevailing westerlies, so that kale, that great winter survivor, carrots and onions for the soup and even some salad stuff—lettuce, radishes, chives and parsley—could be grown.

Blackcurrants and gooseberries, raspberries and, of course, rhubarb, all do well, with the help of some of that precious dung. The old folk may not have heard of vitamins, but they knew what they were about when they planted their little gardens and got them to grow something, against all the odds. At the deserted places, not far from the ruins of the houses, the small walled enclosures that were gardens are still clearly seen. In some the fruit bushes have survived. I took cuttings, once, of some gooseberries which flour-ished splendidly. In one deserted garden I found feverfew, parsley and mint. I was told the old lady who had lived and died there always had 'herbs' for the soup.

By the front door most places sport a small patch of flowers, well fenced against marauders of all kinds—stray sheep, rabbits, hens. Pansies are favoured and batchelors' buttons, bright, low-growing things.

In the mid-nineteen hundreds gardening had been introduced into the school curriculum, for the boys. They certainly learnt to sow peas—those they didn't eat before they got into the ground!—and to weed carrot seed-lings, even during the school holidays. And it got them out of the schoolroom. No doubt many of them put what they learnt to good use later on. And there was also instruction in bee-keeping, by an expert. These were all laud-able efforts to widen the scope of food production on the crofts.

Everywhere, on the unfenced green in front of the croft house, there are great patches of daffodils. Mercifully, even hungry creatures don't seem to favour these so they multiply in glorious profusion to cheer the cold spring days. I often wonder how they came to the places in these heights. Maybe a few were taken from the laird's grounds when he made his 'improvements' long ago and have spread. Or did a kindly lairdess donate them?

In every kitchen window stands a bright growing flower, usually a geranium, carefully tended by the croft wife, however busy she may be. There has always been time to acknowledge the beauty of growing things, to watch the emergence of leaf and bud and flower.

November 10th

This has been a dismally long-drawn-out harvest. It's always sad to see the stooks still in the field at the end of October, each with its small white cap of snow. And that's how it has been this year.

Most of the corn was cut in a brief dry spell, but before it could be put safely into small ricks down would come the rain, the sleet or the snow. Then there would be a day of good drying wind and hopes would rise again, only to be dashed by another deluge during the night.

Of course, we're inured to this sort of thing. It's happened over and over again. We're fatalists. We have to be. There's nothing for it but to glance grimly across the fields, set up the stooks that have been blown over in the night: and stamp off to the shelter of the barn to split sticks for the fire.

Yet the pity of seeing a year's work culminate in this sort of soggy wretchedness always strikes us afresh.

Handling sodden sheaves is a very dreary business. In no time at all you're soaked to the skin and you can't help wistfully remembering the good years, when the grain rattles on the stalk and the only fear is that it may fall to the ground with over-ripeness.

This year much of the grain was cut on the green side and, though it's all right that way for feeding in the sheaf, there's always the fear that it may heat in the stack.

The potatoes are ready for lifting and that is an added worry. With the two harvests overlapping, the pressure of work, when the weather allows work, is tremendous, especially as, by six o'clock, it is now too dark to see stook or tuber. The ground in the tattie-breaks is too soft to bear the weight of horse or tractor-drawn implements. We have to content ourselves by making a start at lifting with the fork.

In some places the hay is still standing in field-ricks, so that virtually three harvests are overlapping. However, the cattle are in good shape and getting a late bite on the hill.

The trees are still in leaf and down by the lochside there is a blaze of colour to delight any eye. On the good days the water is a deep Mediterranean blue and the birches leap up the far hillside like tongues of flame.

We went down to Loch Ness-side the other day to gather some of the last wild harvest of the year—the brambles. They are still exceptionally big and juicy and, though we got soaked to the skin, we carried a basketful home in triumph. We made a fresh discovery—a huge holly tree we had never come on before, already decked with deep red berries. Christmas?...

It seems strange to be thinking of Christmas with the corn still lying out at the mercy of the weather. But winter is on the way, unquestionably. The rowan berries are in steep and rapidly turning into wine!

And the geese are back. When we see those wild, strong gaggles triumphantly honking their way out of the cold north sky we know the year has finally reached its turning-point. There's a sort of comfort in their coming, too, an assurance that there are regions more desolate than ours, that to these hardy creatures our bleakness is a refuge.

December 1st

November brought some of those minor miracles which are apt to be left out of a reasoned forecast of events, and which we accept gladly, with outstretched hands, as a token of beneficence.

All the dreary damp of summer has been forgotten in a spell of out-of-season weather, with drying winds, sunshine and an odd day so still and warm it set the midges dancing. It was like a sudden, unlooked-for reprieve. There's nothing so welcome to exasperated minds and muscles.

In one final burst of stimulated energy we got the last of the corn into the stack and the tatties pitted. Now we can put some, at least, of the turnips into the clamp before the frosts come.

On one or two of the more forward places a start has been made at carting out dung from the midden and letting the plough get a bite of the fine, dry ground. Even a week thus saved from spring can be valuable. And it gives the feeling we've actually dodged a bit of winter.

November is the big month for the selling of stock from the upland crofts. One of the advantages of the late season in the heights is that, although spring is usually so long in coming that it seems it's going to miss us altogether, autumn is correspondingly prolonged and normally there is quite a good green bite about the hill and the fields till well into November.

So we keep hold of stock till the last possible moment. Sound judgement is needed to determine the precise moment when they have reached that peak of bloom which will catch the bidder's eye.

This year the wet has produced a flush of greenery which has benefited both cattle and sheep. Stirks have fetched very satisfactory prices, and one lot of lambs on a neighbouring croft, straight from their hill grazing, topped the sale in a most spectacular manner.

All this is heartening and does make up for the worry and effort of securing the fodder crops. A hungry gap is threatening for late spring, with oat-straw in short supply, but at least we can face the winter with an adequate cash return from the crops of lambs and stirks.

The last of the peats have been carted from the hill now. This is a valuable harvest with coal at the price it is and electricity no cheap alternative.

Now that the fields are cleared of their crops and the lambs despatched to market, all attention is focused on the sheep. From now till the beginning of January is the tupping season. Many crofters take advantage of the Government scheme, whereby a ram can be hired from the Department of Agriculture for a small sum. They are magnificent beasts and ensure a good crop of lambs.

On those places which haven't sufficient grazing to carry a breeding flock, sheep are grazed over the winter, or 'wintered'. The wintering flocks, as well as bringing in some welcome cash, keep the croft land well manured.

Our neighbour, the shepherd

Some people find it profitable to buy in a score or so of lambs now, feed them on turnips and a little crushed oats, in addition to the natural grazing, and sell them again in early spring.

November is far from being a dead season here. It is a very lively time indeed and, when it works its little miracles, as it did this season, it evens up the balance of a stormy year and lets us sail into winter on an even keel.

December 29th

The dead of the year is a pleasant, snug enough time for man and beast. That is the beauty of a life which keeps time with the seasons. While nature sleeps, we can relax with her.

True, it can be dreary trudging round the steading in the morning half-light, with the snow blowing into your face on the back of a south-west gale. But there's great satisfaction in thrusting a bundle of sweet-smelling hay under a hungry horse's nose, and in hearing the delighted crunching as the cows eat their way through a pailful of sliced turnip.

The croft cow, unlike her dairy-farm cousin, doesn't have to be milked in the middle of the night so that her milk may appear on a far-off breakfast table. She can have her winter long-lie, as her mistress can. It's easy enough to slip out correspondingly late to the byre in the evening, so that the milkings may be evenly spaced.

The hens, in their deep-litter shed, come off best of all. They have the bright lights to encourage them and they never need to get their feet wet.

Farming, as it becomes more and more mechanised and specialised, is now a business, like any other. But crofting is still a way of life. We are very near to the bones of things. It's in midwinter that we realise that this is so. Throughout the other seasons we work ceaselessly so that we may live secure through the dark months. That hay we toss so happily to the horse—we can remember how we had to turn it and turn it again, between the summer downpours, and finally hang it, in desperation, on the fence to dry. Now, miraculously, it smells sweet and satisfies a beast's hunger.

That huge white tattie that breaks into flour on our plate reminds us of the hoeing we had to do, in the hot days, when the weeds threatened to get ahead of the tuber stems. Our breakfast egg only appears regularly because we managed to hold those pullets back from laying too soon in the autumn, so that they wouldn't go into a premature moult.

Sometimes we pause before throwing a log on the fire at night, turn the rough wood in our fingers and murmur 'that's a bit of the old tree we had such a job to get over the fence'.

It's now that we feel how closely interdependent we all are—man and beast and small field won from the heather.

Evening leisure brings the ceilidh. Neighbours, whom we may not have seen for a twelvemonth, materialise suddenly out of the black night. Without a knock, sure sign this that they claim us as friends, they appear in the kitchen. Boots are knocked free of snow, sticks and caps are hung on the door-hook, and we settle down to a review of the year's events.

Harvesting achievements, the price the lambs fetched, the more spectacular of the neighbours' doings, are all discussed in leisurely snatches, between sips of tea, a dram or two and pullings on pipes.

The weekly paper and the wireless programme can pass a pleasant enough hour for us in winter, but there's nothing so heartening as an evening spent with neighbours whose lives touch our own at every point, indulging in the endless fascination of talking 'shop'.

The clock ticks through the friendly silences, the wind roars in the chimney and rattles the roof slates. We don't heed the menace of time or storm. The fireside oasis of light and warmth is the snug delight we have achieved.

A Walk in the Wild Places

December in the uplands often has a feel of holiday. The Ness valley may be shrouded in mist, but at 800 feet the sun is brilliant in the crystal snow, the sky is at its bluest, flocks of bullfinches rush into the dark pines and stand there like brilliant decorations, and the air itself is energy. On such a day a walk, even a short one, is an irresistible pleasure.

The garden harvests are in—the potatoes bagged, carrots and turnips pitted, beetroot pickled, apples and honey gathered, onions dried, brambles, sloes and rosehips dealt with. The last green tomatoes are made into chutney and the rowan wine is bottled. Winter greens—cabbage, sprouts and kohl-rabi—are safe under their caps of snow and some chicory is blanching in covered boxes. Plastic cloches cover an always hopeful sowing of peas, beans, lettuce and spring onion. Dung has been collected and spread on the cleared ground.

There is great satisfaction in preparing for winter's siege. We had an early warning signal even in October, when snow fell to a depth of several inches and lay for several days. So it's up to us. Sometimes, and particularly this year, one looks back with a certain longing to the days before the advent of mod. cons., when it was a question of a good peat stack, oil for the Tilley, meth, a bag of candles and batteries for the wireless. Luckily for us, we still have some pine branches from the trees blown down in last year's gales, and the junior members of the family are ardent candlemakers.

Anyway, my conscience is as clear as it can well be when there is always a job looming. Refusing to look closely at what can reasonably be left until tomorrow, I put my head round the door and say: 'I think I'll just take a walk up to the loch'. My husband nods in agreement. He knows what it means—an hour taken at random out of a fine day, an hour which may bring a sense of timelessness, a glimpse of a whole new dimension.

I take the stick carved out of hazel by a neighbour. It is smooth in the hand, firm yet supple and exactly the right length for prodding the moss, for propelling one up a slope or for leaning on before the journey home.

Less than a mile up the road the loch lies, reed-fringed at the far end, with a small green island where the black-headed gulls brood their young, a shapely hill rearing from the far shore.

Before reaching it I am tempted to digress on to the moor. Here three hut circles lie. They had an instinct for a dwelling-site, these old ancestors of ours—on a dry slope, facing just to the west of south, with well-water to hand and the loch close by. I tread round the circle, prodding the stones which formed the base of the walls.

I stand in the entrance gap, looking down the strath, and am away back in time, back to when the sun was master, when one bowed to the new moon, when fertility was life, and death was a re-entering of the womb.

There must have been hardships to living, but what blessedly simple living. When food, clothing and shelter were of one's own procuring and the mysteries were accepted, not explained. Before trade was thought of, when greed had not bred anger on any scale, there must surely have been time to dance under a summer moon and to play with the children round a winter fire.

I go back to the road and look up the sloping ground on the near shore of the loch. Here lie the only fields still cultivated in the traditional five-year pattern.

All the varying shades of green—of oats, grass, turnip and potato-top—are in these fields all season and they are worked to perfection by a man living alone now in his small white house. His cattle beasts are sleek and black. His stacks are snug. He yields to no fancy fashions. But he will leave his ground in good heart.

I reach the loch and there are the tufted ducks as always on parade and heron brooding in the shallows. I hear a strange sound, like the notes of an imagined elf horn, and I look more closely at the ice-fringed water across the loch. A line of wild swans is sailing proudly there. The Whoopers have arrived. My day is made!

I'd like to go back by the far shore, where the roe often lie, and I always have one more look for the smuggler's gear said to have been flung into the mud, long ago, when the excisemen were hot on the trail. But December days are short and I turn about on the road I came.

To the east lies the hill called the 'bodach', the old man, and I can see him very clearly stretched out there, huge and majestic, a long beard flowing down his chest. He is a dimension in himself, a chunk of eternity. The Stone-Agers must have seen him and the Druid priests, the early Christians of Kilianan on Loch Ness shore, the Redcoats a-harrying after Culloden and the smugglers of last century. It will take an earthquake to shatter him.

Strangely enough, it is in the moss below him that the four craters lie, the craters made by bombs jettisoned by a German pilot one night during the last war. The heather has healed the scars now, and in June the small white truce flags of bog-cotton blow up there in the breeze. One likes to think it was a gesture of mercy, anyway, to lay down arms at the foot of the bodach.

As I reach home, my husband is bringing in logs for the evening fire.

'Had a good walk?'

'Mm... wonderful.'

I go to put on the kettle and get out a comb of honey, which spreads the taste of summer on our winter bread.

1957

February 2nd

We've had a green winter so far. There's been the odd day of snow and storm, of course, just to keep us on the alert, with defences well bolstered. But the blackbirds are tuning up in the birches by the loch and daisies are gleaming here and there in the lee of the dykes.

When you meet a neighbour, any morning now, you may be sure his face will light up and his first words will be 'grand weather'…and it will be no casual conversational formula he will be uttering, but a statement that has a wealth of real meaning tucked away in its simple syllables.

Grand weather now means that we can get well ahead with jobs that will ease the pressure of spring work. We can cart out dung and see to fences and drains and be satisfied that the wintering sheep are on the thrive. The breeding ewes have had a good season and, with the departure of the tups, lambing seems to be just round the corner.

The cattle can be out day-long, getting a stray green bite that will eke out a little their ration of straw and turnips and will certainly put heart and health into them. Indeed, so sure are some of them that this winter is only a fake, that they go wandering up the hill at dusk and are positively loth to be persuaded into their warm byre for the night.

The hens take their daily parade round the fields, scratching delightedly at the soft earth and grabbing a beakful of unwary insect or slug. The result is that I can put two eggs into the Sunday cake instead of one.

We can go a little easier on the peat-stack and the wood-pile, too, this weather. That in itself is half the winter battle won. When you can sit back from the fire, instead of crouching over it, during the hour before bed, you know it's time to be looking forward, planning for another year.

With a good extra spell of light both ends of the day, we can emerge thankfully from hibernation and start looking for what we can lay our hands to next. The digging of the garden plot, abandoned since autumn, can be finished off and fresh earth from the molehills in the fields carted to the flower-patch. We can see to brooder-lamps and other rearing equipment, in preparation for the arrival of day-old chicks.

All the small extra tasks, such as the cleaning up of the yards and the patching of roads, which have to be left undone when bad weather keeps us under cover, can be overtaken easily now. The accomplishing of them certainly makes life run more smoothly.

The only ones who don't altogether relish the lengthening of the days are the children. They're in sober mood for they've been told they're to lose the extra hour of freedom they get in the dead of the year. They have to stay in school till four o'clock and they're still home in daylight, however slowly they meander the mile up the road. But soon they'll be able to race about outside till almost bedtime, kicking up their heels like Sheltie foals.

A January like this one has been a happy month. We've shaken off the drowsiness of the deep of winter. We can plan ahead in a leisurely way, looking the new season full in the face, before the hectic scramble and uncertainty of spring catches us up.

March 2nd

We're now into a belated winter régime. Snow, frost and a slippery road making van deliveries uncertain, extra bakings are being done, while the fire is well banked, just in case we should run out of bread. At night, thick socks and gloves and balaclavas are draped round the stove.

The poultry mash is mixed with hot water, to take the chill off it. The geese tap with their beaks on the back door to remind us that their grazing is blanketed in snow.

But it's winter with a twinkle in its eye. A million pin-points of light are glittering in the smooth, white fields, but there's a heat in the noon sun that can make the fiercest-looking icicles drip. And the larks are singing, in a china-blue sky.

We're glad of the crystal-quiet air and the hush that snow brings, for we've had an overdose of turbulence this month. The whole strath has been battle-scarred since the night of the fourth of February.

There are great gaps in nearly every steading roof. Here and there a tree lies prone, its crown flattened, its roots waving in the air like the tentacles of some giant octopus.

At one place, mercifully unoccupied, the entire corrugated roof of the dwelling-house was lifted, like a lid, and deposited against the gable wall of a neighbouring house. Windows were blown in and stacks and henhouses scattered. Sleep was impossible that night. We lay, staring at the ceiling, trying, as each successive onslaught of wind pressed, like a battering-ram, against the house, to calculate at what angle the chimney-stack would hit the roof! Luckily, everything held fast.

Wan-faced neighbours foregathered in the morning to compare notes on the damage they had suffered and to give one another a hand with emergency repairs. Fortunately, there were no casualties among humans or animals.

We had a brief, but almost equally severe spell of gale only a few days before this memorable one, when we were without electricity for about thirty hours. There was a scurrying, then, to borrow lamps and candles from neighbours not connected to the scheme. Momentarily, we envied them their snug circle of lamplight round the glowing fire, their kettle that boiled without the flicking of a switch.

The men from the Hydro Board came valiantly to the rescue. From the window of our blacked-out kitchen we followed their torches weaving across the moor. Neither snow, nor gale, nor cold could deter them. They worked away till they found the fault and, by midnight, in our second evening of darkness, the current was restored and we were blinking at one another in the dazzle.

The larks had been singing on the morning before the hurricane. A week after it subsided we were gloating over the most exciting piece of news of the whole year, news which never fails to thrill us—the return of the peewits. They were only up for a preliminary gambol. We haven't seen them again since the snow came. But they were with us for a couple of days, swooping and flashing over the bogland, trying out their voices exultantly. Any day now they'll be back, getting on with the season's business in earnest.

Meantime, the children, who thought they were going to miss their winter sports altogether this year, are making the most of what snow there is. Small, jaunty snowmen are standing guard by every gate. Through the still afternoon air come the delighted shouts of Saturday sledgers.

Winter's not so bad when you have positive proof, in the rising of larks above your head, that spring is only biding her time. And every steading roof within miles is now securely lashed with weighted ropes.

March 30th

March has been a most genial month. There have been days when, were it not for the small shining caps of snow on the tops of the Strathfarrar hills, we might well have imagined we had taken a leap straight into summer.

It's a great relief to be able to discard the thick, cumbersome garments of winter. We can work outside with a will and feel the sun warm on our bare heads and on arms bare to the elbow.

The moor is alive with returning birds. Peewit and curlew vie with each other for the favoured nesting sites. Snipe dart eagerly here and there.

Grouse skim swiftly across the heather, so intent on their own affairs that they hardly heed the approach of a human. And the larks sing all day long. There's even an odd wagtail about, ready to pounce on the emerging insects.

Weeds are putting in an appearance in the garden plot and there's a flash of bright green across the sward. As for molehills, there are enough to keep the rollers busy any day that can be spared from more urgent operations.

First things first, of course, and already the plough has turned the lighter field giving us the heartening sight of rich brown patches among the dun and the varying shades of green.

The sheep are coming to the lambing in grand shape. Spring-calving cows are slow on the move now and glad of a chance to lie for short spells on a dry, almost warm, patch of ground.

Heather-burning operations have begun. The household stock of matches is forever in a state of depletion. The boy in the hills takes a sort of primitive delight in the ploy of firing. It's certainly thrilling to hear the hiss and crackle of the flames and to watch them leaping away from you, in a wild, elemental rhythm. There's also the satisfaction that you're actually helping new growth, that your destruction has a positive purpose.

At night the fires glow orange along the ridge of the hill and the figures of the men on guard are silhouetted, momentarily, like figures of another age, against the strange light.

Then there's that other spring delight of the active, human male— a day or two spent trying to outwit the fox and bring destruction on him before the arrival of his potential victims, the lambs. For weeks, the slightest sign of his activity is observed. A fall of snow may have provided a valuable clue in the shape of a line of delicate pad-prints, leading, perhaps, to a lair.

Information is pooled, and on a suitable Saturday guns are mobilised and a squad will fan out among the rocks overhanging the loch.

At the end of the day the bag may well be empty, but at least a gesture will have been made. There will have been laughter and wisecracking on the way home and the warm sense of well-being that any communal enterprise brings. Another chuckling reminiscence will have been added to the stock, for next winter's ceilidhs.

It rarely happens, in these heights, that spring is with us by the day of her official arrival, appointed in the calendar. But this year it seems she's made a supreme effort to time her entry. Coltsfoot are blazing in every cranny. Even a primrose, here and there, is blinking, in a surprised way, at the sun. A Forestry squad is busy planting larch along the edge of the old, felled woodland.

As we go out, first thing in the morning, the scent of crumbling, stirring earth comes at us in a heady waft. What April may have in store we don't know, but at the moment we're right in the middle of a time full of promise.

A Highland Neighbour

Our Highland neighbour lives in a small croft house at the head of an unsung glen, high in the hills above Loch Ness.

A friend visiting us for the first time may look across at the neighbouring house and ask wonderingly: 'But how do you get there? There's no road from here, is there?'

But we know better! Along the edge of our fields, over the stile and through the heather goes the narrow, twisting path, with a stepping-stone here, a plank of wood there, to help it across a patch of bog; then over the fence, across the burn by the bridge, or through the water-splash in summer, and we're there. How well-defined the path is to our feet, how many, many times we have taken it, our small daughter leaping ahead from tussock to tussock. Scarcely a week passes but we make the journey at least once and always at the end of it there is the call 'Come in!' from the doorstep or the kitchen. When the visit is over, the quiet, sincere 'Haste ye back!' sounds in our ears as we make our way home, and we know we shall, indeed, hasten back, always sure of our welcome.

Life in these uplands would be well-nigh impossible without a good neighbour. Should one of us fall ill, who will supply the very medicine we are short of, or send one of her household post-haste for the doctor while we hold the fort at home? Our neighbour, of course.

Should we be struggling under a threatening sky to get the cut corn into stooks before the rain descends, who do we see approaching, strong young arms bared to the elbow, yellow pig-tails a-swing, but our neighbour's child, eager to give us a hand, and to tell us Donald will be there in a minute, as soon as he has got the cow home. And her youth and her gaiety give us fresh strength to finish the job.

Helen going to school

Our cow is dry before calving and along comes this same youngster, always smiling, every evening, when school is done, with milk from her early-calved cow.

We buy day-old chicks and find one intended-mother-hen is obstinately refusing to take to her new family. But who is this coming across the heather, nursing a strange-looking bundle? Who but the neighbour child, with a broody hen held in the crook of her arm, and the chickens' troubles, and our own, are over!

It is the same in every difficulty of our life here. Our needs are antici-pated, help is always forthcoming just when it is most wanted, and help given with such simplicity of grace and understanding.

There was the problem of how to get our five-year-old the two miles to school, winter and summer. But it turned out to be no problem at all. The neighbour child would meet her at the burn every morning and shepherd her all the long way through the heather, across the 'back burn,' up the hill and along the road. When she herself left to go to the secondary school she would still be there for the return journey, ready to help our young one over the difficult places, and there would be a hot drink in winter and a cool one in summer and a smile and a happy word in the little house to put her on the last lap of the journey.

They tell us there is 'not the kindness in it' that there was long ago. The sense of community is inevitably becoming less as crofts are abandoned and a money economy spreads its grip everywhere. But to us our immediate surroundings will always remain one of the kindliest spots on God's earth. It is a place where problems are shared and understood and so made easier to cope with, and a place where joys are shared, too. How our neighbour delights in sending over a taste of butter from the first summer cream, a cutting from a specially prized garden flower, the glad tidings of the arrival of a new grand-child!

'It must be very lonely up here!' our visitor exclaims another time. How can I convince him of the contrary? He would have to live and work here, as we have done, to know that the hills are the friendliest places in the world, where the realities of living and dying, of storm and sunshine, of darkness and light, of earth and sky are the things that matter.

We have only to watch the smoke rise, on a summer morning, from the chimney of the little house across the heather, to see the light from its kitchen window shine out on a winter's night, to feel that all is well with our world—thanks to a true Highland neighbour.

April 27th

April has been up to her usual tricks—a chill, white covering of snow on a morning when lambs were due and a wind that could pierce the thickest fleece. Then, a day or two later, sunshine warm enough to bask in and a wind veering to the soft quarter, in the west.

With all its ups and downs it has been a month when the plough could get steadily to work, making a seed-bed once again out of the small, stone-strewn fields. The gulls have arrived as usual, dazzlingly white against the grey streaked sky, to take their share of the pickings. The ancient pattern of awakening has been repeated and given us the lift we depend on.

It has been a busy time. The sheepmen have been the busiest of all, working right round the clock, as the lambs arrive at all hours. But it's work that hasn't had too much anxiety attached to it this year.

The ewes have had an easy winter and are in good shape. The only fear is that some of the lambs may be on the big side, which sometimes makes for a difficult birth.

So far, casualties have been few. The youngsters have got quickly on to their feet and, after a frantic feed from their stoical mothers, have gone gambolling off, sublimely careless of the anxiety their coming may have caused and of the hopes that are fixed on them.

The last of the wintering sheep have been collected, the strays sought high and low and finally rounded up and returned to their owners.

Now the first of the summerings are here. The grass is forging ahead and already there is enough of a bite to allow the sheep to lie placidly cudding, instead of being for ever on a desperate forage.

Calves are arriving, too. Any neighbourly call now entails a visit to the byre to inspect the new hope of the croft—a heifer that will replace, maybe, an ageing cow or a bull calf that will make sturdy beef.

As we bend to admire the small creature lying quietly in its bed of straw and feel the rasp of the warm, black tongue on our fingers, the mother casts an anxious eye upon our intrusion and we give her a pat for her patient share in the renewal of life.

Outside in the sunshine a hen will be strutting proudly after her brood of bright yellow chicks. We throw her a smile and a word of praise, too. However well and scientifically we may plan the year's increase, we cannot do without the mysterious gift of mothering.

The birds have stopped their early springtime clamour. There's almost a hush over the moor now that nesting has started in earnest. The larks still give us short, ecstatic bursts of song, but only occasionally does a crowd of peewits rise angrily into the air, swooping and diving, to scare away a marauding hoodie. Easter has come, this year, at a time appropriate to the heights. When it's too early, it's liable to coincide with a blizzard. This year the children can roll their eggs on a sward of dazzling emerald and make wreaths of the daisy stars. All we're waiting for now is the cheerful, lovable sound of the cuckoo, announcing jauntily that he has brought the sun on his back from Africa. Then we shall be assured, once again, that the earth is swinging in the right direction.

June 1st

May has been a time of hesitations this year. To sow or not to sow, to plant or not to plant, that has been the question all month long. Cold, easterly winds, frost and drought have done nothing to give the ground that cosiness a seed-bed needs.

Still, in the end, we planted and sowed, in hope, and now the rain is falling softly, as we like it to fall, with a slant from the west; and a rift in the cloud bank promises a gleam of that warm May sunshine that will make the damp earth steam and send everything shooting up, fresh and glistening green. The grass, which got such a magnificent start in early spring, has never looked back. That, perhaps, is the greatest blessing of all, for so much depends on grass. Already, the cows' backs are showing a bloom of health and no amount of egg-laying can take the sheen from the hens' tight plumage.

The dryness of the ground threatened an early water shortage so housewives have been busy washing blankets before supplies give out. Meanwhile, the men, oblivious of such domestic worries, have been glad that at least the drying winds have allowed them to make an extra early start at cutting peat.

It is this continual looking forward that keeps us on an even keel. We gladly suffer aching backs as we plant potatoes now, for we can anticipate the satisfaction of having a well-filled clamp to see us through the winter. Also, the thought of a fire to relax at on a freezing night makes us forget that our hands are bulging with callouses when we come from a spell at the peats.

We have been showered with blessings by the authorities these last weeks. The old, rickety wooden bridge above the school has been replaced by a sound, concrete structure. Our road, which, not long ago, was a rutted, pot-holed affair, at which truck drivers looked askance, is now a smooth, black ribbon of a highway. To ride a bike on it is sheer delight. And there is word that the telephone is coming our way this summer. These things do give us a sense of solidarity. For Helen, who is developing interest in the phenomena of the night sky, this has been a memorable month. On a glittering night of frost we saw the comet, hung in the north sky, in stark splendour.

Then, a couple of weeks later, we saw the full moon float, like a giant balloon, above the slope of the hill and watched the earth's shadow engulf its bright surface, till it shone with an angry, perplexed glow. We waited till its own bright rim emerged again and it went sailing on its own harmonious way. The exploding of nuclear bombs seems like the setting off of a few squibs and crackers by a gang of mischievous and boastful boys, when we have these splendid natural phenomena to remind us of the timeless perspective of the Universe. The rhythm is unbroken, come what may.

We plant and sow, with a wary eye to the weather. The martins dart day-long in and out of the broken window in the stable roof, building their nests among the cobwebs under the beams.

The wind has a chill edge to it. The mist swirls among the rocks, to the east. The cuckoo calls, unseen, from all points of the compass. It's an upland May.

June 29th

June is blazing down, at last. After a spell of withering north wind which brought hail and coated the hill-tops with snow, the weather suddenly relented. The wind came from the south and west and carried the scent of summer with it—the scent of fresh grass and leaves and sun-warmed clover.

The drought continues but the night mists bring a little welcome moisture that keeps the green things fresh. The moor is studded with small, bright flowers—milkwort and tormentil, red rattle and speedwell, butterwort and orchids. In the marsh the fat, yellow globe-flowers are lush and splendid in the sun. Helen is kept busy in the long, light evenings looking at all the new blooms and darting from one marked nest to another to watch the progress of the various fledglings—peewit and meadow pipit, sparrow, starling and swallow.

There is also the nest on the hillside, shown to us by a neighbour, where a hen partridge sits, bright-eyed and quite unperturbed, on a clutch of sixteen eggs. At noon the cows stand about in the lee of the steading, swishing their tails languidly. Now and again they break, in a wild stampede, across the pasture, when the sting of a fly goads them to exasperation.

The neighbourly squads of sheep-shearers work their way from croft to croft. Shearing is hot, thirsty work, but it's rewarding to see the beasts—cool, clean-shaven and startlingly white—move off easily, without their heavy fleeces. The summer shepherd has a busy time for, apart from the clipping, he has to be constantly on the watch for sheep that may have been attacked by the fly or have got on their backs and lie, threshing the air with their legs, unable to rise.

Communal work always keeps us happy. The preliminaries—ploughing, harrowing and sowing—are solitary jobs. For hoeing, sheep-shearing and peat-cutting we get together. Jokes crackle, even out of parched lips, and chaffing defeats the pestering of midges. Wisecracks that may be a hundred years old, or more, are still a relief to aching arms and backs. At the end of the day there's tea in the cool of the kitchen and quiet, reminiscent talk as we relax, before the long trek home.

This is the time of year when the uplands come into their own. Where in the world but on a northern moor, in June, could you stand on the doorstep at midnight and see the sun's light still clear in the north sky?

The sheep are small grey humps among the folded daisies. The cattle stay, statuesque, in the cool scoop of the burn. The sheets of bog-cotton glimmer, like snowdrifts, in the half light. To bring the following silence even closer to your ear a curlew, in the far distance, gives a call, like the call from a dream. There's more than a touch of magic about midsummer on a highland moor.

Impromptu Holiday

Ours is a busy life. When you are concerned, just the two-and-a-half of you, with growing crops and rearing beasts on a small Highland farm, you are pretty well tied. But there comes a time, when the last of the seed is sown and the turnips are still just too tender for the hoe, when the lambs are well grown and the chickens past the delicate stage and into sturdy adolescence, when you've made a good start at the peat-cutting and are only hoping for some rain, just a little to help things on—there comes a time, usually on a bright, still morning towards the end of June, when we find ourselves thinking—a little holiday, just a long week-end, would be wonderful! We look at each other, and at our small daughter, playing rather listlessly in the sand-pit, and immediately our minds are made up.

Off goes Jim, to arrange with our good neighbour to milk the house-cow and feed the chickens twice a day (when this neighbour feels like a breath of another airt we shall reciprocate the service) and into the house go I, to unearth the sleeping-bags, the two inflatable rubber mattresses and the old cot mattress, from the cupboard under the stairs. I hastily pack three biscuit tins with food, fill an egg-box, collect bathing-suits, old rubber shoes, the camera and a few other necessary odds and ends and stuff them, with the bedding, into the roomy back of our old, ramshackle van.

After a meal, we are off—just like that! The joy of finding ourselves all of a sudden on the road, going wherever we feel inclined, all ties and worries cast aside, is indescribable. Helen sits behind us, hugging our old black Labrador, in sheer delight. To be up and away, as birds take wing, that is half the joy of it. There is no agonised planning and contriving, no booking of rooms months ahead and then having to occupy them, whether it pours or shines. It is a fine morning, our work has reached a stage, we have a good neighbour, we are off!

Where to go is never any problem with us. The West is in our blood. We simply gravitate towards it as the birds migrate with the sun. We live in the hills, so the sea is what we need. And the Western sea, with the blue hills climbing out of it and the islands strung like pearls across its breast, is the only sea for us. Within an hour, even at the leisurely pace imposed on us by the age and the inexplicable whims of our faithful old 'jalopy', we can begin to smell the authentic smell of the West. Instantly, our blood quickens. Every few minutes we poke our noses out of one or other of the windows and take a rapturous sniff. Helen can sit still no longer. She bounces up and down and reaches over into the back for her spade and pail. The dog sits up and lifts her muzzle, getting the exciting, exhilarating scent.

We decide not to stop to make tea but to push right on to a camping place. Another leisurely hour and we have sighted it.

'There, on that headland, don't you think?' says Jim and we agree unanimously. 'Hold tight!', he says, as he steers us skilfully along the incredibly bumpy track to a spot where the fine green turf meets the white sand, with the little waves foaming up it.

We sit a moment, just gazing. Then out scrambles Helen, already shoeless, and runs across the sand and straight into the sea. The dog lollops after her and we follow, holding hands, as though all the years had fallen away from us.

We soon discover appetites exceeding even our usual. Helen helps her father to gather driftwood and build a fireplace of stones, while I find the source of the little stream we had noticed running into the sand. A spring of the clearest water, it proves to be, and I have the kettle filled as the fireplace is nearing completion. Ham and eggs and tomatoes, bread and butter and gallons of tea—how good they taste in such a spot!

As the sun begins to sink just a little towards the horizon, we start preparations for the night. Helen snuggles down, a beloved doll in her arms, and is asleep in two shakes. Jim and I make a hot night-cap on the ember of the fire, creep into our bags and lie blissfully at ease, perhaps reading till the light fails or gazing at the sea, watching the lighthouses wink out from the headlands. We wake early and lie snug in bed, while the fishing-boats glide past on their way into Loch Broom. How lovely it is to have the wide windows all around us! There is none of the stuffiness of a tent or caravan.

Of course, it's essential to choose a really remote spot for your car camp. Personally, we would never think of choosing any other. But there was one night, when we had retired early, as a fine mist was coming in off the sea, and, to our surprise and their utter consternation, we looked up to see two benighted walkers averting their glance discreetly from us! It must have been slightly disconcerting to come, miles from anywhere, on a van containing a slumbering child and two adults reclining in bed, a book and a steaming cup of tea clutched in either hand!

Towards the end of the last day, as late as we can make it, we pack up and make reluctantly for home. Our holiday has cost us nothing but the petrol for the journey, which was not long. What it has given us could never be reckoned, even in rubies.

August 3rd

We have had our July downpour and, with it, those sombre mists which creep in from the east, blotting out all the loved landmarks and making the world shrink to a grey nearness.

These mists are so muffling and enveloping. They shut us in on ourselves and almost depress our spirits. As we plod about our jobs, the small rain seeps under our collars and we long for a good stiff wind to blow the cloying clouds away and let us discard our dripping oilskins.

Then, suddenly, on our way to the road to meet the grocer's van, we come on a patch of bell heather, bright with bloom. It glows against the grey pall on the hillside and the sight of it revives us instantly.

We wander along, in the stillness, to where the small burn that has been dry for weeks is foaming, in a torrent of amber and white, among the stones. The mosses are vivid green along the bank. It's just a matter of looking more closely. The colours are there—green and purple and amber. And they are the colours of growth. A bright-blue sky may be just too harsh, draining the life from small, growing things. One thing we don't have to worry about in the heights is the possibility of flooding.

On every drying green hang great ropefuls of washing, gleaming like banners in the grey light. The croft wife certainly knows how to rejoice!

With fieldwork at a standstill we can go, without qualms of conscience, to the Wool Fair, the agricultural show or the sheepdog trials. There's nothing like making the best of a bad job.

A couple of owls have suddenly and unaccountably added themselves to the bird population about us. All day long they glide and flap over the rushes in the bog. One morning, as I was crossing the pasture, I noticed one of them circling above my head. He came gradually nearer and I thought for a moment he was going to alight on my shoulder. I stood still and looked up to find his great yellow eyes peering right into mine. His round, cat-like face turned slowly from side to side, as he summed me up. Then, apparently satisfied that I was not edible, he flapped slowly off to join his mate. It was a strange experience to encounter, at such close quarters and in broad daylight, a creature which one usually associates with mystery and twilight.

The crops are not forward enough to have suffered from their soaking. Grass is a lush growth everywhere. It seems to spring afresh every night, in the wake of the grazing sheep and cattle, and, heaven knows, they take their fill. Where would we be without grass, that herb that grows wild and often in unseen places, that herb we have cultivated and tamed and on which so much life now depends...?

There is so much good feeding everywhere that it seemed scarcely necessary for two of the stirks, one misty morning, to lean so heavily on the garden fence (at a weak spot which we had put off mending till the worst of the rain was over) that they were able to break through and demolish, in a couple of shakes, the entire supply of winter greens.

I suppose even the best of diets can become monotonous. We have now reinforced even the defences of the flower-plots in case a heifer, in romantic mood, should feel like a rose for breakfast!

We shall need drying winds and sun soon if the hay is to be harvested in anything like good shape. Meanwhile, we are glad of a gleam of light filtering through a slit in the grey roof over our heads. The smell of the clover, rising in a sudden sweet waft on the back of a stray wind-puff, can compensate for almost anything.

August 31st

After the July rain came a spell of August sunshine and everything leapt into exuberant life. The flower patch, at last, became something to look at, as roses, marguerites and marigolds unfurled their buds. The flower season, in these heights, is late and brief and each plant has a perilous journey to make towards blooming, in the face of its natural enemies. The fact that petals are actually spread at last, on the still air of an August morning, remains something of a miracle. We often stop in our tracks, in sheer wonder, to gaze into the face of some daringly lovely bloom.

The moor itself, of course, is spread with colour now, as the true heather comes fully into flower. To go looking for a strayed ewe or two is a delight, when the spaces are vivid and scented like warm honey. You find yourself forgetting the wanderers and looking, instead, for the odd sprig of white heather to bring luck to a friend.

Grouse are exceptionally strong on the wing this year. Often, a great sturdy covey of a dozen or more will rise from before our feet as we make an innocent sally down towards the well. It always pleases me that we none of us carry a gun and that hardly a pop is to be heard from any in these forgotten uplands.

What is the pleasure in tasting a slice of perhaps indifferently cooked game compared to that of seeing the bird, alive and free, whirring over the heather-tops, uttering his valiant shout—'go-back, go-back.'...?

Sentimental...? Yes, perhaps, if it's sentimental to prefer life to death...

The weather of early August put heart into everyone. Arrears of work are quickly made up when the sun shines. The clipping of the sheep, which was interrupted time and time again, when fanks became quagmires, was finished at last. The turnip-singling squads worked rhythmically up and down the steaming drills and a start was made at the hay.

Then, when hopes were high of a quick harvesting of this precious crop, came a 24-hour deluge, which turned the fragrant swathes into a sticky, tangled mass. Lucky were the folk who had managed to get at least small field-ricks made before the devastating downpour came. The corn has withstood the onslaught well and gleams, pale yellow, in the watery sunlight.

The kitchen garden has done us proud this year, in spite of everything. We've had raspberries which could only be described as luscious and the blackcurrants are clinging like fat, black grapes to the bushes.

When jam-making time comes round one's thoughts turn, reluctantly, to winter. Blackcurrant jam is so good, spread on scone or bread, at a winter tea-time. I'd rather eat a succulent berry, straight off the bush, with the sun's warmth still on it!

Already, there are signs that summer is on the wane. There is a sharp pungency in the evening air. We can no longer go to bed in daylight and there's a brittle look about the rowans as they emerge from their morning swathe of mist. Spiders' webs gleam on the fencing in the early sun.

Here and there, in the wood, a shaft of pure gold shows among the birch leaves. Toadstools, of fantastic size, appear in the strangest places.

In every house where there are children there are sad expressions on small faces as the opening of the school session comes, inevitably, round. In close on two months' summer freedom the young ones grow and bloom, like all other living things, at this season. One wonders, sometimes, how they will keep those long brown legs still under rigid desks and those darting eyes fixed on the narrow, printed page.

There is one other happy token to record—a pair of swallows rearing a second brood of nestlings in the byre. That makes one think that real autumn must still be a long way off.

Highland Healing

The use of 'herbs', plants of many kinds, as an alternative to chemically produced medicines in the treatment of illness or injury—herbalism—is becoming commonplace today. It has been known to Highland people for

Blaeberries—good for the kidneys!

centuries as, through a long process of observation and experimentation, they discovered which plant cured a specific affliction.

As a store of knowledge built up much of it was written down, in mediaeval times. A family of MacBeths, with a name-change to Beaton and, later, Bethune, became famed physicians to the Lords of the Isles. So valuable was the information recorded that in 1878 a small group of medical students at Edinburgh University established the Caledonian Medical Society, to promote the study of Celtic folk medicine.

Feverfew, which I found growing in an abandoned croft garden, helps to relieve the pain of migraine and of rheumatism in the joints. I often chew a leaf as a preventive measure! The nettle, which makes a delicious soup, is full of iron and can also be used to rub on rheumaticky knees! Bishopweed, which used to be grown near monasteries and inns, is good for the treatment of gout. The daisy has curative properties for disorders of the eye.

The dandelion—'Brigid's flower'—has many uses. An infusion of the whole plant makes a stomach tonic, the leaves are good in salad, the flowers make wine, the roots, dried and ground, are a good substitute for coffee. All these I have tried! I've heard that, in New Jersey, the dandelion is grown on a field scale, commercially.

Sorrel can be given, in an infusion, to reduce fever. The leaves of coltsfoot were often dried and smoked in clay pipes when tobacco was scarce or expensive. This practice was said to relieve asthma. Foxglove leaves were moistened and applied directly to the skin as a cure for eczema and boils.

We all know the relief that docken leaves give when rubbed into nettle stings.

The leaves of the hawthorn, which we chew in spring and call 'bread and cheese' because of their flavour, were said to keep high blood pressure in trim. Sphagnum moss, which is highly absorbent and even antiseptic, was used as a field-dressing during both world wars. The tuberous vetch was a useful plant. Its tubers were dried and chewed like gum to ward off hunger, a useful attribute when times were hard.

A favourite plant of St Columba's, on Iona, was St John's wort. It is known to contain a substance which allows adrenalin to flow and can be used in cases of depression. Blaeberries are said to help dissolve kidney stones. Raspberries were prized as medicine for pregnant women. Meadowsweet,the 'queen of the meadows' is better than aspirin for curing fevers and headaches.

The juniper, said to be the first plant to emerge after the ice-age, produced berries which were used as an astrigent. Sloes, the fruit of the blackthorn, made a cure for sore throats and winter coughs. The vitamin C contained in rose-hips is usually enough to ward off most winter ills.

These are some of the plants which helped in the treatment of disorders in times now past. It's good, I think, that their uses are being rediscovered as our systems begin to baulk at the constant application of chemically-based drugs.

September 28th

We woke, the other Sunday morning, to find a dazzling sight. We followed one another to the kitchen window to peer out and there, on the shoulders of Ben Wyvis and the peaks of the Strathfarrar hills, lay a bright cover of fresh snow. We looked down the strath and saw the neighbouring fields of barely ripened oats, the coils of hay still waiting a final gathering.

To find snow on the standing stooks is no unusual occurrence, for it is often late October before the corn is led. To catch the gleam of winter when the oat-crop is still pale gold makes one realise what a miracle each upland harvest is. In the heights one is never dismayed. The fact that the odds are so heavily against it makes the achievement of any sort of harvest a satisfaction.

It's grand to be getting a good-sized tattie again. Those that you dig with the fork, a few at a time, are somehow so much sweeter and fresher than those you take, later on, out of the clamp. As you gather them, at leisure, you have time to count what each seed has produced and to savour the pungent smell of turned earth.

There is one wild harvest we are missing this year—the fruit of the rowan tree. Hardly a berry is to be seen anywhere, though normally, at this time, they are hanging in heavy, glistening clusters on the trees. The frosty winds of late spring must have shrivelled the blossom.

It seems we shall have to do without that glass of rowan wine we find reviving on a winter's night. It is so easy to make. Simply steep the berries for ten days in boiling water, along with a small piece of root ginger. Stir the mixture each day, then strain it, add a pound of sugar to a quart of liquid and—bottle!

The result, if one can refrain from imbibing till the stuff is well matured, is a smooth, pungent drink, said to contain the secret of eternal youth. A guest of ours once gallantly mistook it for liqueur whisky!

Alas, this year it looks as if we shall have to make a witch's brew out of potatoes, or nettles or something.

The children are not too sure about school yet. It's still irksome to any youngster who, for close on eight weeks, has been as unfettered as a lark, to stay in one place for hours on end. When the wind begins to bare its teeth they'll be glad that their classroom is small and cosy and secure.

When the swallows gather in chattering groups along the steading roof and the robin's clear notes are heard, with a slight shock of surprise, in the wood, it is time our own preparations for winter were complete.

That gleam of snow on the high tops, glimpsed from the corner of an eye, spurs us on. Through the still air we catch the creak of wheels on the road, half a mile away. We look up and see a neighbour's white mare plodding along, the cart behind her piled high with brushwood. Along the old peat-road that winds into the hill, a tractor noses its way and returns, in an hour or two, with a trailer-load of peats. For all the handiness of the electric gadgets there's hardly a house that doesn't rely, for real winter comfort, on an open fire, a living, leaping thing to keep you company.

Our modern conveniences are very much at the mercy of the elements here. The wind and the frost are always liable to take control. Remembering that electric cables, like water-pipes, may become the playthings of frost and gale, we are laying in, as well as peat and wood, a stock of paraffin and candles, just in case.

November 16th

Some October days are among the loveliest of the year. There was the Saturday, for instance, when we went down the wooded slope to the shore of Loch Ness, to gather brambles. The sky was that intense, luminous blue which only autumn can produce, and the water of the loch vied with it in blueness.

The sunlight filtered warmly through the yellowing leaves of birch and rowan and hazel. The rocks shone black and the birch bark was polished silver. Only one colour was missing—the red glint of the rowan berry.

We stopped often in our picking to watch the small birds that are strangers to our own bare moorland—a wren, a tree-creeper, a dazzling, debonair bullfinch.

We pounced with amazement and delight on some woodland flowers still blooming, beside the toadstools and the fallen hazel nuts.

We cling to such October days, for it seems as though, on their backs, it might be possible to bypass winter, the winter we've been preparing for, and land without more ado in spring.

Of course, October can show another face. Sudden showers of ice-cold rain, flung by a wind that springs out of nowhere, send us scurrying to the barn, turning up our coat collars and blowing on our fingers as we go. Standing in the doorway, while the north sky turns dramatically black, and then is lit by a gleaming rainbow, we wonder, for a moment, is this autumn or April, that cruellest month?

It's autumn all right, for up there, on the latest places, the stooks are still standing out in the fields and some of them are ominously dark in colour. Suddenly, the sky clears. We look over our shoulders at the fresh white powdering of snow on the tops of the blue hills, as we hurry back to scrabble for some more tatties in the cold, heavy earth. The crop, on the whole, is not a good one anywhere. The growing season was just too wet and sunless.

It's time the cattle were sold, before they lose condition. Every market morning now, there is commotion up and down the strath, a shouting of men and a scurrying of over-eager dogs, as stirks and weaned calves and farrow cows are gathered into the fanks to await the float.

There goes all the work and anxiety of months and years to take its chance in the market-place. The black-faced lambs have still a week or two to enjoy the freedom of the hills.

With the early dark comes the compensation of the ceilidh. As you weave your way by torchlight along the shortcut to a neighbour's house the smell of the fresh peat-smoke comes at you in a reassuring waft.

You speculate together about the radioactive cows in that fabulous south country, where, it seems, anything can happen,* and you wonder

*A serious accident had occurred at Windscale Nuclear Power Station in October. There was widespread radioactive contamination of the surrounding countryside.

101

about it all and you're glad that, whatever comes, you're in it together. The old solidarity is there—man and beast, rock, hill and star.

When the guisers arrive you ply them gladly with nuts and apples and give them more than a bright sixpence for their song. You know just how fitting it is to keep a welcome for this gay, laughing acknowledgment of the supernatural.

December 27th

On the croft, Christmas is usually a time when a snug, carefree life within doors can be enjoyed by man and beast. The weather is often astonishingly mild by day, with skies of pale, clear blue, and a softness in the west wind that makes one think of spring. With outdoor work practically at a standstill, apart from the carting of fodder for the animals, we have time to work away in the house at preparing festivities for the children.

New Year is for the grown-ups and is a comparatively simple matter. As long as one has something in the bottle and a hefty black bun in the cake-tin, the natural exuberance of friends and neighbours takes care of that festivity.

For Christmas, there are puddings and pies to be made, gifts to be worked at in secret and stowed carefully away and decorations to be devised. But, with the lamp lit and everyone 'in for the night' by half past four these happy tasks are easily accomplished. The evening world is reduced to the charmed circle of the lamp's golden light. The peats glow on the hearth. Out in the byre, the cows lie contentedly in their deep beds of straw. The horse stands motionless in his stall, dreaming of spring grass. The sheep, with their uncanny instinct for self-preservation, find themselves shelter and sustenance in the folds of the hill. The hens scratch happily away at the dry litter in their cosy, lamplit shed. All the long months of outdoor work have resulted in this winter snugness. Everything is battened down till spring.

But last Christmas things refused to stay battened down! About the third week in December came the first of the north-easterly gales, bringing the blizzard conditions which were to last, off and on, till nearly the end of May.

We were awakened one night by the sound of this fearsome wind roaring up under the roof-slates. A little later it seemed as though the whole house, with its two-foot walls of granite and whinstone, was shaking like a jelly. The floorboards seemed to be heaving like the planks of a storm-tossed ship. We got through the night and prepared to face the day.

In the normal way, we are practically independent of shops. The weekly van provides us with everything we do not produce ourselves. But at Christmas a little shopping is inevitable, and this, of all days, was our Christmas shopping day!

Placing the soup-pot on the hob and a hearty pile of sandwiches on the kitchen table, I left my husband to cope with the animals and set off, clutching small Helen firmly by the hand for fear the gale capsize her. The sky away to the north, beyond Ben Wyvis, had a black, evil look about it. But the wind was at our back and in no time Helen was deposited in the safe shelter of the schoolroom and I was wafted the rest of the two miles to the bus.

Town was a thronging mass of shoppers. The shops were bright and warm, but I was soon bewildered by the dazzling array of wares. There was something unreal about it all, a sort of jauntiness about the tinsel and the gaudy cardboard robins and the effigies of Santa Claus that jarred. I made my purchases as quickly as I could and bolted to the bus. Already I was longing to get back to the clean freshness of the heights. A home in the wilds has a magic element of security about it, especially in midwinter. You cherish it, as it cherishes you, and you ride out every storm together.

By mid-afternoon, I was struggling up the hill, a bulging shopping-bag in either hand. At the school gate I found Helen waiting, with her father, who had come to meet us. Snow was falling fast now and drifting into fantastic patterns as it fell. We plodded on together in silence, saving our breath.

As we reached the gate, I looked up. Something was missing from the familiar landscape. 'The shed,' I gasped, 'where is it?' My husband grinned and gestured with his hands. The familiar red corrugated sheets were lying in a heap, like a collapsed pack of cards. We reached the house and found the large galvanised water-butt lying across the back-door step. A huge limb of our oldest and dearest rowan tree hung limply from the parent trunk. It was a desolating scene. We went in and shut the door on the raging blackness, spread our fingers to the fire and drank cups of scalding tea, supremely glad to be alive and sheltered.

Next morning the storm had more or less blown itself out. Helen was despatched to school for the last day of the term and, the cow and hens seen to, I got down to Christmas preparations in earnest. I gathered fir boughs and trails of ivy and plucked the Christmas cockerel. Then, with pick and shovel, I went to dig up the canister of rowan-berries, buried so easily in the autumn but now, with the ground like iron, so difficult to retrieve. But I came on it at last and opened it in the kitchen to find the berries glowing fresh and red as the day they were gathered, and all ready to be made into decorations.

After an early dinner, we set off with a bottle of home-made rowan-berry wine and a Christmas cake as gifts for an elderly neighbour. There was still the tree to get from the derelict woodland up the hill, but that would have to wait till next day and we prayed another storm would not intervene.

We reached home at dusk, just as Helen arrived from school. 'Mummy, what's that thing leaning against the front door?' she asked, round-eyed and startled, 'something dark and funny. I saw it as I passed.'

We went through the kitchen and opened the front door, and into our arms, prickly and aromatic and dark green and mysterious, fell the loveliest Christmas tree we had ever seen! We took it into the lamplight and saw the frost crystals shining on its branches. It was the surprise and delight of it that made the moment! But how did it get there, how in all the world? Then we saw, tied to the trunk, a small piece of crumpled paper. Scrawled on it in pencil were the words— 'Here is a tree. Billy' Just that. But how like a neighbour's boy! Billy, of course. He had known we wanted a tree, he had known the storm made it difficult for us to get over for one, with all the jobs about the place become doubly laborious, so he had gone to get one for us himself.

That night, when Helen was tucked up safely in bed, I took my lantern and went out to the byre to milk the cow. The young black-bird, who had taken up his abode in the steading since the first of the wintry weather, flew up onto a rafter at the opening of the door. As the milk began to spurt into the pail, he looked down at me with his bright, gleaming eyes and uttered a tiny inward warble of song. How shadowy and shy, how charmingly companionable he was! Milking done, I stroked the cow's glossy neck and went to gather the warm, golden eggs from the straw next door. The horse gave a low whinny as I passed his stall and as I came in, the dog nosing my hand, under the enormous stars, I felt a glow of thankfulness that our Christmas was in the heart. How could it be otherwise, when we had kindly neigh-bours, the comforting presence of stalled beasts and the firm companionship of earth and sky?

Came Christmas Eve and a party in the village hall and—a snow-storm of renewed intensity! We peered out through the frost-encrusted windows. Would it be wise to attempt the journey? Probably not, but the party had been looked forward to so eagerly, for so many, many weeks.

By mid-afternoon we had the animals well fed and bedded, the cracks in the byre wall stuffed with old sacks to keep out the driving snow, Helen and ourselves swathed in layers of coats and waterproofs over our party clothes, and we were off. Heads well down, we struggled foot by foot along the short cut through the heather. Within ten minutes we were so plastered with driven snow that we looked like three live snowmen. We reached a neighbouring house and, the breath knocked out of us, we simply had to seek a moment's shelter. We were given a drink of tea and the loan of a stout walking stick apiece and, before our dripping clothes made too much havoc in our kind host's kitchen, we set off with renewed energy. Soon we saw other dim figures approaching from various directions through the whirling madness of the storm and, within minutes, we were there.

What joy it was to peel off our cumbersome garments and thaw our toes and fingers at the huge blazing fire! The hall was quite unrecognisable as its usual, work-a-day self. Coloured streamers and lanterns, a glittering, loaded tree and the wondering faces of a crowd of youngsters made it seem like a little lost piece of fairyland. But, was this reality, or the black, raging inferno outside? This, we decided, and plunged gaily into the Dashing White Sergeant!

Carols, the haunting tenderness of Gaelic songs, crackers, hot pies and cream cakes and oranges and a visit from Santa Claus made a wonderful Christmas Eve of it.

When the good-nights were said, we muffled ourselves up again and prepared to set off, in convoy this time, on the homeward trek. To our astonishment, we stepped out into a still, glistening world. Not a breath of wind stirred over the vast white spaces round us. The hills were like picture-book mountains, enormous and shining and remote. The sky was brilliant with stars. We crunched our way contentedly home, lit the lamp and rigged the tree and tumbled into bed.

Christmas morning! We woke early and lay listening for the sound of the wind. Was it rising? Would the road be blocked again? Would another storm prevent the children from over the hill coming to share our Christmas? We feared it might but, putting this thought to the back of our minds, we kindled the fire, made tea and smiled at Helen's joy as she delved into her stocking.

Then, out to feed the animals and in again to see to the roasting of the chicken and the steaming of the pudding. Towards three o'clock we gathered at the kitchen window to scan the horizon for a sight of the children coming down the short-cut. There they were, five small, bobbing figures, kicking their way lustily through the snow. A

THE CROFTING WAY

neighbour had brought them in his van as far as the snow-bound road would permit and had promised to meet them at the same point later on. We blessed him and took the children into the warmth of the fire.

Then we danced to the mad tunes that Billy got out of his mouth-organ and played the old Christmas games and sang the old songs of Christmas round the decked tree and ate and drank and were very merry.

When darkness fell, I slipped out to the byre for the milking. The cows lay contentedly cudding. The yellow straw shone like gold in the lamp's light. The hay in the stalls smelt sweet and good. The blackbird sang his tiny, lilting carol. It was Christmas within and without.

As my husband set off to shepherd the children to the road, we lit fresh candles on the tree and drew back the curtains so that the light would shine out across the fields.

Later that night, as we lay warm in bed, we heard the wind rising ominously once more. But we only snuggled deeper under the blankets. Come what might in the way of gales, blizzards or drifts, we could cope with them all. We had had a wonderful Christmas!

During that year my husband, like so many crofters of former times, took a spell working away from home to supplement our income. My writing was going quite well and I was contributing short stories to B.B.C. programmes and so on, but still this did not provide a steady supplement. The work of the croft was on an organized basis and I knew that, in an emergency, help from neighbours would always be forthcoming. Loneliness was compensated for by the happiness of reunion.

Though wage-labour was always an alien concept to the older Highland people, yet necessity often drove their descendents, with large families living on small crofts, to look for it. And the boys would seek apprenticeships in trades, becoming skilled joiners, stonemasons, smiths. The girls still living at home would often go off to work at harvests in the south, bringing their wages back. Perilous journeys they made, on foot, by rough hill tracks, and were sometimes waylaid and robbed.

At times sources of employment arrived, as it were, on the crofters' doorsteps. In the early 1800s the building of the Caledonian canal provided labouring work for the men of many communities along the shores of Loch Ness. Hard labour it was, done with pick and shovel and barrow, on a meagre diet of oatmeal and a small ration of whisky for those 'working in the water'. It was almost within commuting distance of their homes and, though they were lodged in primitive huts, they could, and often did, get back to their crofts at ploughing, peat-cutting and harvest times.

In the mid-nineteen-hundreds there was work to be had in road-building and on the hydro-electric schemes. The Forestry Commission provided jobs in the planting of huge breaks of conifers.

There had been, as we have seen, some estate work, in draining, wall-building and so on, One huge dry-stone dyke that marked the boundary of the hill-grazing is still partly standing. And on our own ground we sometimes come across the heaps, now mostly grassed over, of small stones broken by Iain Mor, Big John, the old man who plied his trade as stone-breaker, to help in the patching-up of the roads. Younger men could get almost full-time employment at work on the roads, filling holes, trimming verges and so on. And, of course, our 'Post' had an important, essential job and worked a splendid croft into the bargain.

1958

February 1st

Our New Year ceilidh jaunts were made under ideal conditions this year. By day the sun shone from a china-blue sky and in the evening the light of a huge moon was reflected from the frosted surfaces of field and hill and loch. Everyone was on the move and visiting was a delight.

Now, when the last hand has been shaken and the last dram drained, we find ourselves isolated behind soft walls of snow. We had a hearty New Year. Doubtless it will be good for us to tighten our belts a bit and bring fresh muscles into use.

Everywhere there is a great wielding of shovels and, in between whiles, a scanning of the horizon for a sight of the snow-plough coming up the road. So many vans visit us these days in the good weather that we have got more and more out of the habit of planning ahead for supplies.

We need never really worry. Only yesterday, when we had re-signed ourselves to the prospect of a meatless dinner, a neighbour, on his way back from the hill, appeared on the doorstep, knocking the snow from his boots and holding aloft a freshly-killed rabbit.

'Got him with the stick,' he said, with a cheery grin. 'He'll make you a stew.'

Now that the shrieking of the north wind has died, a great, white stillness fills the days. The ring of an axe, from a croft half a mile away, sets the dog's ears pricking.

There is little movement anywhere. The branches of the rowans bear their blobs of snow, like blossom. The cattle and the hens are content to stay in their warm quarters, quietly rustling the straw and contemplating their destiny. Only a shepherd, looking strangely large, like a figure in a dream, his dog lolloping through the soft drifts behind him, moves across the hill, bringing his sheep to the sheltered slopes. Now and again a pack of grouse whirrs low over the dazzling surface of the moor.

We miss the laughter and the clear calling of the children on the road, morning and evening, for between home and school the drifts are deep. But Helen is in her element. Being now of a size to make use of the battered old family ski-things she has become a winter sports enthusiast. And she's lucky. For her, there is no wearisome travelling to the enticing slopes. Right at the doorstep she is shod with magic as she plunges away over the diamond-studded spaces. A fall or two as a ski encounters a submerged molehill and many a long uphill plod— these are just part of the game.

Only when the sky fades to mauve, the snow glimmers with greenish light and the thought of tea at the fire becomes really attractive can she be persuaded to lay her skis by, in the barn, till morning.

As for ourselves, the snow gives us pause, which is a good thing. When the beasts are fed, the path to the steading cleared and the wood chopped we still have time, in the lengthening light, to marvel at the shapes of the sculptured drifts.

There is the solidity of stone about them, with the blue shadows stretching from their chiselled edges. Yet the impermanence that is the heart of them makes us try to hold their beauty firm in the mind's eye. We're glad the snow has come, as long as the sheep don't suffer. Isolated in a world in which the basic elements are all-important, we discover our weakness and our strength. We are toughened and awakened to fresh thought and effort. The snow will fill the springs against summer drought and give the ground and the roots of all growing things the blessing of sound sleep. Under snow, they say, there is bread.

Poaching

A rabbit does indeed make a tasty stew. Many times starvation must have been kept at bay by a hot, nourishing meal of 'coineanach'. It does not seem that much use was made of their skins. I have a suit, bought in a well-known big store, which is made of (I quote the label) 67% acrylic, 21% polyester, 12% rabbit hair. It's a light, warm fabric and has an attractive fleck in it. They are attractive creatures, rabbits, sitting up washing their faces in the morning dew. Their depredations in gardens and field crops are disastrous, but nevertheless we missed them when myxamatosis struck. They are reappearing now. It's not so long since even the killing of a rabbit was a crime. The midwinter snow always brought out one or two local guns to have a go at the white hares. Perhaps a small gesture of defiance?

Summer would take an intrepid pair up to the hill lochs, one to trail the 'otter', a device for ensnaring trout, the other to keep watch for unfriendly intruders. Perhaps a poacher turned gamekeeper?

A roe deer for a New Year family dinner was another matter, undertaken, nevertheless, in early daylight and the spoils gathered at night.

With many estates changing hands so rapidly you were never sure on whose land you were walking, shouldering rod or gun.

That old adage: 'a fish from the stream, a deer from the forest...' as a

THE CROFTING WAY

Highlander's right is no more than a memory now, but the instinct lingers. I'm hungry, my family is hungry, I must kill what I need. The antics of the well-fed who came up to kill for 'sport' made many a good tale at a fireside ceilidh.

March 8th

We've come smiling out of another blizzard. It was bad enough while it lasted, though not nearly as bad as in other places, but we were ready for it. And it disappeared magically on the back of a south-east gale.

Then—we had an early glimpse of spring, soon followed by a return to frost and a powdering of snow. The withered grasses and the bare-armed trees shuddered at the touch of a bold north wind. But the brief glimpse put heart into us.

It was on Valentine's Day that spring put in an appearance. That's the day, they say, when the birds choose their mates and, sure enough, the larks were soaring and spilling their song recklessly into the blue air. We stopped in our tracks, eyes and ears greedy for the sight and sound of them. Every year, this miracle of the returning larks amazes us. We know quite well it will occur. We begin to look for it from the end of January, if the weather is open. Yet when it actually unfolds before us, it brings the same excitement.

The early work went with a swing that day, for not only was there lark-song in the air, there was also the authentic smell of spring, the tang of crumbling earth, of earth that is eager for seed.

Thoughts, everywhere, were turned to the possibility of ploughing. Of course, we knew quite well that the wind would probably swing to the north and encase everything in frost again. And so it turned out. But there was real joy in getting out the oilcans and making the ploughing gear ready. Later in the day, as though at a given signal, fires sprang up along the line of the hill. 'Charlie and Jock are burning the old whins,' we said, as we sniffed the aromatic smoke.

It was a prosaic enough statement, but there was a lilt in the voice that uttered it, for there's magic to those fires. They destroy old growth to make way for new. That's plain enough. But they do more. By purifying the ground they seem to lay old ghosts, to banish fears, to bring us nearer to the certainty that renewal is what matters.

So, by the evening of Valentine's Day, we were all lifted into a state of optimism. Meeting a neighbour on the road, we saw in his glance the light that we felt was in our own. 'It's been a grand day', was our mutual, happy greeting.

Our neighbour Jock, who makes walking-sticks and beehives

The peat-stacks and the wood-piles have dwindled alarmingly as a result of the cold spells we've endured. And the tattie-pits, this year, have not their usual reassuring bulk. But the hens, bless them, lay on determinedly.

On a morning of black frost, when your fingers stick painfully to the handle of the feed-pail, there's nothing so cheering as the sound of a hen placidly announcing that she has just deposited a golden egg in the warm, polished straw of her nest.

However fiercely winter may continue to batter us, we shall not be dismayed. We know it has only a rearguard action left to fight. Light lingers in the fields till six o'clock these evenings.

We've heard a snatch of lark-song and smelt the stirring earth. Soon, we shall be looking for the triumphant flash of the returning peewits and winter will be in full retreat.

April 5th

March was a hard month. It came in deceptively like a lamb, with pale skies and little scurries of soft air. The larks sang from first light and long after dusk the peewits were clamouring about the shadowed fields.

Then the wind swung to the north again and all hope of starting spring work was gone.

There was much visual beauty in the days. Never, I think, has snow sparkled as it did last month, under a deep blue sky and in the light of a dazzling sun. Mornings and evenings were splendid. We simply had to stand and watch the superb crimson sunsets and marvel at the length of the glittering icicles along the steading eaves.

But it was a cold, silent splendour. As it continued the larks' song came only as a thin trickle of music through the sharp air. The peewits went back to the lower ground, only an odd one venturing up again to settle warily on a molehill protruding through the snow, looking bewildered, thwarted in his courtship for lack of a daring mate.

A few early lambs staggered into life on the hillside. We await the full lambing season with trepidation. No ewe can give of her best when all she can scrape to eat is a few frozen shoots of heather and some burn-side gleanings of withered grass.

Winter feed of every kind ran short. Lorries struggled gallantly along the icy roads, delivering loads of hay to bridge the hungry gap.

With the ground like iron again and all thoughts of ploughing put aside, we're back to the winter occupations—carting sticks for the fire and forcing numbed fingers to the perennial job of repairing fences.

Ceilidhing, normally abandoned at this time of year as outdoor work is prolonged well into the lengthening evenings, is still indulged in. But there is an unreal feel about it. It's impossible to relax when one's mind is on the hazards of a difficult lambing-time and fingers and feet itch to be at the essential work that can't be tackled. An anxious note will creep into the talk and breath is held and ears cocked towards the wireless, as each weather forecast is announced.

The children are beginning to tire of making snowmen in the playground. But how can one swing a skipping-rope or chase a ball when the ground slides from under the feet? Still it's healthy weather, for it defeats the germs. Young cheeks glow and eyes are bright.

In spite of everything, this is not really winter. There's a heat in the midday sun that tans the skin. One has the feeling that, once the air softens and the snow really melts, everything will burst miraculously into life, like Japanese flowers immersed in water.

This morning I saw a pair of curlews rise and go gliding over the moor. Their long, bubbling call was the happiest music I've heard in a long time.

May 17th

April is often 'the cruellest month'. This year it was, perhaps, more cruel than usual. You never cease to expect it to be a time of release from the toils of winter, when the mere fact of stepping outside into the sweetened air is an intense pleasure. Yet, in actual fact, it most often turns out, as it has this year, to be a time of anxiety.

Never, it seemed, would the ground dry out enough to let the plough get a proper bite. Now, the seed-bags are standing in the brown furrows, but the seed will be a long time sprouting.

The withered heather itself will hardly take the flame, for the snow is still lying in stubborn patches on the hill. The cattle beasts, thin and woebegone after their long winter, stand shivering in the lee of the steading, turning their backs to the harsh wind and the squalls of sleet. The lambs frisk defiantly, to keep themselves warm, while their mothers are anxiously absorbed in seeking for a bite.

Yet we know, as one recognises a recurring nightmare, that we've been through all this before. Soon it will be time to wake up and we shall find that things are not as black as they look. It's amazing how everything rights itself in the long run.

Meantime, we have to content ourselves with the odd day when the air is unexpectedly still, the sweet scent rises and the warmth of the sun can be felt, like a tangible blessing. Then, heads bare and sleeves rolled to the elbow, we cast about for a sign. And we find it—in the blaze of the coltsfoot along the dyke-side, in the flash of emerald growth below the dun tangle of withered grass, in the sprightly strutting of a wagtail across the mud in the yard.

The peewits dive frantically at us as we pass along the field-side, sure proof that nests are well on the way. The oyster catchers' gallant piping makes us raise our eyes to admire their dapper plumage and bright orange bills. The swans are on the loch again, riding the choppy water, under the grey storm clouds.

Our little school, its roll reduced to two, has had to close its door. Helen is now spirited away in a bus each morning to a school five miles away—and is spirited back each evening at half past four. She was happy in the quiet classroom and on the rambling journey home that took such an unconscionable time when there was always something new to see in the familiar landscape—snow-patterns to make in winter, nests to watch in spring, flowers in summer, wild raspberries to eat.

But I think she has absorbed a background that will keep her on an even keel in any hurly-burly.

There is television, now, in a hill-top kitchen. The telephone line has reached our gate. But there is no sound of children on the road. We are acquiring the gadgets for recording life, but we are left with fewer and fewer human beings facing the raw realities of living.

It's a pity, for the echo, at second-hand, can never match the actuality. An April morning may be an anxious time—but it's still an April morning. If you step firmly into the chill of it you are sure to come on a sign and a wonder.

A School Closes

The closing of a school is always a sad occasion. With two pupils left and no younger ones waiting for a place, it was inevitable. The Director of Education came personally to acquaint us of the decision and to discuss future arrangements for the girls. We were grateful for his concern.

There had been a school in Abriachan for many years. The earliest recorded teacher was James Rhind in 1766, when there were nine girls and twenty-five boys on the register. He was appointed, as were many subsequent teachers, by the Scottish Society for the Propagation of Christian Knowledge.

The first school building is now a rickle of stones beside the road, the one built after the Education Act of 1872 stands close by. At one time, between the two world wars, it catered for over a hundred pupils and had three teachers. Many of the children were orphans, boarded with crofting families. Latterly the roll had been falling quite rapidly.

Today, there are minibuses and even taxis to transport the children to schools in more populated parts. Some of them suffer from sickness on the tortuous roads, some from minor forms of bullying when the driver's attention is distracted. Those walks to and from school, in the days when there was no danger from deranged adults, were a form of healthy exercise.

The playground games were healthy, too, with much running, hopping, skipping, jumping, games of skill with handball as well as football and shinty practice for the boys. For the girls, singing accompanied many of the games, the rhythm and tune fitting the action naturally.

There was little competitive spirit in these activities. Today, in some places, teachers are encouraging a return to this type of play. It does a little to counteract the inactivity of hours in front of the computer or the television at home, when, sadly, for town children, street games are out.

For the children of the crofts certain jobs would be awaiting their return from school—feeding the hens, collecting eggs, bringing in sticks or peat for the fire. Playtime at school was an eagerly enjoyed part of their day.

The last two pupils in Abriachan School—Helen and Janet

In the bigger schools to which they were conveyed there would never be quite the same intimacy of companionship, when they had to mingle with children of very different backgrounds. Indeed, at first, a certain amount of hostility was evident. The jokes and jibes that everyone understood were lost on a crowd of strangers. But things settled after their first introduction to this wider world.

September 18th

A Highland moor on a fine September morning—where in the world, I wonder, could you come on a fairer place than this?

As the white mist slowly lifts from the hollows, the sun climbs above the rise to the east and floods the hill slopes with light, making the heather bloom glow. The blue of the sky deepens and a light breeze skims over the shining surface of the loch, bringing with it the honey-scent of the farther hills, the scent of warmed heather and pine.

Against this background the life of the croft moves steadily on towards the climax of harvest. A day or two of this God-sent weather and all the dreary weeks of grey skies and downpour are forgotten. There's a smile in every eye and an extra ounce of strength in every arm.

Actually, in these heights, the crops have not suffered anything like as badly as those on the large, low-ground farms. With judicious and speedy handling our small crops of hay were got safely into field-ricks during the prized, bright intervals. Then, when a steady spell of fine weather came along, it was a simple matter to build the ricks into stacks.

The corn stood bravely up to the summer storms for they caught it when it was still green and resilient. Only now is it beginning to pale in the yellow sunlight and to grow brittle with ripeness.

The turnips are plumping nicely and the tatties, though a mixed lot, are better than last year.

The soakings have kept the pastures fresh and succulent, so that the sheep and cattle can spend hours contentedly cudding and putting on gloss and weight for the autumn sales.

It's difficult to believe that this is autumn. At noon, when the horse stands swishing his tail in the lea of the steading, it seems more like midsummer. The children, the girls in cotton frocks and sandals, run in from school clamouring for cool drinks. They long for Saturday so that they can go paddling in the burn.

But the rowan berries are glistening red and the robins, in the birches at the edge of the wood, are singing their clear, rather sad little song. The swallows skim happily over the sunlit fields then settle, chattering, on the byre roof. In the morning, when we step outside, we can see the long trails the cattle make in the dew-soaked grass as they move slowly forward, breakfasting as they go.

The level beams of the early sun floodlight the cobwebs festooning the fences. In the evening, the moon that stares at us out of the velvet sky is huge and yellow, portending harvest, with the carts swaying home under the last loads of tight-packed sheaves.

October 23rd

The long golden days of our Indian summer have given way to tradition-ally boisterous autumn weather. There's the gleam of snow, now, on the tops of the farthest hills. Even the west wind has an edge to it that turns the rain to sleet. A harvest field is a delight to the eye when a glint of sun strikes the rows of yellow sheaves. An hour later, when the wind is driving the rain slantwise into the heart of the stooks, the same field becomes a place of desolation. The strongest arms grow tired of turning the same sodden sheaves over and over again. As time goes by the stoutest hearts grow tired, with the knowledge that each passing day reduces the feeding value of whatever will eventually be harvested. Then there is the nagging worry of the tatties. They should be lifted now, before the swirling floodwater washes the ground from the tubers. When two harvests overlap it is always a testing time for patience and endurance. But we have our certainties and one of them is that harvest is always, somehow or other, achieved.

Prospects for the hay looked bad enough, yet the stacks have risen. They are not stacks of perfect hay, perhaps, but they are not black or reeking. There they stand, comely in design, bastions against winter, satisfying to eye and mind. The peat-stacks, too, are standing sentinel at the gables of the houses, and the wood-piles grow a little higher each day.

One harvest it has been a delight to gather is that of the rowan berries. Never, I think, have I seen such enormous clusters of brilliant fruit as this year. After last season's dearth they are a special joy.

The time of the ceilidh is here. Though it can't assume its carefree atmosphere until the anxiety of harvest is over, still the pleasure of gathering round an evening fire is very real.

Soon, we shall be making room at the hearth for that queer collection of visitors, who, with their calico masks, their turnip head-pieces and their horsehair tails, look as if they'd just arrived from another planet. We shall press nuts and sweets into camouflaged hands and beg for a song, before the guisers disappear into the night.

The geese are back. There's nothing quite like the thrill of seeing the long, wedged lines of them coming in out of a black north sky and of listening to their high clamour. Aloof they are, yet akin to us in their seeking for shelter from the cold.

The fieldfares are late in reaching us this year. The larks, bless them, are still with us. The other morning I watched one launch himself into the temporarily blue air above the drenched corn stooks and pour out a full volume of song, for all the world as though it were a spring morning and time to set the plough going.

November 27th

November in the Highlands can be one of the loveliest months, and this is the way most of it has been with us this year. Each calm, sunlit day is a small miracle in itself, for it wards off, as if by magic, the approach of winter. The grass is still green enough to tempt the cattle beasts out into lingering about the fields, well into the darkening, though they're glad enough to be brought into the shelter of the byre last thing. The hens, their combs aflame in the yellow sunlight, strut delightedly about the green places, packing their crops with the insects the warmth has lured out. All this feeding means a saving of winter fodder and the promise of extra eggs in the dark days. The corn-stacks are standing, now, beside the haystacks. They're a bit dark in colour, maybe, but the wonder is that they are there at all. The tattie-pits have a fair enough bulk to them and the peat-stacks are reassuringly solid.

It's a real pleasure, on a still November afternoon, to lift the tatties from the brown, crumbling earth and to see their skins drying before your eyes as they lie in the pit, waiting to be covered. As you straighten your back you watch the midges dancing in the golden light and you look up and see a couple of swans flying in to their quarters on the loch and you wonder what it was you were worried about the week before. Everything is coming out even, as you knew it would, really. And there's this added bonus of fragile beauty to each day. There are the colours—the browns of earth and bracken and tree-leaf, the gold, the yellow, the green, brown and red of innumerable other leaves, the blue of the loch water and the sudden patches of rainbow that hang about the blue-grey sky. The bright colours and the living sounds are doubly precious when you know that, any time now, they may be obliterated by the first of the blizzards. Meantime, the sharp tang of frost in the morning air is a spur to work and, at the end of the day, the dampness of dusk makes the fire in the hearth twice as welcome.

There's the glint of a star in the sky, now, when Helen comes home from school. When she sets off in the morning the star has hardly paled. But here and there there's still an odd sprig of heather in bloom on the moor and, in the garden, a primrose is flowering quite happily. Even in November there's a forward look!

Song-Making

In the long dark evenings of November time was found, long ago, before the days of radio and television, for the composing of those songs that helped life along. Song had always come to people as naturally as everyday speech. Some of the earliest melodies are thought to have been based on the songs of birds. Words for the songs came naturally to everyone, too, though each community would have one or two specially gifted song-makers who could claim the title of 'township bard'. They composed in the oral tradition. The people often requested songs, regarding them as a form of therapy. Satires and humorous songs would relieve tension in any critical situation which might arise between neighbours or in dealings with chiefs or landlords. And local and national political events were often dealt with.

Sometimes 'flytings' between township bards occurred, jealous fighting when the composing became competitive. This served to sharpen their skills. Màiri Mhór nan Orainn (Big Mary of the Songs), a Skye woman, composed many songs during the latter part of the nineteenth century, which helped the people greatly in their struggles against overweening authority in the time of the Land Wars. Though she was illiterate in Gaelic she could recite hundreds of her own compositions.

The old bardic tradition goes back, of course, to the very early prechristian times of the Druids, when the art was taken very seriously. Official or semi-official poetry and song certainly played an important part in Highland life, but those that touched the peoples' lives most closely were the work songs. Alexander Carmichael, an excise officer who travelled extensively in the Highlands and Islands last century, made a vast collection of the people's songs. He also found prayers, blessings, incantations, all giving a spiritual dimension to life. Every activity, from the kindling of the fire in the morning to the 'smooring' of the fire at night, had its special prayer, blessing or song. For communal labour—reaping, rowing—a fairly incisive measure was needed, to keep the rhythm of the work going. A man still living remembers how, when energy was beginning to flag in a squad engaged in singing turnips, a monotonous job, he was asked to play them a tune on the pipes to spur them on!

The women were mostly involved in more solitary tasks—spinning, milking, churning, grinding grain in the quern—for which quieter songs, with much repetition and sometimes nonsense lines, were suitable.

The one communal women's task was the waulking, or shrinking, of the cloth. A group of women, perhaps a dozen, would sit, six on each side of a table, pounding the cloth rhythmically as they passed it from hand to hand till the right consistency was achieved. Many songs were composed for this work, often humorous or satirical, poking fun at the men, who were not allowed to take part.

The idea that the Highland people were, or are, gloomy or morose, is entirely false. Humour, tenderness, compassion, shine out of these songs. Among the most beautiful are the lullabies, children being the most precious of assets. And dirges for the dead show the respect always paid to progenitors.

Luckily, with the advent of recording methods before the last of the traditional singers died, and the tireless efforts of collectors, many of these beautiful old songs have been preserved. And a new generation is beginning to value them, as the archives are unfolded today.

1959

March 12th

To wake in daylight, with the ring of lark-song in the air outside, is one of the delights of early spring in the hills. As you draw back the curtains you see the peewits capering madly about the morning sky. You go down with a light heart to begin the day. With the larks and the peewits clamouring about the roof-top you know for sure that everything is turning towards the sun again. After the long immobility of winter, the mere fact of being able to move freely about the fields, along the moor path, up the hill track, is a small thrill in itself. The beasts themselves share in this thrill.

The cattle wander off to the furthest limit of their grazing and stand staring at the boundless acres of freedom beyond the fence. The horse kicks up his heels in a splendid burst of a gallop, then rolls on his back, delirious with joy. The geese march off in the morning to their small private paradise on the moor—a peat-hag filled with amber water, where they splash and feed all day. Even the hens strut boldly away, though never losing sight of their familiar places, to scratch the fresh, pungent earth of the molehills and to gobble up the worms and insects lurking there.

The sheep are coming to the lambing in reasonably good heart this year. They've learnt to survive practically everything our climate can throw at them. This winter they were snowed up for weeks and had to scrape the frozen hillside for a living till their feet were raw. Then they were blown upon for days by the southerly gales and had to huddle for comfort in what hollows they could find among the heather.

Now their biggest ordeal—that of bringing forth the lambs they have carried through the bleak days—is before them. The blackfaced hill ewe must surely be one of the hardiest specimens in creation.

Up here it is early yet for ploughing, but in the lengthening evenings we can take a spade to the garden plot, even if it's only for the joy of seeing and smelling the black earth as it falls off the blade. And we're loath to come in to supper, for the peewits swoop about the fields long after dusk and their cry still sounds urgent in the gathering night.

April 16th

The cry of a brand-new lamb lingering in the sharp morning air. A curlew gliding through the dusk, its long call haunting the shadows. The grass in brilliant patches of emerald about the sheltered hollows. Coltsfoot dazzling yellow in the noonday sun. Buds swelling on the rowan branches and even the five-year-old hen announcing the laying of yet another egg. These are some of the signs and wonders of April on an upland croft.

After a winter in which the snow has lain deep and long, everything seems to spring quickly into life. The primroses practically flowered through the snow, as the crocuses do in the Alps, and the catkins were gleaming like frost crystals on the wintry willow branches.

The middens are emptied of dung now and the little steep fields are enriched once more. Ploughing is almost completed and the earth is slowly warming for the seed.

So far only the odd lamb has put in an appearance. The main crop will not arrive till near the end of the month. It's just as well, for the snow is still lying deep on the Strathfarrar hilltops and who knows when a fresh scurry of flakes may come whirling out of a sudden black cloud.

Still, there's a gleam about the month which quickly dispels worry. You see it on the face of the loch in the blue noon and on the green grass-blades that are precious as jewels. It's there, too, in the flashing swoop of gulls as they leave their circling high above the ploughman's shoulders, and even on the broad black back of the crow, swaying precariously on the topmost branch of a slim silver birch.

You can quickly forget the numbness in your fingers and the ache in your back as you watch the new lamb you have helped into a still chilly world stagger to its mother's side and start taking nourishment, its tail bobbing deliriously. April is a month full of hard work and uncertainty, but it's lit with these flashes of light which keep you going.

May 14th

May has brought the cuckoo-snow but not, so far, the cuckoo. He's a crafty bird, the cuckoo. He's probably sheltering in the close-set pine-wood lower down the strath before venturing into our wide heights. No doubt we shall soon see his rather ungainly brown form alight on a fence-post and hear the twin notes that call the magic tune of summer.

The seed is sown now and the fields have that neat, well-tended look which graces them only at this time of year, before any kind of growth has burst through their smooth surface.

Though the snow still lies gleaming on the high tops, the clouds keep piling up behind Ben Wyvis and a wind with an edge like a saw-blade keeps driving them our way, yet the buds on the rowan are bursting and the grass gets a little greener every day.

When a lull comes and the air softens for a while, we take an evening walk purely for pleasure, though an eye is, of course, perpetually open for the lambing ewe, any sheep in any kind of distress, or the fence in need of repair.

The sky is green where the sun has left it, a buzzard slowly circles and cries its desolate cry above our heads. This is an old land, patiently waiting for summer. It seems, at such a time, particularly near to us.

As we turn on the doorstep because the glint of a star has caught our eye, we look at the land again, as it lies under the night, and we say to ourselves for the hundreth time, that we could never live happily anywhere else.

June 11th

The corn springing green and slender in one field and in the next the grass shining and rippling in the breeze; the plovers perpetually scream-ing in alarm as you pass too near a brood of young ones on your way about the place; blossom lying like blobs of cream among the fresh rowan leaves; huge yellow butterballs in the marsh; the swallows dart-ing in and out of the broken sky-light in the byre roof to their nests under the rafters; curlew gliding over the drifts of bog-cotton that are dazzling in the morning sun and still glimmer through the long dusk of a mid-summer night. These are some of the things that June brings to a Highland croft.

There are big jobs to be done, of course. The lambs have to be marked, the peats to be cut and an early onslaught made on those persistent enemies—the dockens and other noxious weeds.

Much of this June work is shared by neighbours and goes with a swing. Gathering the sheep is no hardship when you walk the hill in company and the little soft breeze brings you the scent of myrtle and the lichened boulders are warm to the hand when you stop for a drink at the burn.

Even the cutting and piling of the peats can be reckoned a pleasure when a couple of well-tried companions are sharing their store of tales and wisecracks. At midday you can ease your back on a springy couch of heather, watch the pipe-smoke rise into the still, blue air and listen to the curlew's drifting summer call.

At midsummer in the hills every heart is young. How could it be otherwise when there is no night and the last cuckoo has hardly finished calling from the birch tree at the edge of the wood, when the first larks are wide awake and making the cool air ring with song?

The oldest eye has a light in it at sight of the tender braird. The oldest hand can grasp a work-tool when the sun is there, warming the blood. As for the young ones, to run bare-legged and barefoot in the June freedom of hill and moor is enough for them.

July 16th

With the passing of summer's peak we're looking anxiously for a drop of rain. Farmers are, of course, never satisfied! In fact, it would take more than a drop to put the ground right. Two or three days' good soaking is what it needs. The pastures are growing bare and burnt and the root crops are slow to put on flesh.

Wells are at their ebb. It looks as if we may soon have to resort to the old practice of doing the washing in the burn. On a warm day this can be a thoroughly enjoyable way of tackling a problem. You choose your pool of amber water, from which the astonished small trout have flashed in dismay, and wash your clothes there, laying the linen on a flat stone for scrubbing. Then you move upstream to another unsullied pool for the rinsing. A frog or two will goggle at you in amazement and a heron may give you a disapproving glare, before making off in high and dignified dudgeon at your intrusion. You'll spread the clothes on the dwarf alders to dry. When you fetch them home they'll be smelling of myrtle and sun-warmed thyme.

In spite of the drought the hillside, that tough old portion of earth which can withstand all the vagaries of the weather, is breaking early into flower. The bell-heather is blooming on the lower slopes, making splendid patches of colour against the green of young larch and pine.

Holiday-time in the hills is a time to be young and barefoot and free to run on the cool moss at the burnside or to lie hidden in the flowering grasses. That is how the croft children can spend their summer days.

August 27th

Now, the drought has been well and truly broken. We stood, one afternoon, at the door of the byre, gleefully listening to the rain hissing on the baked ground and watching the drops bouncing off all the hard surfaces.

The rain didn't turn into one of those interminable downpours which flatten the growing corn and turn the ground into a quagmire, so that all work comes to a stop. It was gentle rain which seeped into the earth and brought the springs bubbling up again. Now everything is freshened and the air smells of clover and honey-scented heather and ricked hay.

Yes, the hay is actually in the rick and that is certainly a small miracle. Hay that is quickly made stays fragrant and nourishing all through the sapless days of winter. It's a big burden off the mind to know that it's there, waiting for the beasts' needs.

The oats themselves are almost on the turn. Unless things go very far awry, that's another crop that should be harvested well before the snow comes this year.

To have the hay and the peats secured so soon and in such good order makes you feel you could tackle the rest of the harvest twice over. It's a long time since there was such blessing on a season.

September 24th

This summer will, I think, soon become a legend. At winter ceilidhs we shall tell the tale of it, savouring our words, with a shine in our eyes and warmth in our voices.

Seldom has a harvest been gathered so early and so happily as this year's. All down the strath, field after field smiles back at the sun, its rich golden crop standing in tidy stooks.

Of course, there has been another side to things. The scarcity of rain has made the burns dwindle to a tiny flow between the parched stones and in places the ground is baked so hard that it has cracked open and has almost the look of an alien land.

As one well after another dried up water has to be fetched, by all sorts of means, from far-off, mossy places in the hills. How good that water tastes, scooped in the hollow of a sun-burned hand from the cool deeps, and how good it feels, swilled over neck and arms, before the long journey home with brimming pails. The pastures are on the bare side, though this high, peaty soil retains whatever moisture comes along and, actually, a second flowering has appeared on the clover.

There's a promise in the air, as there is in spring, and over the harvest fields the larks are rising and singing, for the sheer fun of it.

October 22nd

The other morning, as I stepped outside, pail on arm, and set off on the well-worn path to the well, I drew in a breath and immediately stopped in my tracks to marvel at the sweetness of the air.

What was that fragrance which made the mind tingle with memories of spring? I tilted my head for another whiff and remembered...it was the smell of rain! It had actually rained a little in the night.

Then, in imagination, I heard water running in a steady trickle into the butt. I heard the burn roaring in spate from the hill. I caught the sound of gum-booted feet slushing through mud in the yard. In reality, the sun was shining on yet another day of blue and gold.

This long succession of vivid days has made everything seem unreal. Were there ever such bulging stacks of corn at the field-side, such stout-hearted cabbages in the garden, turnips and hay so succulent and sweet?

The sheer abundance makes older heads shake slowly in amazement. And when the tatties come up huge and gleaming from ground that is fine as dry sand, eyes open wider than they have for many a year.

It's difficult to believe that winter lies ahead when pale primroses are in bloom in the garden.

When the early mist lies white in the hollow of the burn, when cobwebs glisten on fences in the morning light and sheeps' feet leave long trails in the dew-soaked grass, when the sun hangs like a red balloon before it fades into the evening sky, then we have to acknowledge the presence of autumn.

November 19th

Winter is here at last. We were sure it was on its way when the long strings of geese came flapping in across the pale north sky and when the rowans, having shed the last of their tattered leaves, took on the gaunt look they will wear till spring.

Yet still the air was soft enough to set the midges dancing and the cows lingered in the fields till dusk, loath to come in to shelter.

Now, however, winter is really baring her teeth at us. With the snow whirling horizontally across the moor, an icy wind at its back, we begin a frantic search for thick woollen garments. The soup pot is kept simmering at the side of the fire and the bringing-in of the fuel becomes one of the day's most important tasks.

Seldom have the crofts here been better prepared to face winter.

With the corn and hay secured in first-class order, the tattie-pits bulging at the field sides, and the peats dry as bone in the stack, it is almost a pleasure to contemplate the coming of the dark days.

There is real satisfaction in tossing armfuls of sweet hay into the horse's rack at dusk and in placing a pailful of juicy turnip-slivers under the house-cow's nose.

So often it has happened in the past that a season's hard work has produced a poor barricade against winter—sticky hay, mildewed straw, sodden peats and potatoes smaller than the seed they sprang from.

This year the work has brought bounty, so we can sit at the well-banked fire in the evening, listening without fear to the wind raging round the house.

December 23rd

The short days of December are sometimes among the most beautiful of the year. There's the odd spell of storm, of course, but that is to be expected and has been provided for.

The wonder is that there are so many days when it is a positive pleasure to be outside. The sky may be shrouded but the grass shows a brilliant green and the air flows fresh against the cheek.

This is time for making journeys and the best of all ways to journey is with horse and cart. A touch of night frost will have stiffened the ruts on the side road and as you set off you know that the rumble of the wheels, the creak of the axle and the ring of the horse's hooves will have announced your departure to the world at large.

You pass the loch where the swans are sailing in winter peace and you notice that the slender bare twigs of the birches are mauve in the pale light. You walk for a while at the horse's head and you sense the strength and warmth and patience of him, as you feel his breath against your hand.

On the way back you stop to load some fallen pine branches. Your wood-pile at home is already a substantial one, but this is a fine excuse to linger a little while among the still trees, to smell the resin and to listen to the whirring of innumerable small wings as the chaffinch flocks flit past. Then the darkness will be on you suddenly and before you near home there'll be a star or two twinkling in the pale green sky and you'll find lamplight in the stable. When you've given the horse feed and drink and have spread some gleaming straw between his feet, you'll come in to the warm kitchen, well content with a winter day which has given you time to look and listen and think.

Hogmanay

In this age, with our well-being more or less assured all the year round, with electricity giving us light and heat and summer food in the depth of winter, we tend to forget how precarious is our hold on this old universe of ours. Yet a breakdown in the electricity supply can reduce a great city to a state of panic.

Our ancestors had just the one source of heat and energy and well-being —the sun. They knew that it was great and beautiful and to be relied on utterly, and they looked upon it with both awe and joy. So as—at what we now call New Year—it began slowly tilting its glorious face towards them again, they rushed to sweep and garnish and purify their homes, to greet their neighbours, and to feast and dance and sing in mutual congratulation that life was to be continued and renewed.

We, their descendants, have lost most of the contact they had with the mysteries of earth and sea, darkness and stars. Some of the excitement comes through in the customs we still cherish, though they can't be as real to us as they were to our forebears of even a hundred years ago.

Have you ever heard two shots shattering the stillness that follows the last of the midnight strokes? You should be standing at the open door of a Highland croft house to hear them. One kills the old year and the next welcomes the new.

Then you listen and hear another two shots, and another, and you smile to yourself and say: 'Alec's at it, west the glen', and: 'Neil himself is there, too'.

You're glad that you're all in it together. Solidarity is the greatest comfort.

In older times the ritual of purification of the home was carried out in two ways. Water from 'the ford of the living and the dead' was sprinkled in the rooms and given as a drink to each member of the family, and juniper branches were lighted and carried flaming through the house, the smoke fumigating both places and people. Fire and water—the sacred elements— did their work.

On Calluinn (New Year's Eve) the custom was for a young man of the district to dress himself in the skin of a bull and to go from house to house, followed by a company of his fellows.

He would go round each house 'deiseil', that is, sun-wise, and in the fire a part of the hide was singed and the company would inhale the fumes. The power of the bull was thus communicated to man and assured prosperity.

Before midnight the house was swept, the hearth scrupulously cleaned and a sprig of rowan nailed to the door.

The first-foot was eagerly looked for, though it might be breakfast-time before he came if the house was ten miles across the moor. It was hoped he would be tall and dark and would carry a gift of fuel as well as food and drink.

In face of the world's threatening one had to be careful to propitiate. One wore new clothes and a genial mood. One carried a silver coin. There was no harm in helping the omens along.

A visit to a neighbour is a rare and valued thing when lives are hard and isolated and the great joy of New Year is still to be able to indulge in visiting for days on end. Often a whole year's news and gossip is exchanged.

In some parts older folk still celebrate January 12, their New Year date before 1877. It makes a grand reason for prolonging the festivities!

On New Year's Day itself the shinty match was and, in a modified form, still is, the thing. In the old days the piper led the way to the field and every able man took part so that sometimes, with 50 or more a-side, and in spite of the pledges to abide by the rules, the game would sound more like a battle.

But it was all part of the fun and there would still be energy for dancing and singing and feasting after dark.

These were the rites that the sun inspired…rites evolved by a people in touch with a universe they loved a lot, feared a little and venerated greatly.

Through those which we still practise we can feel the depth of our kinship with our ancestors and grope our way back and forward, from our little electrically-controlled corner of Creation.

II
AFTER CROFTING

After Crofting...?

When, eventually, reluctantly, owing to various circumstances, we had to give up working the croft, we were fortunate enough to be able to go on living in the area. I had been doing some teaching in Inverness. The former schoolhouse in Abriachan, which had been available to rent by teachers working for the local authority since the closure of the school, became vacant just at this time and we were able to move in. The family of the former occupant had worked the Post Office from the house, so we took over this job as well.

There was a good quarter-acre of garden—room for our bee-hives and some chickens and, eventually, a goat. We could be largely self-supporting. A succession of short-term tenants had meant that the ground had been neglected, but after some months of hard work—draining, rotovating, digging out rampant weeds—we got it back into production. Even the age-old apple-tree bore fruit and we planted a plum-tree to keep it company.

So, with vegetables of all kinds, fruit, honey, eggs and milk, we lacked little. And there was lilac and wild cherry-blossom and a hawthorn hedge. We missed the crofting desperately but there were many blessings to count. We also looked after a small museum depicting crofting life, which had originated as part of a project done by the pupils of my school.

Helen finished at school in Inverness and University in Edinburgh, travelled the world as students do, married and settled on a small farm twenty miles away. The grandchildren came in summer to eat strawberries and cream and to swim in the loch.

I was invited to write again for the Scotsman about life in the area and was also able to contribute something to the debate going on then—25 years ago—about the reform of landholding in the Highlands.

1973

August

It comes late, the flowering in these old uplands just beyond the Great Glen, but it is well worth the waiting. The damp, midsummer days have made the heather shoot and now the purple sheen is spreading slowly up the slopes. In the wet ground by the little loch the white flags of bog-cotton still blow, reminding us always of the crofter's wife, our good neighbour, who used them for stuffing her babies' pillows. And the scent of bog myrtle is everywhere.

The sheep are dazzling white from the shearing and the lambs have settled again, grown accustomed to the sight of mother in her strange, ungainly shape. Fewer and fewer are the flocks on the high ground now, for much of it is to be planted with trees. One wonders sometimes about the rapacious appetite of pulp mills. Wool and mutton are surely commodities to be prized above paper. We live in a paper-ridden world, maybe, but we must first be clothed and fed.

The Forestry Commission are, however, willing to make concessions to the environment. We are apprehensive as we hear the whine of power-saws and watch the great caterpillar monsters, with their loads of fencing posts, crawling over the face of the hill opposite. For many years, it has been our day-long delight. We've grown accustomed to the lift of it. The sun soars above its cairn in summer and on winter days sits glowing on its topmost shoulder. In spring the light pours down its flanks, to the accompaniment of lark-song, and in autumn it's ablaze with yellow bracken and red rowans. There's a path across it where the people trekked up to the peat-banks beyond, and shelter in its hollows for sheep and roe and mountain hares.

But 'they' assure us that they are going to leave certain standings of natural birch—those miraculous trees which are frail mauve skeletons in winter, green shade in summer, and rich gold beacons in the autumn frosts.

They promise, too, that they will not be planting over the remains of a smugglers' bothy on the slope on the far shore of the loch. Only the tumbled walls remain, for the heather thatch has long since decayed, but the small burn still flows past and the look-out stone is immoveable.

This upland stretch was one of the great places in the heyday of the illicit stills—remote, almost inaccessible and full of people with the wit to outdo the craftiest of excisemen. Bribes for the giving of information were offered, but seldom accepted, unless by arrangement, for the replenishing of worn-out gear. Many are the tales, which still go the rounds at winter ceilidhs, of those heroic days when a man could still strive to go his own way and 'we' were mightier than 'them'.

This year, also, we have rescued from the planting a stretch of hill which bears traces of the first prehistoric settlers in these parts. Nine hut circles, some of the 'scooped-out', some of the 'platform' type, many 'field clearance' heaps of stones and the remains of a dividing dyke are clearly visible on the dry, west-facing slope and it is hoped that some digging can be undertaken next summer to try to recover pottery and establish dates.

One wonders how long it will be before the fields of the few remaining crofters of today, those fields won at such cost in muscle-power from the bog and rock by their forebears, will be obliterated, if not by the planting of trees, then by the inroads of rushes and bracken. The houses will doubtless stand for long enough, with concrete projections stuck on to their walls of natural stone, as havens for those weary of the spinning world. Each summer more of the weary brave the narrow hill road and find here, I think, what they came to seek—the absolute stillness or the sound of the wind in the heather or of water lapping the shore of the loch.

Our favourites, this year, were the two young men in the small brown tent that merged so well into the hill as to be almost invisible. They asked only for eggs and milk. We wished that the crofters of yesteryear had been here to supply that simple need, with bannocks and great girdle scones and cheese and butter into the bargain!

The young men scorned the idea of going, in their old car, the five miles to the nearest shop and I didn't blame them. Hard tack with water is enough to keep you going when you don't want to miss a moment of summer in the hills. To breathe the scent of the moor, to feel the strike of the sun through clear air, to gaze into the faces of the tiny roadside flowers, to lie and watch the roedeer come to drink at the burn flowing deep in a cleft of the hill and the grebe ceaselessly diving for food for their young among the rushes by the loch shore—when these things satisfy no-one is poor.

We're thankful so many young people like these now come knocking on our door. To them this is a world new-born. We know how old it is, but we thank goodness it's being rediscovered every day. Discoverers like these are a summer flowering that will not wither.

September

In the uplands summer does not fade. Instead, as the calendar signals the start of autumn, the richest colouring of the year appears, with the hill-slopes covered in heather flower, the birches still green and the rowans sporting a gloss of scarlet fruit. True, there are the morning mists, but when they lift and the early sun dries out the webs of gossamer on scabious and harebell and red clover, then the colours come up as though conjured out of the still air.

The rowan berries are the first of our wild harvests. We gather them as they reach plump maturity, soak them in water for ten days with a small piece of bruised ginger, and stir daily. Then they are strained and to each quart of liquid is added a pound of sugar and the result, six months later, is a very palatable wine, said by those who like a touch of magic in their lives to contain the secret of eternal youth.

Certain it is that the rowan was always considered to have magical properties. Isn't there at least one at the door of every Highland house to keep the evil spirits at bay? Didn't they even fix a branch above the byre door to guard the precious family cow?

The berries, mixed with apples, also make a jelly, slightly bitter on bread or scones, but most acceptable as a relish with hare or venison. And buried in a tin in the ground they can be brought out at Christmas as a decoration should holly berries fail.

This summer we have seen more people from the crowded world than ever before. From England, France, Spain, Italy, Belgium, Denmark, Sweden, Germany and even Japan, they have come, in their search for the byways and the heights.

One and all, they marvel at the bright air, the clear water, the flowers, the butterflies, the fish, the vast variety of birds, the deer, even the rabbits. We are privileged to talk to many of them as they come to buy a stamp in the minute Post Office which my husband looks after in the front porch, or as we take them to the small Croft Museum and Interpretation Centre which was set up here by Inverness High School under the Highland Village Scheme for Conservation Year 1970.

This consists of a collection of crofting implements and household gear, documents and photographs relating to the social and natural history of the area, specimens of rock and plant, the substance of the place, and of a crofthouse and steading, restored and furnished in the style of 100 years ago. The overall aim is to show how the life appropriate to the place was lived before the impact of mechanisation, commercialisation, tourism and exploitation.

We sense the appreciation in our visitors' eyes and voices and it brings real warmth into our exchanges with them. Here is humanity looking for its common origin and rejoicing in a glimpse of it. But at the back of our minds there is a fear. The fear is that it may soon be too late to catch even a glimpse of the old simple pattern of life that was lived to the rhythm of the seasons, of sun, storm, wind, rain, snow and the shared help of neighbours.

Meantime, as we wake each morning to the quiet and the fresh air, we sing a small inward canticle of praise. Our garden is large and somewhat of a wilderness. But the bees can forage in flowers undamaged by chemicals. There are nettles for the butterflies to lay in and some cabbages earmarked for caterpillar grubs.

I have made 50 pounds of jam from the raspberries that clutter the old orchard and soon the wild roses will give hips for jelly and syrup. There are certain disadvantages to a garden in the heights. A frost in the third week of August killed the runner beans at a stroke and blackened the potato tops. But the peas are bursting from the pod and the carrots are crisp and sweet.

There never was a year like this one for mushroom growth. Boletus are everywhere and in woodland not far away one can gather chanterelle by the pound. We remember a Czech friend who stayed with us one summer. He would go out for a couple of hours of an afternoon and come back with a huge kerchief stuffed with fungi of all kinds.

Sitting at the kitchen table, he would slice them up with a bread knife, adding slivers of onion, fry them gently in butter, toss in two or three switched eggs and the result would be a supper dish of dream-like succulence.

And everyone survived the night! I wish I could gather fungi with such confidence. I am sure of three or four varieties and would add more to my list if the trial and error process were less fraught with danger.

October

'The last remaining wilderness on the north-west edge of Europe' is how the propagandists describe the Highland area. We can only hope fervently that those in authority will see to it that it is allowed to retain the quality of wilderness by exercising wise and far-seeing control.

We remember the couple from Barcelona who arrived on our doorstep one evening in July. They were pale with exhaustion after crawling in their tiny car up the A9 and searching fruitlessly for somewhere to lay their heads at their journey's end. In desperation they had taken our turning.

'We thought it was all quiet in the Highlands, with little traffic and lots of beds and breakfasts,' they said. 'It can be,' we answered, anxious that no-one should be let down and making swiftly for the telephone. Fortunately a friendly neighbour was able to make them welcome for 48 hours. When they came to say goodbye they looked ten years younger and were only sorry they could not stay a whole month in the quiet.

Of course the good things are to be shared. But there must be no grabbing and hogging. The Highland people themselves, to whom hospitality is second nature, should be the ones who say how far a

135

welcome can be stretched. Highland hospitality is real, bred in the bone of a people to whom, in older times, it was often a question of survival. But it cannot cope with excess.

Obviously most of those who come to look at the hills and moors and lochs will be car-borne, and for them roads and beds are the first necessity. Increasing numbers of younger people, however, are eager to wander off the beaten tracks and, though most of them have the instinct to respect the wild, for some there is much to be learnt.

Fortunately the means to guide them unobtrusively do seem to be developing and the various authorities involved—the Countryside Commission, the Forestry Commission, the Scottish Wildlife Trust, the Nature Conservancy, as well as smaller private enterprises—are manned by informed and dedicated enthusiasts. But there is a danger inherent even in this necessary amount of organisation for leisure.

It is vital that the visitor should realise that the Highland area, with its quiet grandeur, is not merely a playground. True, vast acreages have been made over to the 'sport' of killing deer, grouse, pheasant, salmon and other creatures. But there are still, in those parts of the wilderness made to blossom by the generations, many people earning a satisfying living from raising crops and producing plain food. Calves do not thrive on a stomachful of plastic wrappings and sheep and cattle will stray into cultivations when fences are broken and gates left ajar.

For those of us who are privileged to live and work here the hope is that somebody, somewhere, in some seat of power, will decree that the means of making a livelihood, not an overnight fortune but a modest livelihood, will be established in the little places, so that not all the young ones have to scurry to the coasts and leave the hinterland empty again. Why should they not quietly learn to weave carpets in Lairg, to make furniture in Kinlochewe and in the evenings cultivate their gardens? Uneconomic, the pundits will say and go back to nursing the headaches of thinking in millions.

It is clear that planning for the Highland area must be on a scale suited to the background if the country is to keep its identity. On the table is a postcard just received from Venice. A young Italian woman who stayed in a croft house here this summer writes: 'I miss the meagre atmosphere of the Highlands', and I know just what she means. I know Venice, too. But only in uplands like these do you get a glimpse of the bones and elements and the basic simplicity of things.

Meanwhile I can tell you that the fieldfares have arrived to feast on our harvests of berries and that the first long arrows of geese have come over in the clear mornings. It's good that we are a winter refuge for so many.

This week we are off to glean a particular little hidden corner of untamed wilderness on the slope towards Loch Ness. There one can get the feel of the habitat of primitive man, A vixen will be standing bright-eyed in a clearing, giving you two seconds' stare before she streaks to cover. A roe fawn may be couched in the warm bracken, staying utterly still till you pass. A kestrel will be hovering above the yellow birch leaves, sending the small woodland creatures scurrying to cover down below.

The hazel nuts are ripening. In years gone by the women would walk barefoot to Inverness carrying basketfuls to sell for a few pence at Hallowe'en. There is a great profusion of wild fruit—sloes with a bloom on them like that on hothouse grapes, huge glistening brambles, rosehips and one enormous old hawthorn weighed down with dark-red berries. These all had their uses, culinary and medicinal. Sloe syrup was the thing for winter coughs and hips and haws were squeezed out and the contents eaten raw to ward off colds. Folk knew instinctively about vitamins without putting a label on them.

A Highland autumn always makes up for the uncertainties of spring. This year the corn is heavy in the ear and the days are blue and gold beyond belief.

1974

January

If a gateway stands for expectancy and a raising of the sights, then January really is the gateway of the year. Just inside our own garden gate a deep crimson primula is blooming. The pre-Christmas snows must have kept it snugly happed against the old granite wall, and now, in the strengthening light, it positively glows.

By the twelfth of the month, date of the 'old' New Year, now scarcely remembered in these parts, they used to say there was 'an hour on the day'. This meant a lot to people working with candle and oil lamps in byre and kitchen. It means a lot to us today, an extra hour when one can be active outdoors or in and so postpone the time when the fire must be poked and sat at.

It is strange, yet not strange, for us, on a trip to town, to go into a candle or lamp-lit shop to make a few essential purchases.* Nails to fix the shed roof which blew off in a gale, wool to knit socks and gloves to keep the blood warm, an axe to replace the one worn out with much chopping—these are things bought with a sense of purpose in an atmosphere of calm.

There is an underlying serenity in the shops that defeats the frustrations of shortages and delays. If we can't get one thing we make do with another. Limitations are acknowledged. On the ironmonger's counter are lamps and lanterns in the style of those in the museum. We finger them wonderingly and think how beautiful they are—purpose-built, functional, with the curve and contour of purpose.

The afternoon streets, even on market-day, are quiet. Only essential business is being done. The road home is quiet too.

One has the feeling that in each house, behind the one lighted window, each family is gathered, as evening meetings are cancelled or curtailed. Perhaps the members of the families will get to know one another better, with shared responsibilities and ploys.

Of course, one realises that there are inconveniences and dangers to living when the habitual comforts of power are withdrawn and short-time working will bring harsh problems of every kind. Yet one cannot help finding that the general slowing-down of what had become

---

*This was written during the industrial disputes of 1974, when power-cuts were common and many industries were forced to close down for part of the working week.

the breakneck speed of the race must have a salutary effect on the human being.

We have the great good fortune, of which we are continually aware, of being able to function, here, at some remove from the crises of the world. The innate sanity of the human race lingers in the eyes and attitudes of the older people of the hills. The notion of a three-day week is dismissed with a shrug by folk who, like the Almighty, need all of six to build their world.

There is disappointment that the elders of the tribes 'with all their education', education by which such store was always set, cannot see to it that there are fair shares for all. But leaders have been lost before and one has always had, in the long run, to rely on one's own strength and resourcefulness. And there are still enough neighbours to be relied on to help dig out a truck if the snow-plough runs out of fuel or to share a last loaf if the grocer's van can't manage to slither up the ice on the unsalted road. Somehow, some time or other, we've seen something not unlike it before.

As for today's talk of recycling, that was in operation generations ago, when the roof thatch was renewed every year and the old, soot-encrusted one ploughed into the ground, and when human soil, as well as that of the stalled beasts, was used as fertiliser. There were no tins or plastics then to clutter up the roadsides and the insides of sheep and cattle. Let us hope there will be fewer from now on.

Unused energy thrashes about just beyond the window-pane, with seeming derision. The wind roars in the trees, the snow piles in immoveable drifts, the sun glares through the racing clouds. There is power out there asking to be challenged.

Some 20 years ago, when we worked a croft here, we did harness wind and water to our needs. On the top of a larch pole, cut and carted from up the road, we fixed wind sails and a dynamo which generated light. On nights of gale we rejoiced in its whirring and switched on all the lights and made merry. During a prolonged spell of still frost the batteries sank and we sat around the Tilley.

We diverted the flow of a small burn to fill a tank, thus creating a head of power to drive a 'ram', which pushed the water up to the house. Again, in time of exceptional drought, the power waned and we had to carry pails for a while or use the butt at the kitchen door. We were thus on intimate terms with our sources of energy and acquired an understanding of their ways and a healthy respect for them. To this day, with mod cons at our command, we still automatically turn off switches and taps, even in times of gale and deluge.

This is January. Nothing anyone, anywhere, can devise can stop the slow bowing of the earth towards the sun. There are still forces on the side of life—witness the flower blooming under the snow—and life must include the human race.

February

February is a chancy month. It's a time for risked beginnings, for sudden setbacks, for the scanning of portents and, withal, a time to sing. The snowdrop florets were just piercing their green sheaths when frost struck them rigid. A chaffinch had stuttered out an octave or two and gales sent him to cover in the plantation. These are the shifts and uncertainties of youth. It is, after all, the early adolescence of the year.

In the old Celtic world the 1st of February was celebrated as the festival of spring. It is difficult to imagine this when, as the month moves on, one is still looking at bare birches on a frost-bound hill. But the Celts had seeing eyes. Being utterly dependent on the power of the sun, they would watch it riding higher and the rays, like life-lines, striking more nearly the vertical, seeming to pull growth out of the earth. Then they would feel the life in themselves stir, too, and there would be the need to look up and to shout and dance.

February 1 is the day, too, of St Bride, that motherly little saint who combines the virtues of pagan and Christian. Benign small goddess of spring for whom the meadows bloomed, she was also the one whose chosen beatitude was 'Blessed are the merciful'. She's a saint one would like to have known.

The 2nd of the month is Candlemas. This marked the end of the period of Yule and also the end of the three winter months from Hallowe'en, the time of 'little sun'. It was a day for observing and recording the signs. Still today the older folk look about them at Candlemas. They scan the sky and prod the ground and pronounce.

There is an old Scots quatrain which says:

> Candlemas Day, gin ye be fair
> The half o' winter's to come and mair;
> Candlemas Day, gin ye be foul
> The half o' winter's gane at Yule.

This year Candlemas was a conundrum. There was grey sky, an icy wind, but a chink of gold at sunset and a thrush shouting from the top of a fir.

It must have been a great comfort to have these festive days scattered through the year. There would have been always something to look forward to and to remember, something by which to reckon the events in one's own life—'she was born a year come Candlemas'. In the big places there was perhaps some abuse of festivity, but for most of the folk, who were country folk, the Red Letter days were a wholesome break in the monotony of work. And the uniformity of the customs associated with them bound people together as few things do today.

We may eat pancakes on Shrove Tuesday but few of us probably do it with the same relish as those who were consciously feasting on the rich things from which they'd be abstaining during the period before Easter. This time of fasting, though it was part of the Christian ritual, was probably dictated by necessity. Cattle, too, endured the 'hungry gap' in early spring. When stocks of corn and hay were running short, the people would bruise whins or any other edible growth in the hollowed stones, sometimes called 'knocking stones', which are still seen at most old crofts today.

By Valentine's Day some say the birds are mating. But that must be in warmer climes than ours. Here they are mostly flocking still. One of the delights of an early gardening spell is to be aware of a crowd of long-tailed tits gambolling in the trees above one's head.

Bride, Candlemas and Valentine: words like a ring of bells announcing spring. How dull, in a modern calendar, are labels like 'Bank Holiday'. A holy day spent reclining on a green bank sprigged with celandine—yes! But just a day when those marble halls cease gorging and disgorging their endless diet of printed paper does not seem worth singing about. It does, of course, remind us of how far we are in thrall to the banks, else why record their closing days along with things of such import as the rising and setting times of sun and moon, the days of equinox, midsummer, the shortest and the longest day.

Now, this year, we must ring another date in the diary. Come polling day we shall be sitting, from what will seem like dawn to long past dusk, in the old schoolroom, recording the votes of this scattered populace. There will be a fire in the grate and tea on the hob and we shall while away the gaps between the arrivals with good talk with the patient, good-natured local arm of the law. There will be time for greetings, too, from folk not seen the winter-long, for every serious occasion must have its touch of ceremony.

We must be prepared for blizzards at this uncertain time of year, have shovels at the ready and lay in stores against the possibility of blocked roads and marooned voters. As long as the outcome is a clearing of the air and a chance to get on with living it will perhaps be something of an improvised Red Letter day to celebrate.

March

It's in mid-March that I'm writing this. I'm sitting on the patch of rough grass and heather between house and hill. There's a shine on the grey stalks of last year's growth and between them young emerald shoots are piercing through. The pines at my back are stirring, but the breeze is slight and mild today.

One marvels at the resilience of these old trees. All winter they have been rocked by gales. They just take and give, take and give. Only if rot attacks their innards do they succumb.

The bees are out on a cleansing flight. They revel in this brief escape from the confines of the winter-bound hive. Attracted no doubt by the white paper I am using, three have just looked along and investigated the pad. One stays, seeming to enjoy her walk on the smooth paper. Her eyes are big and bright.

In proportion to the work she does she seems so very small. How apt it is that 'small is beautiful'. Usually a washing on the line or a shining window-pane is the bees' objective on these occasions and many a housewife has cursed them roundly when her work was to do over again. But it's good to have a rapport with the creatures who share one's life.

On a stone sits a ginger cat, his white chest gleaming, his young eyes round and very innocent. One could scarcely see in him the pitiful skeleton that was dumped at the roadside last August. It took us three days to tempt him with food into temporary captivity in the shed and a week to chase the terror from his eyes. The first tentative purr and the rubbing of an arched back against one's knee was like the sun bursting through a rain-cloud.

With a sturdy black fluff of a kitten already to rear we were not sure how the larder would stretch to fill another mouth, but Ginger is not fussy, and I reckon he'll earn his keep in nature's way. As he sleeps in straw in the outhouse, he'll soon be on the early shift to protect the cabbages.

I look up to rest my eyes on the sky. It is a young blue with streaks of pale cloud—and the long-awaited signal of spring is there. A small brown bird is rising, plummeting, rising again and his song is cascading over the moor. Resisting the temptation to rush and tell the world, 'the larks are singing!' I stay, watching and listening.

Every year we wait for it, every year it happens, yet every year it seems more of a miracle that the brown stretches of these uplands, still bare and battered by the onslaughts of winter, are the chosen breeding grounds of these and so many other small, frail creatures.

I watch him and hear him establishing his right to life and wish that humans could do it half as gracefully. I envy him somewhat, him and his mate. They can make their home at will, as long as they defend it. No building regulations hem them in. They get by cosily with one room.

I think of our house. The March sun shows that rooms need cleaning. There is painting to be done. There's a whole garden to be combed clear of the winter debris of leaves and branches. What energy must be expended before the creative acts of planting and sowing can be begun!

One feels earth-bound and encumbered. Yet envy never did the spirit any good. Thanks to you, small bird. Sing on and dance and may your season be a happy one.

In the field across the road, I can see another mad March happening. Two brown hares are careering in erratic circles. The circles become loops, the loops figures-of-eight. It is like an elaborate ritual dance and the dancers are so completely obsessed by their own antics that they seem quite unaware of anyone watching them. One is reminded a little of youngsters on the pop scene mesmerising themselves into oblivion.

The lark sings on and from the ground; in counterpoint comes another of the young sounds of spring—the bleat of a blackfaced lamb. His early appearance is really a bit of a madness in these parts, though his whitefaced cousins are arriving thick and fast in lower, sheltered fields. But doubtless he'll survive. His mother will be adept at finding dry hollows under juniper or whin should storms blow up.

Over the rim of the hill a couple of buzzards are circling, with nesting no doubt in mind. I watch them and hear their strange, mewing cries and there, across the face of the sun, a drift of blue smoke wanders.

It is the seeming March madness of man, the madness of ancient wisdom. The old growth of heather must be destroyed to make way for the new, and the firing exploits are of course necessary and controlled.

But what an outlet they are for the frustrations of winter. There is magnificence about a whole hillside ablaze, when you know the destruction has a purpose and you have the means to control it.

April

To be sunburned before the cuckoo comes is one measure of this incredible Highland April. To be sowing cabbage seed and planting potatoes, sleeves rolled high, till dusk, is another.

Friends from the flat lands to the east came seeking the sun in our heights and were not disappointed. They found us decked in daffodils and deep red flowering currant, with a sky of Alpine blue. For days the sun never flagged, rising in one red orb and setting in another and the moon, not to be outdone, was huge and russet too.

Now the curlew calls from first light till well into the darkening. And it is curlew for real, no longer the starlings' imitations which had us rushing out to see the glide of the great moorland birds and in again in a fury of disappointment, shaking our fists at the cheeky impersonators. They've had me lumbering in, muddy gumboots and all, to answer a faked telephone ring! Now, thank goodness, they're busy nesting under the house eaves, though even that means streaked window panes and early morning chattered awakenings. I never could really appreciate a starling.

The wagtails are darting about the shiny grass, real dandy creatures, and our fantails are hatching a second brood in the dovecot. Up at the hill loch the island is a clamour of black-headed gulls, jostling for nest space. Mallard and tufted duck glide busily in and out of the reed beds and the coot hold their own boisterously. With pochard and golden-eye and a pair of whoopers, oystercatcher, plover, sandpiper and snipe all on or near the dazzling blue water the place is a small chunk of bird paradise these April days.

The blackfaced lambs are getting a good warm start to life, though soon the rain will be needed to give succulence to the grass. We shan't have to shout for it. A whisper will do. We know it must be waiting in the wings, somewhere to the west. Meanwhile, for this unexpected early benison of sun we can only give unstinted thanks.

The sun brings out the humans, too, and early visitors to the Croft Museum included a couple from the Punjab. It was strange to see jewelled turban and silk sari, bright dark eyes and sleek brown hands moving among the homely implements. Yet foot-plough and quern, flail and girdle, even the dairying dishes and the shoemaker's kit, were all instantly recognised as replicas of those in use in their homeland. Peat and thatch were quickly appreciated. And when we told of folk from a croft here whose sons had spent their whole working lives in India the bonds of recognition were real. Photographs were taken and there was teasing and laughter with the children. One sometimes feels that these contacts at close personal level, if realised on an adequate scale, could achieve more than the signed documents exchanged by politicians.

Three of these early spring days we have spent, a small band of us, clearing winter debris from the old churchyard at Killianan, on Loch Ness shore. By removing dead growth now we are able to ensure that the carpet of wild hyacinths, which has spread over it through the generations, is seen in May-time glory. Already primrose, celandine and daffodil are decking it in spring gold.

Before the bracken rises one can see the outline of the old church foundation, said to have been dedicated to Fianan or to Adamnan. In an enclosure lies a grave slab of medieval times, sculpted with cross and fleur-de-lis. A pair of shears incised at the foot is said to indicate that the grave contains the remains of a woman, and legend has it that she was a Norwegian princess. Whoever it is lies there, she must lie easy, for it is a magic spot.

In spite of the ever-increasing volume of noise from the road nearby, there are times when the quiet is such that one can visualise the sixth or seventh century monks, calmly engrossed in their devotions, their cultivations and their missionary enterprises. One can imagine them aware of the great creatures in the big loch which lapped their sanctuary, accepting them as part of their world. One can see the brown-clad figures climbing the hill to parley with the Druid priest who ministered to the folk up there, perhaps exchanging knowledge on the properties of plants, on cures for human ills, on the science of sun, moon and stars. There is a strong aura of peace about Killianan. I'm sure there was a wisdom stronger than strife.

In the wood behind the churchyard is a large, flat, heart-shaped stone, known as Columba's Font. A hole in the middle of it is always filled with water, even in times of drought, though no apparent source can be discovered. Within the memory of some still living the women would come, surreptitiously in later days, to fill a bottle with the liquid for use at times of childbirth or christening. Bitter it must have been to taste, but perhaps that is symbolic, too, of both the pagan and the Christian acceptance of life. The veneration of the ages can be felt around the stone, enclosed as it is by slender hazels, with the nuts of knowledge thick upon the ground.

Killianan and all it stands for give a sense of depth and continuity to the whole area, making the crashing of traffic seem irrelevant to the purpose of the world.

May

This year I first heard the cuckoo call, three times, from a birch half-way up the hillside. It was at dusk and that is lucky. To hear him first at dawn, as one usually does, is said to bode ill. Perhaps it is because there are more ill omens than good that each normal happening has a special shine.

The cuckoo does bring magic to May, even though most of his habits are unattractive, he is ungainly in appearance and eventually one does tire a little of his calling. Mostly he keeps his distance and the sound of him does turn our thoughts to summer. He did not bring snow this year, anyway, but some much-needed rain. This put an end to very real fears of fire damage to the many woodlands which now surround us.

With holidaymakers on the move there is always danger from picnic fires and discarded cigarette ends. The Forestry Commission vans patrol the roads, depositing firebrooms at strategic points. Officials of the commission are showing great sensitivity to the amenity of the area. They are planning diversity in the choice of trees, promising not to blanket the slopes in conifers but to plant in blocks and to include birch, rowan, gean and willow in their planting. They are respecting the sites of ancient monuments and allowing access by stile for walkers on the hill.

What has disturbed us lately has been the planting by other forestry concerns of acres of arable land which carried good crops until quite recently and made excellent grazing. With talk of food shortage facing the world at large surely a move could be made towards lessening the wastage of paper, which must be apparent to everyone when a small piece of chocolate is often wrapped in three separate layers.

When one remembers the lives spent in turning these uplands from barren moor to land fit to grow food, one is saddened. They were our neighbours who drained and fenced, took out huge stones, ploughed, harrowed, sowed and harvested. They had little use for paper but they could tell good oats from bad, good hay, good lambs and calves, good potatoes. When the fields revert, it is for ever.

As the cuckoo wings in, the geese wing off and that really is a signal from summer. As you're digging the last of the potato ground, a billowing, arrowed band of geese passes overhead. You look up as the full-throated sound of them breaks the stillness and, listening hard, you can hear the creak of their great wings. You shade your eyes to watch them disappear into the white north sky and then your spade bites deeper into the earth.

The beauty of this aerial movement and its attendant sound contrasts strangely with the one we dread—that of low-flying jet aircraft.

One very still, frosty day in winter I was putting food for the birds on a ledge attached to a tall fir tree in the garden.

Suddenly, I was aware of the topmost branches of the tree moving in one direction, as though sucked into a vacuum. Seconds later there was an explosion of sound. I looked up and saw a jet plane banking and disappearing over the ridge towards Loch Ness.

I went in, sat down and wrote a letter to the RAF authorities, pointing out that this is not a desolate area of bare moor, but a place where, mercifully, there still live children and old people, not to mention those in their hale middle years—and stock, too, liable to be put into a state of real alarm by these incursions.

As a result I received a courteous telephone call, a letter and a visit from an RAF officer and the noisome flying has been much less frequent, though still occurring from time to time.

These last weeks we have been well and truly wooed by our would-be councillors, both regional and district. One thing at least they have in common—the need for a strong stomach to cope with the drinks of tea and of stronger stuff and the plates of scones and biscuits which visits to the scattered homes of their electors involve.

Once again the votes are recorded in the old schoolroom here and we're thankful it's May-time. On the winter election day we finished up at ten o'clock huddled over the dying fire and happed in blankets to keep out the icy draughts!

All in all, this is the quiet month. The anxieties of lambing-time are over. And this has been a good lambing year. The ewes call confidently to their young. The lambs, alternately dozing and capering in the sun, grow almost visibly from curly, wobbly blobs to long-legged, boisterous, recognisable creatures, romping in gangs and brashly demanding sustenance from their long-suffering mothers.

Birdsong grows less as parents of both sexes cope busily with the appetites of their fledglings.

In field and garden the seed is set. The April sun and now the May rain have brought some of it through in record time. Our only fear is that late frost may nip some tender shoots. But then we remember—we heard the cuckoo in the evening. What is the use of omens if you don't believe in what they tell?

June

The long caress of the April sun coaxed these old woods and moors to bloom and blossom as seldom before. Now, in case we became light-headed enough to think of planting outdoor tomatoes, cucumbers or other follies, comes a timely reminder that we are after all a northern land. Frost has blackened the early potatoes.

Still, it was good to have lettuce and radish in mid-May, even though the winds were then chill enough for snow and one felt more like eating a dish of steaming mashed turnip.

We are fortunate here in having so many different kinds of terrain and almost of climate, each with its special quality of healing, right on our doorstep. A mile and a half away, down near the shores of Loch Ness, on the south-east-facing slopes, the wild strawberries will soon be red, the blackthorn sports white foam and the woods are roofed in green and carpeted in the haze of hyacinth.

One thinks of Deirdre and her bower and one wonders how many other unsung Deirdres lived carefree summers in these glades. With fruit, nuts, fish and game to hand, clear water everywhere and a cave to retreat to in winter, life could have been good before the advent of wheel and power.

There were two famous caves near the loch shore where tinkers would sleep among the stalactites and stalagmites. They are still marked on some maps, though they vanished during a road-making programme in the thirties. Every summer a tourist or two has to be told the sad news.

There is also the 'Robber's Cave' in a granite cliff known as the Red Crag. Here last century one Samuel Cameron, an outlawed cattle-lifter, held the sheriff at bay. Pointing a pistol at the worthy fellow's breast, the outlaw made the officer promise to declare him a free man at the cross of Inverness. The sheriff agreed and kept his word, and thereafter Cameron lived a blameless life with his large family.

In other nooks and crannies the amateur distillers met and hid their gear. Rocks have always been a refuge.

A walk along the shore of the big loch brings rewards of many kinds—driftwood with the shine and finish of silk, planks fit for house repairs (one such now makes us a bathroom shelf!), pebbles and blocks of granite with the dazzle and richness of jewels, bones which polish to the consistency of ivory.

It is sad that the people processing in their cars, seeing the water, the hills and the trees mainly as subjects for their cameras, have no opportunity to get on intimate terms with them, to spend even one hourless day, as children do, guddling for pebbles, eating tiny strawberries, lying on the moss watching the flicker of light in the canopy of birch leaves, following the flight of a dragonfly, gazing at caterpillar, slow-worm and ant.

Within a stone's throw of the passing throng there is an intensity of life absorbed in its own processes. To watch it is to be aware of one's own kinship with it. And to catch a glimpse of a new dimension. What are one's personal problems compared to those of the ant struggling to shift a piece of provender ten times bigger than itself? Can one hope ever to create anything as perfect as the nest of the willow warbler in the bushes on the bank? Who ever made a song as fresh and lively as that of the chaffinch suddenly rippling into the air above one's head? To watch and listen is to achieve a cure for distress more lasting than the one contained in pill or potion or found on the psychiatrist's couch.

Climbing the hill to reach 800 feet in 1° miles one is quickly among moor and pine and the small fields wrested long ago from the heather. Here is hill air with the scent of bog myrtle. This is where the whins are a dazzle of gold and the small plumes of bog-cotton spread like snow over the wetlands.

So here buzzards glide and snipe ('sky-goats' in Gaelic) flicker and bleat in the half-night. This is the place for movement, and kinship with the buzzard means the urge to climb every hill in sight and to rove from summit to summit. Chunks of time are needed here for the therapy to work and an abandoning of schedules.

To set off at dusk and wander the tops till after sunrise is what gives a totally new outlook in the heights. Why not, when one can catch up on sleep of an afternoon, stretched under a flowering gean in the shelter of a dyke?

Hill, tree and water are here waiting, not to be looked at dimly through a glass but to be known closely, to be touched, tasted, breathed in, delightedly discovered. If every child in the land had a hill to climb, trees to wander among, a loch to plunge in, I guarantee that hooligans and vandals would be few.

It's too late for that alas, and there is no real substitute. But it is reassuring that there is a growing respect for the power of the wilderness in the healing of human lives.

August

A queer summer we've had of it so far—winds, even at gale force, and hardly a day without a cloudful of rain, yet not enough of a soaking to prevent the drying-up of many drinking sources. The April sun, which beamed giddily across the sky from day to day is part culprit. Burns have had to be tapped and water carried.

That's a timely enough reminder of how dependent we still are on the uncontrollable. Perhaps we might yet be persuaded to make sacrifice on the altar of progress of some cherished commodity. Why not the surplus private car? Perhaps funds could be channelled, say, from endless road-making to the provision of adequate water supplies.

The bees have had a thin season. The flowers are there and in their glory, in colours defying the grey-white sky—yellow bedstraw, red foxglove, blue harebell and so many more. Yet the wind and the showers kept the bees too often hive-bound. Still, we are promised a warm week in late August and that might just coincide with the blooming of the heather.

The fruit crop is good. The gooseberries in the lea of the west wall have never looked so plump and golden, raspberries are lush and black and red currants a-shine. Only the strawberries, profuse as they are, need a touch of the sun. Best of all, kind friends have brought small gifts of sugar, so that the crop need not all go to waste.

Summer is summer no matter what the colour of the sky, and summer means the advent of the young. We hear the gate crank open, we look up from hoeing or fruit-picking or stamp-selling, and there they are coming up the path in bleached denims, patched sweaters and always the same clearness of eye. From many parts they come and all on the same quest—looking for the bare bones of their world, for some place uncluttered by the wonders of technology.

They are not easily dazzled, these young. They look closely and clearly at everything. Man must go to the moon, they say, but he must also live in a clean place here on earth and eat clean food and make things that please him. They do give us faith.

We will remember the four French students who pitched their tent in a hollow by the burn. They had worked hard at jobs uncongenial to them in their home towns and had saved enough for some weeks' wandering. They used public transport to avoid adding pollution, though they could have shared a car. They gathered wood for their fire and mushrooms for their pot, and they left a small stone table and seats as their signature on the landscape.

The old come visiting, too. For many of them, if they were here when young, there is a sadness, a sense of paradise lost. The rocks remain of course. The burns still flow. From the shouting-stone there is the same strange echo through the hills. But the trimness of cultivation has gone, along with the small houses demolished by time. And these people are looking for the vanished races and their ways.

I spent an afternoon sharing a relived childhood with a small middle-aged lady now married in Glasgow. We wandered round the ruin of her croft home, where the granny spoke only Gaelic, where she herself had papered the walls and fetched sand from the burnside to scrub the dresser.

To her delight she found still intact the outbuilding where they took their Saturday bath, and listening to her I could see her wandering up the hill on an early summer evening to let the breeze dry her hair and to keep a tally of the lambs.

The bog-cotton which they used for stuffing pillows and the flowers and mosses which all served as medicines or dyes, giving a sweetness and a savour, and excitement to life, these are still here. But who uses them now? And the fields that were full of potatoes and corn? She gazed disbelievingly at the swamp of rushes. 'The drains are all choked', she said.

We looked for the well but couldn't find it among the overlying bog. She began to mistrust her memory. Then, brightening, 'The cherry-tree,' she said, 'the cherry-tree where the cuckoo always called!' By the burn we found a stump, recently sawn off for firewood. 'It must have died,' I said. 'Yes. Yes, trees do die.'

We walked back a little sadly. 'I came up this path every day to school, taking milk to the master. It was good milk!' We turned, looking back.

'There were so many of us then and there was so much to do, we never wearied. There's where the boys played shinty. We'd fetch our messages from the van at the foot of the brae on Saturday and on Sunday night there was a prayer meeting in the big schoolroom. There were classes in the evening for folk who'd left school and wanted to go on learning.

'Berries and nuts grew everywhere and sometimes we'd find a wild bees' honey-comb. We'd work to do in the fields after school and it was hard, but everyone helped. Sometimes neighbours quarrelled but you always knew you could count on them in trouble. And there was guising at Hallowe'en and ceilidhs…'

She was smiling when she left. She'd had her childhood. Nothing could alter that. It's the undertones of that kind of childhood so many of the young are looking for today.

September

As we adjust to the coming of September we wonder, a little sadly, where the sun has been since April. We can remember one evening in

June when it was hot enough to walk up to the loch wearing a swim-suit with one garment on top, to revel in total immersion in that incomparable element—loch water.

'You don't swim there?' say visitors who know only the joys of blue salt sea and yellow sand. 'Indeed we do,' comes the emphatic answer. But their faces do not register acceptance. How can one convey the experience to them?

As one's feet leave the steady floor of rock and sink slightly into the ooze one pushes gently off among the swaying reeds and at eye-level one meets the calm stare of a tufted duck, before she glides off to join her brood. The small trout jump happily ahead and the swifts scream and circle in their absorbing insect hunt. There is no sense of alienation or intrusion. One feels totally accepted by the brotherhood.

A swim in the loch is an essential ingredient of summer. Another is tea in the garden and, if possible, dinner and breakfast too. Breakfast is the thing. One emerges quietly, preferably barefoot, to sit in the long shafts of yellow light, toes in the grass and face tilted to the gentle sun. The tea has the taste of nectar and bright chaffinches and a clear-eyed robin share the crumbs. The day's chores seem a million miles away. And what are chores when one feels strong enough to lift the world on one's shoulders?

This year we have not breakfasted outside. But there are other summers. Though the sun has rarely dazzled us since April the garden crops don't seem to have suffered much. The greens are shining and plump, the onions stout and golden. Peas and early potatoes have been succulent and sweet. Only carrots and beet are disappointing. The spring drought took the growing out of them.

Jam-making has been limited by the lack of sugar, but at least there is the knowledge that the birds have not gone short. Many a small beak has been stained with ungrudged raspberry juice.

Nothing, of course, can spoil the splendour of the heather. Indeed, under a grey sky it has a special warmth, matching the brilliance of the rowan fruit. And the bees at last are taking their fill.

We're reluctant to acknowledge that summer is slipping away, but we can't ignore the signs. There is the chattering of swallows lining up their families in preparation for lift-off. And the newly-arrived fieldfares compete with them for perching space. The robin is trilling his shrill little song. The young one who follows me around the garden is getting a sharp look in his eye, as his chest feathers turn from russet to red.

As the birds prepare for winter, so must we. We are lucky enough to have learnt some lore from the crofters who have now almost all gone under the hill. They were indeed wise in their time and only now is the spendthrift world catching up with them. We remember how they would cut every shred of grass for hay, using a sickle where there as no room to swing a scythe. So that's what we do now. And, what's more, we load the boot of the car with the lush reapings from the roadside verges on our weekly return trip from town.

Bridget, the goat, will turn it into milk and crowdie for us in the months ahead. She thrives on a diet of nettles, thistles and practically every known weed, thus fulfilling a dual role of provider and cleaner-up of the wild patches. She also supplies first-class fertiliser for the food crops. She's a friendly and intelligent part of the scheme of things into the bargain. Watching her nibble and chew, her lips closing delicately round the live nettles, her alert, amber eyes looking for the next bit of nutrient she can absorb, one thinks more than a little sadly of the acres that are allowed to rot, while the price of milk and cheese soars. Who ever heard of a world shortage of nettles or an increase in the price of docken?

Then, on further reflection, one is cheered. For surely we shall one day reach a point where necessity will bring the families back into the wilderness, not to seek temporary refuge from urban stresses or to indulge in killing sports but to produce food and health and balanced living and help save some of the human race from becoming robots sustained by chemicals.

'Oh, the lovely valley that was in it!' said the old Irishman from Donegal, shaking his head at the prospect of choked fields and falling fences beyond the garden gate. If only his verb could be in the future tense. Land, the most precious asset in the world, since it is irreplaceable, is sold off in leisure plots. Surely soon there will be an authority with the courage and wisdom to make ownership of land carry the obligation to cherish and improve it.

October

The lingering hope of a summer, even an Indian one, finally faded and we came abruptly to our senses when Ben Wyvis emerged from the mist the other morning resplendent in a coat of snow. Rime on the cabbages and snow on the ben, while the birches have not lost a green leaf, is a measure of the strange feel of this season. There's nothing for it but to harvest when we can and to step confidently onto the merry-go-round of nature.

No power of ours can beat back the wind-driven hail, but to walk through a storm is to generate heat enough to make the toes tingle. Then, when the bright calm comes, as it always eventually does, we have energy to reach the rowan berries before the fieldfares strip them from the trees.

It is a great lift to watch the eager feasting of these birds and we don't grudge them a drop of rowan juice. There's plenty for them on the more inaccessible branches. They richly deserve their fill and one is glad to see them replete after their long storm-driven flight across the North Sea. Their coming reminds us, too, that this land is still a haven, with its back to the more cruel kinds of cold.

With strict economy and the use of saccharine in tea we have managed to save enough sugar to make at least a measure of rowan wine. It lifts the gloom from a winter's day as nothing else can, with its bouquet made of the memory of bright red fruit and blue October sky.

This very year, of course, the brambles are tantalisingly profuse. We shall eat them warm from the sun, anyway, if it is not possible to preserve many for winter. And we shall encourage a taste of the savoury by pickling whatever crops we can. It's good to be rid of the more cloying forms of sweetness, anyway. Our few combs of honey will be treasured, of course. Their sweetness has the pungency of life itself.

The alder leaves are still green and already, behind each one, there is the tiny swell of next year's bud. When nature is so lavish and so willing it seems ridiculous that anyone should starve. A handful of seed gives roots and greens to feed a family through a winter. There is health and satisfaction for that family in the sowing, the care, the harvesting and the storing of the crops, as well as in the eating.

But if the family let their garden become a trampled midden, turn it into a playground, with swimming pool or ball-game pitch or sell it for speculative 'development', then they may reap pleasure or money, but they cannot live on those.

It's a mere twenty years since a man here looked at his stacks of oats and thought, those will see so many beasts through the winter, that will mean milk and eggs for the family, a feed for the horse, survival for us all till the spring grass comes. He was rich and content.

If he considers their value now in terms of a new car for pleasure trips, a freezer for the kitchen and colour TV for the family, then he is poor and desperately worried. There are limits to be acknowledged.

A man lately home on holiday from Canada brought a photograph for the museum records. It was taken on his parents' wedding day some sixty years ago. Seventy souls are in the picture, aged between eight and eighty.

They are ranged along the front of the house. The old couple sit in the middle, he white-bearded as a prophet, she wearing a lace cap and shawl. The newly-weds stand, to the front but to the side. The bride holds her husband's arm and carries a posy.

There is a piper in full regalia. The dresses, the blouses, the cravats are spotless. Everyone looks steadily ahead. The eyes are serious, but calm, the mouths are firm.

One feels that these members of the human race have an inkling of what it's all about. There is no look of hankering for the impossible, but rather a pride in the possible. There's the sense of togetherness and continuity. This was clearly a real occasion, to be recorded and savoured to the full.

Later there was to be feasting and music in the barn, as our Canadian recalled. But one feels that those men, and those women, too, would soon be talking again of what the summer would bring, of harvest hopes and the doings of far-off friends.

That house is empty now, the barn and byre are roofless, the fields unfenced and bare. Many of those in the picture went to Australia and New Zealand, we were told. One cannot help imagining what they could have made of their lives in their home acres had they been given the chance. And what benefit we would all have reaped from having them and their descendants around.

November

We have had all the warnings now. The geese have come over, ahead of the storms, in ragged, weary-sounding formations. The first gales, those that boom out of the north, lift the roof-slates and send the smoke swirling down the chimney, the first real gales have blown. The garden ground is littered with red and yellow birch and rowan leaves. It really is time to batten the hatches and look winter in the face.

A fallen pine is certainly best cut into logs and kindling for the fire. This year, above all others, is the time to re-establish peat-cutting rights eroded by the march of progress. We are delighted to hear that a neighbour has won his three-year fight to keep his peat-bank clear of trees.

When every place had a peat-stack half as big as the house there was little fear of the dark cold days. Now, with the price of coal rising and the threat of power-cuts, as well as breakdowns, it's a different story.

Though the gales are fast stripping the trees, there is still green growth in sheltered corners. Late spring in the uplands has the compensation of an equally late autumn. Many years there can be a reasonable bite for sheep and even cattle until almost the end of the year.

And there are still harvests to be gathered. Hazelnuts strew the ground. Sloes, elderberries and rose-hips hang on slender bare branches. There is a huge and ancient hawthorn tree still decked with dark-red fruit. And the brambles are all the better for a touch of frost.

This year I have bramble and elderberry wine in the making. The brambles are simply steeping in sugar. The elderberries have been immersed in boiling water, left overnight, and strained; and to the liquid have been added sugar, sliced lemon and a boiling of raisins with ginger and cinnamon. This concoction should ward off coughs and colds, even if it doesn't turn out a classic vintage.

The potatoes have been a crop to rejoice over. Twenty-eight tubers lay close below the surface on one plant and a third of them were the size of grapefruit. Boiled, they melt in the mouth. Two of them, with a slice of butter and a poached egg, make a memorable meal.

The hens, bless them, are red-combed and brisk after a summer moult and a spell of broodiness. The morning thrill is to find the clutch of golden-brown eggs in the shiny straw, warm and smooth to the touch, though ice-cold rain may be splattering through the chinks in the hen-house wall.

In the hives all is quiet now, with guards in position at the entrances to keep out predatory mice. It's good to imagine the clustered bees keeping warm together as they slowly absorb their stores of honey.

There is still, in these heights, the worry of a long-drawn-out harvesting of the oat crop. Many a year the stooks have been out in the fields until each was capped with snow. Yet somehow or other it was ricked and stacked in the end. I can remember a crop of potatoes left in the ground all winter and lifted not much the worse in spring. The earth is a kind nurse.

Worrying for the sheep-men are the ridiculously poor prices some lambs are fetching at the sales. Our forbears were well enough endowed with brawn and brain on a diet of fresh oatmeal, milk, cheese, eggs, potatoes and some greens, with the occasional rabbit and, just now and again, one of the laird's salmon that 'jumped the fence' from the river beyond the hayfield!

We'd probably be all the better for a return to a simpler diet and we could save materials by cutting out a lot of kitchen gadgetry. Freshness is the vital factor and that can be achieved only by home production.

Whatever cares beset a community they can always be put aside for an hour or two when the folk get together. This is what we did in the big schoolroom at Hallowe'en. A harvest, good or bad, must be feasted and the coming of winter wished away. There were peats on the fire, oat sheaves in the dark corners and witches glowering into their cauldrons.

The children have not lost the art of guising and of the fashioning of turnip-lanterns. There were some really splendid efforts. And the old tricks of snatching an apple in the teeth from the water-tub and of grabbing a bite from a swinging, treacle-smeared scone still have all their appeal.

We have luck in the community—a resident fiddler and a piper and, best of all, three young brothers who are shaping as first-rate traditional fiddlers under the expert guidance of their teacher from over the hill. With a couple of singers, a guitar, a banjo and a *fear an tighe* who cemented it all with fun we had the ingredients of a ceilidh.

Outside, the moon did us proud, hanging round and yellow, like a huge lantern in the sky. There was frost among the stars.

The magic stirred.

December

As December wraps the real dark of winter about our shoulders there is inevitably a tendency to find a reason or an excuse for jobs that can be done indoors, or at least under cover.

The wine is bottled now, the onions are hanging in splendidly plump and aromatic clusters, roots and tubers are snugly clamped. This is the time for brewing great pots of broth, perfumed with leek, thyme and parsley. The smell, wafting out to the garden, takes the stiffness from frozen fingers, brings back a whiff of the growing days of summer and leads the mind to plan next year's garden.

We shall abandon, I think, the sowing of runner beans. An early frost nearly always does for them before they're eatable. Beetroot must be started later. This year the spring drought held them back and then they bolted.

We must renew the plastic cloches which do tear in the gales, but which are so valuable in bringing on the welcome early bite of lettuce and carrot.

These plans light up the mind when all that can be done outwith the house is the tidying of bee gear, the securing of the henhouse roof with strategically placed boulders, the lining of the shed walls to keep out the worst of the frost.

THE CROFTING WAY

There is great satisfaction in putting a pailful of sliced turnip and chopped kail under the nose of Bridget the goat, watching and hearing her enjoyment of it, and in bringing her armfuls of the grass we gathered from the roadside in summer, now sweetly dry and scented with wild flowers. She is still turning it into milk, though she has to spend most of the worst days of storm cooped in her stall.

The art of the old lifestyle on the crofts was of course to see that winter could be faced and lived through without panic or disaster. There was no question then of packing the store-cupboard and the deep freeze; thrift was a necessity.

When money entered so little into life, inflation could not be a factor. You saved your own seed, or exchanged it with the man from over the hill, fed your beasts with what you could grow and mucked your fields with the very best of fertilisers—dung. The treading and grazing of cattle kept the ground in good heart and the rank weeds at bay. Lime was burnt in kilns, now starkly ruined. There was balance and control.

Of course there were disasters—crops that failed through drought or flood and beasts that died. But then there were folk drawn together by community of interest as well as natural human fellowship, and everyone helped out. A basket of eggs would appear like manna on the morning doorstep. A cartload of turnips or oat-sheaves would come swaying, unheralded, over the horizon.

There would always be someone with a few more peats than he could burn. No-one was willing to admit to hardship. Trouble was always tacitly understood. If the worst came to the worst, a cattle beast was bled and the blood mixed with oatmeal so that a human family might survive.

We must expect no increase in our standard of living over the next few years, they tell us. Does the spine shudder at the thought of no advance from the fish-finger, no dafter antics from the little men on the coloured screen in the corner of the livingroom?

Let a child savour a mealy potato that crumbles on the tongue, a carrot fresh from the ground that he can crunch till the juice flows through his teeth, and he will be hooked for life, discarding fish-fingers along with iced lollies and bubble-gum as insipid trash. There are still adventures he can live out on his own, without prompting from cardboard characters. It must surely depend on what is meant by standard.

Here there are some due for a seasonal increase. With less to be done outside and with certain indoor jobs agreed as optional (a small layer of dust can safely be left in corners till the spring!) there are

158

occasional days which must be set aside for celebration—for walking abroad to look and listen.

Calm in December is a gift straight from the gods. The midday sun rides easily along the ridge of the hill beyond the window. The birches are purple shadows, lit to silver at the crown. Three wild swans fly out of the north, their necks outstretched, looking for a haven. To the west the far high hills are white with snow. The moor, bare now of heather bloom and myrtle, is brown and ageless.

The foundations of the old dwellings are clearly visible. For 3,000 years folk have lived here, loved and hated, fought and died. In the peat a sword was found once and a swift, light leather brogue and a flint scraper—tokens of a life that was hard won and cherished mightily. Surely it cannot fizzle out now in a scrabble for more 'goods' than anyone knows what to do with and which pile up to choke the earth with rotting.

In the plantation by the loch there is the quiet of close-grown trees. This is the dead of the year, the biding time. Yet the young branches are vivid green. Suddenly there is a rushing of wings. A flock of bull-finches whirls into a tree, lacing it with colour, making a December festival.

1975

January

Here we go—stepping gaily into a new year with grass in the sheltered places lying like splashes of fresh green paint, buds swelling on the hawthorn and last season's pansies and next season's primulas blooming happily together in the gardens.

On New Year's morning itself we were practically first-footed by the bees. Emerging sleepily, after a few hours' slumber since the departure of our human visitors, we were greeted by a familiar droning, and there were the bees, going busily in and out of their own small doors. This can be perilous for them, of course, as activity may make them consume too much of their precious stores. So our first job of the year was to boil their candy.

This really was a time of truce, though we're well aware that the old enemy, winter, must be preparing an ambush, waiting for the familiar reinforcements of frost, gale and snow. Meantime, it's hard to resist the temptation to dig and plant, when the daylight lingers until nearly five and the small birds are gargling the rust from their throats. They'll be trying to nest, I shouldn't wonder, those that haunt the hollows. But the hill birds are more wary. Hawk and buzzard still sail austerely through their domain of cold air in the heights. They are not easily beguiled.

With the cost of keeping any livestock becoming rapidly prohibitive we are scanning the horizon in a search for substitutes for the more conventional foodstuffs. They used to feed horses on pounded whin, we remember, in the 'hungry gap' of old-time springs. There are whins in plenty along the roadside and some of them in dazzling bloom. The goat will eat them as they are.

We often think of a charming Czech family with whom we once spent some summer weeks, communicating via the father in the delightful French which he had kept hoarded in his brain unused for 25 years. In the garden of the little house a few miles out of Prague every inch of ground served a purpose. One stretched a hand out of the bedroom window and gathered peaches for breakfast, peaches warm with the morning sun. The cherries were over, the apples were to come. Among the fruit trees, on the patchy grass, young turkeys strutted and gurgled.

In pens and hutches lining the back-yard were chickens, ducks, geese, rabbits and even a couple of sheep. The feathers and wool were almost as much prized as the eggs and milk these animals produced and all were treated with the greatest respect and care.

On outings in the ancient family car, roadside grasses, herbs and flowers would be cut, sparingly and avoiding any damage to the roots, for two-legged as well as four-legged consumption. The woods would be searched for fungi, mosses, berries, pine-cones and dead branches for the fire.

The fields of sunflowers were perhaps our greatest delight—*tournesol* as the French call them. One could imagine actually catching them as they just turned their heavy, burnished heads, following the sun on its majestic course through that dazzling sky. Sensing our joy, our host stopped the car and dashed out to pick two huge specimens which we carried home in our suitcase and kept until they withered at last. We tried hopefully to grow sunflowers here, in the sunniest, most sheltered spot, but alas the golden heads had only bloomed when the early frosts killed them.

One crop we mean to try this year is the cultivated dandelion. Sitting hugging the fire on a blustery evening, scanning the seed catalogues, we admit to being intrigued by the idea of fostering a plant usually howked out as a rank weed. But we are assured it really is multi-purpose. The leaves can be eaten, we know, as salad, or blanched and used like chicory; the flowers can be made into wine, and the roots into the equivalent of coffee. It sounds as if it couldn't fail.

Another mid-European friend, staying a summer with us here, was perplexed and horrified at the general under-use of natural resources. 'You let that dead wood rot,' he would say in his faultless English, 'when it would make a lovely fire. And you burn coal when there is so much peat. And the moor where no-one goes—it is covered with mushrooms and berries. You could live like lords...' Many a time we bless him. It's salutary to see, and to be seen, as ithers see us!

Perhaps pounded these wild foods would eke out the hen's mash. The hazelnuts which litter the ground in the woods down by the big loch must surely be as full of nourishment for beast as for man. Perhaps a way could be devised of shelling and crushing them.

We have always had an idea that more use could be made of the heather which grows by the acre from doorstep to doorstep in the croft lands. The bees make good use of its bloom of course, and the rich, brown honey results. It will give ale and wine for human consumption. The ruminants do enjoy a chew at it, especially when it is the only growing thing protruding through the snow. It was also used to make thatch, bedding, ropes, pot-scrubbers and brooms, all of which achieved their various purposes most adequately and were so easily renewed at the cost only of a little time and skill. But could it be cut, dried and stacked for use as winter feed, we wonder.

The other day we watched the reaction of Bridget, the goat, to the heather on her small grazing plot. She seemed to enjoy the savour of the withered flowers as much as that of the fresh green lower growth. And she consumed the bundle we cut and put in her rack for supper. Of course, goats are exceptional feeders. Perhaps more of them could be kept, as they were in the times of Highland austerity.

February

As a fanfare for February, winter whistled up a gale or two and a couple of mini-blizzards, but they cannot be taken too seriously when the sun rides a little higher each day above the rim of the hill and the outdoor afternoons are stretching almost into evenings.

When the cloud cover breaks, one can duly salute the sun. Tilt the head back, eyes closed, and you can feel real warmth on the eyelids. It is enough to send you searching under the hawthorn hedge for a sight of the snowdrops—and there they are, slim white spears ready to break from their green sheaths.

Then there are the sudden, unexpected bonuses—five waxwings perched like bright toy birds on the bare branches of the alder, happily replete after a feast of berries. We blessed them for cheering a grey Sunday.

And the reality of the sun and snow signs on the television weather map may mean half a day of magic, with the hills glistening white under a brilliant sky, drifted snow lying in shapes of such perfection as cannot go unheeded and each small hole made by stick or boot with its own hidden blue shadow. The loch is covered in wave-moulded ice and in the calm you can hear the huge floes creak as they move to their own rhythm.

This is a time for looking inward. Though the world may be a global village and it is essential to feel our kinship with the people of Peru, yet in order not to be overwhelmed by the sheer size and complexity of things it is also essential, I think, to stand firm on our own doorstep, to look hard at our own corner and to hold on to the realities we know. The isolation of winter helps, lapping us in its folds, hemming us in. Dependent we all are on almost everyone else, yet we are still dependent on ourselves.

Waking on a wild morning, we draw back the curtain and there, as we thought, is the snow hurtling horizontally across the face of the hill. We turn the light switch. No power.

Sparing a thought for the men who have been struggling, maybe for hours, to find the fault in the line on the high exposed ground to the west, we go down to light the fire.

There is the immediacy of the feel of pine-cones and twigs for kindling, the smell of resin as the flame leaps and the cheerful bubbling of the kettle. We are in touch with wood, flame, heat, water. The bread stock is low, it is near grocer's day and the road is closing, but we have milk, eggs and flour, and pancakes make a breakfast for the gods.

By dinner-time the fire is a solid glow and the broth pan wedged firmly in a corner. Goat and hens are snug in the straw, cheerfully cudding and pecking, the cats stretched out at the hearth. As dusk comes, with the power restored to dazzle us, we almost wish for an evening without the 'electric'.

The greatest tranquillity comes in sitting, toes stretched to the warmth, staring into the fire, with candles casting soft light on folded hands and faces. Then it is bliss to be cut down to size, to let the elements have their say, to watch and listen.

By contrast, Bride's Day was another of the bonuses—a day like herself, quiet and mild, with the light streaming from a milk-blue sky. There was a feel of Eden in the garden—the fantails strutting round their loft with soft, persistent cooing; the bright-combed hens, along with chaffinches and sparrows, eagerly snatching up the scattered feed; the goat cavorting like a kid, bees dancing in the warm air and the orange cat lying sunning himself, like a small happy tiger, gazing sleepily at the action.

It was a day for the sheep to go traipsing over the tops, shunning shepherd and dog, for the starlings to try out all their repertoire, from curlew to snipe and back to peewit, making the heart leap till the trick was recognised.

The hills to the south put on their italianate air, mauve shadows filling the folds, while to the west there was the alpine look of withdrawn white peaks, tinged with sunglow. After dark the burn sang sweet and clear under the huge chandelier of stars. There was the scent of untouched earth.

This was not winter, nor was it spring. It was a time right out of season, a time with the magic identity of legend, clear as an image from the greatest bard, yet real, close at hand, to be seen and savoured by us mortals of today. A time to keep hoarded in the hand.

March

It's a day when to be breathing is plenty and if work is in the fields then it's a feast; a day for the children to be busy outside till dusk, a day to open windows for the sick, for the old to go pacing the garden walk.

A lark shakes winter from his wings and his throat as he erupts from the brown moor, announcing spring. The blackbird had beaten him to it by several weeks, trying out his own quiet inward notes from the shelter of the hawthorn hedge. But that was just a private advance intimation, for he is a garden pet who shares the hens' mash with the robin and a chaffinch or three. The hill lark is a mountaineer, his kingdom bounded only by that of the buzzard and the hawk.

Shading our eyes against the noon sun we stop in our tracks to watch and listen. The light filters through his vibrating wings. How so small a creature can let loose such a volume of sound is what gives one pause. It's good to pause a little at this time for, lowering our gaze earthwards, we see the pile of work that looms in the garden.

The ground is still on the heavy side, but there is clearing everywhere to be done. Last summer's weeds still look healthy, for the frosts have not done their usual job. There are bonfires to be made and dung heaps to be shifted. Soon we shall be completely in thrall. The earth is a taskmistress, but one we gladly slave for.

The joy of collecting a pitcher of milk, a handful of eggs and a basket of greens every chilly morning is a real reward. And each renewal of plant and bush seems more miraculous than the last. As the back begins to ache one tends to wander round, to peer into the heart of the snowdrop florets, to stroke the buds on the currant bushes, to smooth the trailing leaves in the strawberry patch.

Then, inevitably, one afternoon when even the wind is warm, there is the temptation to go stretching the legs on a walk across the moor. There, lately, on such an expedition near the old hut circles, we found flints. Tiny, chiselled scraps of golden, amber and rose-pink flint, they lay exposed, after thousands of years' burial on the crests of the newly-turned forestry furrows. The imagination sprang alive. We saw the people of the flints, felt the skill in the fingers that had worked them, heard the talk and the laughter as they used them to scrape and fashion skins for clothing, to pick marrow from bones for a feast, to make tools for all the business of living. And they must have seen the colour and the shape in the flint and seen that it was good.

They must have had time to wander, too, to see the image of the hill reflected on the surface of the loch, the beam of moonlight broken into fragments by the waves on a night of storm, to hear the lark sing and know that it meant a fresh burst of living. These things must have made them happy, or sad, for when, later, they evolved a language sophisticated enough to express emotion, it was the impact of their surroundings on mind and heart that they recorded.

Perhaps a man, on a solitary hunt, may have stooped to drink from a pool, seen his face mirrored in the still water and paused to wonder who he was and what his years in the hunting grounds meant. They were not always easy, that is clear. There was danger and distress. But he could invent the ever-happy grounds for later on, when his bones would be at rest.

Meanwhile the pressures on him would have been those of necessity, not of greed. A handful of berries would satisfy a summer hunger and in winter his belly could flatten between hunting trips. One skin would cover him so why would he have two? He would not have needed more than one house when that was enough to shelter his family. He could foresee no end to the things that served his purposes—to stone and wood, clay, bone, hide, grass and the wild harvests of moor and loch. He used them sparingly enough, with no thought of exploitation. If the peoples in today's world still living lives fairly close to the primitive Eskimos and the Australian aborigines appear happy and have the gift for laughter, then surely these ancestors of ours must have been content with their lot, too. We're glad to link hands with them, as we finger the small, fragile tools they fashioned.

Who, today, would have the skill and patience to make any comparable thing? Being in thrall to the machine we have only to move levers or assemble parts and there's small scope for the working of mind or heart in that.

But it can't be too late. There are small stirrings everywhere. The centres of industry are self-destructible. People are emerging, on foot, to look at hills and trees, stones, birds, snowdrifts and the smallest hidden flowers. They're learning all over again, as primitive man had to learn. Humility comes into it, and respect, and that's the beginning of the wisdom the world needs.

April

The April showers are laced with sleet. The ground is cold-shouldering the seed. There's a bleak look about the hill, the heather dank and brown and the birches still in winter mauve. Perhaps the most cheering sight, in late afternoon, is the blue wood-smoke swirling from a neighbour's chimney. It's good, yet, to be able to thaw out fingers and toes at tea-time.

But the daffodils are yellowing and the tally of lambs rises daily. It is heartening to hear their cries and watch their capers. They're as thrilled as were all their predecessors with the chilly world they've inherited. There will be losses. There always are. But the fittest will survive. It's the way of the world.

The curlews glide and call in the grey air and in the evening there's the flicker of snipe. A flock of peewits stand, at dusk, in a snow-flecked field, heads held to the wind. It's an upland spring, like so many before it, like so many that will follow.

The Easter folk have come and gone. Tight lips, suppressing shivers, crease into tentative smiles as they acknowledge our unconcern about the elements. Piling wood on the fire, we offer tea and scones as a substitute for the picnic in the car. It is good to see the faces glow as we tell about last year's April and the long days spent working in the garden, sleeves rolled high.

It is uncertainty that keeps you on your toes. You take each season as it comes. Taking each day as it comes, you find this one is a time for clearing ground, that one a time for slipping in a handful of seed, the next a time for repairing gear under cover. So, slowly, the work proceeds and in the end there'll be a time for feasting.

The Easter folk expected the skies to clear, only for them go home with a love of the mist and the wind. 'We'll shake the kaleidoscope,' said one. 'There are always new patterns.' As we see them off and go back to scanning our arch of sky for portents, we bless them for their company and for the exchanges of fellowship: 'Thanks for your ceilidh,' as the old people used to say.

It is the never-failing renewal of life against all the odds, a thumbsup in the teeth of the storm, that builds confidence. There is much change and rumour of change all about. The enormities that accompany progress clamour for attention. There is the roar and grind of the huge container lorries that cruise along the main road down below. As one pauses, agape, to let them pass, one tries to visualise, with a sense of incomprehension, the gigantic constructions to which they're carrying essential parts. If they kill and maim a few unwary humans on the way it seems this must be accepted as in the natural order.

Yet the small things manage to survive and it's to them one turns with a real leap of delight—to the dazzle of coltsfoot on the bare verges, to the primrose and violet hidden in the ditch, to the brightening buds on larch and hazel.

There is movement in the uplands, too: movement one can follow from beginning to end. There's the slow striding of the sheepmen across the face of the hill and the controlled racing of their dogs. A pause and a shout of command and you know the look of satisfaction on the human face as a lamb is re-united with its mother.

A trailer-load of dung rumbles past and you read, as on a printed page, the tale of ploughing and planting and eventual digging of great mealy potatoes. Turnips and straw are shifted, too, to clear the winter fields and satisfy the huge spring hunger of cattle and sheep. Young flocks which have wintered happily in the high fields are returned to their owners' lusher parks. Stirks are marketed and the small men astonish the dealers with the quality of their few, well-cared-for beasts.

All this movement goes serenely on under a black sky and a lashing of hail, because the capacity for faith is inborn. This is the lambing-snow, harsh and cruel. The cuckoo-snow is still to come. But still there's the trust in sun and wind. A few days' blow and shine and the ground will be workable, we say, looking each other happily in the eye. It always is, in the long run.

And, sure enough, there comes a day of grace, a jewel of a day, when even the withered grasses take on a shine, the loch has the glint of blue glass and the gulls are clamouring at their nesting-sites. Winter will still linger a good while in the dazzle of the high tops but in the quiet hollow by the burn the sun is warm on the hand. Small signs and tokens are gratefully received. This is the kind of spring we know and understand.

May

Snow on the garden and a cuckoo shouting faintly from the birches on the hillside—that was our May morning. Not one for rising before the sun, however urgent the quest for beauty. The snow has vanished by noon, of course. The cuckoo retreated to return in a day or two's time, his call still coy, like a diffident invitation to the dance.

The lambs look to be thriving. A couple of sturdy twins have adopted the goat as playmate and sneak off from parental control whenever they can for a friendly gambol. There's a coal-black youngster, too, who's as frisky as they come and blithely unaware of being odd-man-out. The daffodils and primroses have scarcely ever bloomed as profusely as this year and in the intervals of brilliant blue they outshine the sun.

The geese have gone over, heading north in huge, wind-scattered skeins. One feared for them on their great journey. But their instinct

Helen with a calf

is as strong and as sure as their wing-beats and their voices, and one knows they must be right to go.

There is much nesting activity. The starlings clatter in and out of their hole under the eaves. Wagtails dart about the grass, collecting goat-hairs. Chaffinches guard their domain with shrill song. Farther afield, the moor and hill and loch birds are quieter now that nests are built, eggs laid and incubation in progress.

Every evening, regularly, as though to timetable, the black-headed gulls fly down the strath from the loch to feed in the pastures. The fantails have proudly hatched a pair of young.

So life goes on busily renewing itself, with never a thought of waiting till conditions are wholly favourable. The birches are slowly greening, the bright new grass stems cover the withered yellow ones, the larches sport their brilliant buds.

At the back of the wind and beyond the gloom of the cloudbanks there must be the heat needed to bring out the more sophisticated forms of growth we humans have developed. Meantime we gaze at the bare, heavy garden plots, hands that itch to get at the planting still thrust unwillingly into pockets. There's at least one comforting thought—surely water will not be scarce this summer.

This is the hungry gap, when we eke out the last of the potatoes and turnips and kail and it seems as if the new greens will never be ready, though some are struggling gallantly along under cloches. We remember the May storms of twenty years ago, when the crofts hereabouts were worked to the old rhythm. Folk then took the long view and we bless them as always for their legacy of stoic patience. A tightening of the belt was in the order of things and didn't do much harm. A boiling of nettles was an excellent dish for man and beast and the children would suck the primroses for sweets. Then, when the cow calved, what rejoicing there was, with great bubbling jugs of milk, white puddings, made with gelatine, the first butter to spread on the oatcakes and cheese in the making. Only those who have gone short of it can really savour the goodness of natural food.

When few beasts were kept there was a close link between human and animal life. The family depended on the cow, the sheep, the hens, the pig, as they, in turn, depended on the family. By modern standards of hygiene it was deplorable, of course, to have cattle under the same roof as people, to have hens perched on the house beams and lambs sleeping at the fire. But the breath of a healthy cow is sweet and when you came in from a day's battling with the spring cold you were glad of the warmth of sleek, bulky bodies.

There's a crofter on the far coast of Sutherland who has a cow directly descended from the one his family brought to that bleak spot when they were evicted from a green inland glen. That is a measure of the man and beast link.

Sheep were kept snug inbye and the wool transferred from their backs to those of the family. How one weeps to see pictures of beasts jammed into trucks and whirled through nights and days across alien hills to end, some of them, in grisly mountains of frozen flesh. From the madness of the world we turn with relief to the cultivation of one small garden. Soon the swifts will come swooping out of nowhere, with warm air on their backs and there will be a thrust of growth as everything makes up for a lost spring.

June

June—and the hillside birches that are the backcloth to our lives are massed in green. They respond to the revolving sun, casting long morning shadows to the west and in the evenings standing separate in the yellow light.

We've had our long-awaited glimpse of summer brilliance. It was good to be assured that there really is a sky above the ceiling of grey cloud. We'd almost forgotten that look of limitless blue, with the gaudy old sun rocking its way from horizon to horizon.

The peas have shot through the ground, and there are radishes to crunch. Mint, chives and thyme give savour to the dullest dish. Each day we survey the lettuce seedlings and will them to grow. The little alpine strawberries are flowering, and there's good bloom on the apple trees.

We go a little daft when things get really on the move—work to the point of exhaustion and then take a spell stretched on the ground, letting the sun beat on the eyelids. The thing to do is to lie on the ground itself, scorning rug or cushion, and to walk barefoot when you can.

We have so much to learn from the East in this regard. Let's listen to those small, patient people. Grow a tree, even a minute one, in at least a pot of real earth. Handle it gently. Water it. Watch it. If you have an emperor, have him descended from the sun. If you have a flag or emblem let it sport stars and moons and the leaves of trees. Keep your eyes open to the passing of a cloud, the movement of a branch, even glimpsed from a square of window. There is arrogance in the crushing of a single blade of grass. Watch it continually. See how it moves towards the sun, shines, fades, withers, dies, and you learn about the whole pattern of life.

The roadside flowers are appearing—lady's smock and eyebright and tormentil. And there are butterflies. Each day we're thankful to have the luck to live where there are flowers and butterflies.

A brother from Canada stayed with us once in May. Canada! In the mind's eye the word evokes vast clean prairies between the forests, the mountains and the lakes. Yet he would come in to breakfast from an early walk, a shine on his face as he said: 'There are flowers!'

Friends from Suffolk came one day. Suffolk! Another word with magic overtones—thatched houses, cottage gardens, farmland and sea. But the magic faded when they said: 'We scarcely see a butterfly'.

The old soothsayer of Easter Ross, the Brahan Seer, foretold the day when not a smoke would rise from the chimneys in these parts. That came about in large measure, when many of the places went 'electric'. He also prophesied the 'black rain', and one wonders if that might be the fall-out from chemical plants. And at what that would entail one can only make a shuddering guess.

Meanwhile there is a garden growing. The earth crumbles to the touch at last, and there's sap under the dry surface. The children run on the grass, stoop to peer at ladybirds and daisies and tilt their faces to the sun. One can live on the scented air, a cup of milk and a cress sandwich. Sadness, one feels, must be somewhere else, on another planet, maybe. This is a time to dance.

But of course one knows about the folk in those other places, the jammed cities, the disputed lands, the dried-up plains. Before it's too late could we each discard some hoarded possession, some cherished plan, pare life to the essential and send a share spinning across the world? It would lift a load from our own shoulders, for possessions breed anxiety and envy, cage-bars and guns and other ugliness. And it would make us human again.

Not long since no door in these parts was ever locked, no old person unvisited, no child left hungry, though the cupboard held no toys.

The earth gives, tirelessly, pushing foxgloves through the cracks in a falling house. Could we stop a moment to look? With less to hold and guard perhaps we could feel more akin to the Asian wading in his rice-field, to the Lapp tapping birch bark for sustenance. A sharing of discomfort might make the distances grow less.

I'm reminded of the women from Jamaica whose eyes lit as they handled iron pots and box-irons in the museum here. 'We use them still,' they said. Their faces were sad as they looked at the small fields beyond the window. 'But you don't make anything grow here?'

It would have taken me all day to give an answer they could understand. But a frail bridge was building.

August

Three weeks of sunshine to one of rain is about as good a recipe for growth as we can get. That's what we've had this year and the garden crops are bulging in the rows. Going out on a bright blue morning to gather salad stuff one can almost see the greens getting greener and pods and roots swelling.

Only the strawberries suffered a little, the sun having ripened them early just before the needed rain fell. But they're still yielding many a bowlful of dessert, and the Alpines, bearing their crop higher, are fruiting to perfection. Eat some straight from the plant on a morning wander and it's like absorbing a mouthful of scented sunshine.

The bees have kept us busy this year, swarming merrily in apple tree and fruit bush. Very accommodating bees they are, who cluster in accessible places and are easily gathered. Only one small cast made off across the heather and could not be traced. One hopes they find solid shelter where they may not perish.

In a hollow tree farther down the hill a colony has survived for several years. Meantime the hives are healthily full of brood, with honey in the making, and we've been happy to be able to give needed bees to friends. For a queen bee we received the surprise bounty of a box of superb farm vegetables. There's solid satisfaction in the age-old custom of barter.

Ground warm to the touch and steaming gently after a shower has made this a year for mushrooms, both wild and cultivated. With mushrooms for breakfast, strawberries at dinner and honey on the tea-table, one listens with a feeling of guilt to the tales of austerity coming from the radio in the corner of the kitchen.

It's that other voice again. If only it wouldn't keep insisting that things must be assessed in terms of monetary gain. Why not in the realities of fruit, milk, honey, eggs, wool, grass?

Potatoes are too dear to buy so we plan to grow more earlies next year. There's nothing like a steady look ahead. Another plot of ground is needed. Casting an eye over the half acre we see there's only the site of the old rubbish dump at the top of the garden. I take the strongest fork I can find and a couple of pails and dig.

Perhaps there'll be hidden treasure. We once came on a cache of school slates which must have been dumped there when jotters were introduced into the classroom. Friends tell me of beautiful old bottles they have found in similar places. The only ones I come on are smashed into fragments which nick the fingers.

Bits of elegant china cups turn up and one imagines the dismay their breaking caused. The soles of children's boots bring pictures into the mind, as do the half rims of porridge bowls and the rusted peat tongs. The only real treasure is in the pailful of black cinders thrown out with the ashes when coal was plentiful and cheap and which glow day-long on a winter fire. With a good dressing of manure we reckon the reclaimed plot will grow at least a bag of tatties.

The sun shone on the two main midsummer labours here—the clipping and the making of hay. The shorn ewes have settled down again, dazzling white and looking much the same size as their astonished offspring. And the hay has come in sweet-smelling and streaked with green.

A kind neighbour has brought trailer-loads of grass cut on his rough sward to supplement the roadside gatherings. We proffered strawberries as scant enough thanks for such a prize of a gift. The shed is filled to the roof now, for the goat's winter breakfasts. Meanwhile she's chewing her way through the rich banks of undergrowth, demolishing weeds and scrub with a light in her amber eyes and giving more milk than cats, hens and humans can imbibe.

There's little time to walk abroad at present, with everything growing so abundantly and needing to be thinned and cut and weeded. But the summer treats are to hand. There are breakfasts on the grass, with the fantails crouched among the daisies, the hens grabbing crumbs and the cats, replete with milk, blinking in the early sun.

There's the delight of sharing the high air, the quiet, the shapes of hills and the scent of myrtle with the few people who leave the highway to come, on foot, to find these things and of seeing the lines of tension ease from their faces as they take time to look about and to exchange a thought or two.

And the wilderness is on the doorstep. From the gate we can watch the harriers quartering the field across the road. The roe-deer scamper through the scattered pines beyond the garden wall. A garden in the hills is something of a miracle, surviving only with constant vigilance and beating of the bounds. Heather and rushes, beautiful in their own place, would so easily take over all the ground again. And each evening we go the rounds, securing gates and patching fences against the possible marauding of straying sheep and cattle beasts.

Already the darkening is earlier now, when what we really need is a couple of extra hours of light to deal with the jobs in hand. There's no stumbling on melons as we go, but yellow raspberries picked by moonlight have a flavour all their own.

September

This has been a summer to sing about, a festive season if ever there was one. Later on, sitting at the fire, we shall recall it, compare it to others —that of 20 years ago has already come to mind—but for the moment it is unique, like one of the first summers of the world.

We are still immersed in the wonder of being woken by the sun, of working among food crops which are almost embarrassingly prolific and of strolling out after dark, sleeves still rolled high, to listen to the owls and greet the stars with surprise.

These old hills must be clapping their hands, for it's their turn now, with warmth in their bones, to put on their bit of magic. And how splendidly they have done it. Bluebells, scabious and yellow bedstraw shine on the lower slopes, the myrtle is still green; and the heather, rich with the scent of honey, stretches in swathes to the horizon.

There must have been rain, though one was scarcely aware of it, for things are sappy and there has not been a real breakdown in water supplies. We have grown so accustomed to warm air and skies of every possible shade of blue that it may be we shall be caught napping over preparations for winter. The scarlet of berries glimpsed through the still green leaves of the rowan, and a robin stuttering about the garden— these are the only signals that should alert us to the approach of autumn.

It has been a season of surprise and satisfaction. Surprise at the blossoming of things that only managed to put forth a leaf before, satisfaction in that things have ripened in orderly sequence and the old ways of thrift have come back into their own.

Peats have been carted home between hay and harvest, and there has been time to gather the wild crops of raspberries, blaeberries and meadow grass. A sunburnt young face, stained blue with blaeberry juice, is a recipe for laughter with a bacchanalian ring!

We are so rich, with all the fruit and sunshine we have feasted on. And there has been loch water, smooth as satin, to swim in. Garlands have been made of marigolds and the sunflowers are six feet tall.

With no August frost the runner beans have been a real crop this year and small, unexpected plantlings—potential bushes and trees—are sprouting everywhere. Banks of willowherb adorn the wild patch at the top of the garden, making a rose-coloured paradise for the bees. They are busy there and in the heather all the daylight hours, and must be piling up a good surplus of honey.

Needless to say, the weeds have been equally prolific, but with a goat about the place nothing is ever wasted. A pile of nettles, dockens, tansy and sweet cecily goes into her rack at supper-time, along with pea-pods and turnip-tops. To see the glint in her eyes, a marigold protruding from her lips, is to make one give another shout of laughter and clap her back with thanks for a glimpse of the old days of gods and heroes.

This is the time of year when many exiles come back, bringing wives or husbands, children and grandchildren to meet their origins. Most are in shiny cars, some on foot. We often wonder, did they find what they were after when they left? Watching their faces as they look around, we think they mostly wonder that, themselves.

After a browse through the album of old photographs in the museum collection, their eyes ease and glimpses of past days emerge. There was Bill, whose horse pulled the snow-plough to let them get to school in winter. There was Kate, who made the best crowdie you ever tasted.

Brose was monotonous, but the delight of salt herring and mealy potatoes never palled.

The treats are remembered—the trip on the steamer and the picnic on the hill—and the day the telephone link to Inverness was installed and, as the old school log records, 'one of the children engaged the Town Clerk in conversation.' With Hallowe'en and New Year and the 'harvest play', as the summer holidays were called, as red letter days, looked forward to and relished long afterwards, the year swung by to its own rhythm. The bad times seem mostly forgotten, for the good blotted them out with the wealth of their goodness.

So the exiles are drawn back, and we who live here now find the whole place enriched with their memories. There were the old, the cantankerous, the God-fearing, the schemers and the kind; the young, the meek and the wild. There was loving and hating, quarrelling, envy and acts of quiet devotion. There were wedding feasts in the barns, coffins carried shoulder-high and nights of dancing on the bridge.

It is all there still, if you take it quietly, leaving the road and following the little overgrown foot-tracks between the sites of the old houses. Here, for the finding, is all the legacy of a group of people set down in a hollow of hills, not ghostly but warm and alive. This summer, of all summers, we came nearest to the dancing on the bridge.

October

Summer didn't end until near the last day of September and then it went off in style—a sunset of winter brilliance, a blaze of stars in the night sky, with the northern stretches palely floodlit, and in the morning a white blanket of frost.

Over breakfast we heard of blizzards in the high hills. Eyes looking from faces still browned by summer glinted with a moment's alarm. We remembered the old fable. Had we been grasshoppers the summer long, or ants? Had we danced and sung too merrily, not scurried with our loads and stored them tidily away against the rainy days that inevitably come?

But no, we had lifted carrots, onions and beet on a golden day when they dried as they lay exposed—beautiful and tapered and round—and they were snugly secured.

Potatoes were safe in the ground and the greens would weather happily. The tomatoes are almost embarrassingly lush—plump and red like an apple in the hand. There will be fewer green ones for chutney this year.

The honey is stored and the bees tucked up, with ample for their winter needs. All in all, we do not think the ant would have been too cross with us.

Hearing of southern harvests, we count our blessings. We had the sun but not the drought, and our peaty ground holds moisture like a sponge. So the garden has bulged with goodness all summer. The alpine strawberries are still impudently fruiting, the berries snugly hidden among the bushy leaves. We must have more next year, for there is a special joy in out-of-season fruit.

'It's always next year in a garden,' someone said the other day. That's it, of course. New plans kindle in the mind. And life responds so cheerfully. Lettuce seedlings are already thrusting under cloches, and carrots and spring onions are biding their time.

The corn was stooked by mid-September and now we have had rain to swell the turnips. So fodder should be ample for reasonable needs. As long as one does not look for miracles, all should be well.

Soon we shall be out securing the wild harvests of sloe, bramble, hips and hazelnuts. And this must surely be the year of the fungi. Boletus are everywhere, chanterelles in a few favoured corners, along with puffballs, and mushrooms the size of soup-plates cover the sheltered pastures. With an evening fire at the cave-mouth one could surely survive happily in this wilderness at the season's end!

The equinoctial gales blew not too harshly, though they sent the swallows packing. Few leaves came down, for there is still sap enough to hold them tight to the branches. But there was a shower of small green apples. They will simmer happily with the rowan berries soon. And one surprise bonus was a load of plums which tumbled from a kind friend's tree, and are now in shining pots of tangy jam.

There is one small sadness to record—the death of a dove. The sudden fierce swoop of a hawk caught him unawares. It is as old as the world, of course, the story of doves and hawks.

He was a bonny bird. He would come to my call, along with his mate, wings alight in the early sun. He would strut round the feeding ledge on his neat pink feet, in his eagerness scattering seed, which the hens gobbled on the grass below. They would make beautiful patterns in the air, the two of them, and soothing sounds, circling the house with peace.

But his mate survives. She has two half-grown young in the small loft. They must take their chance. But we hope the hawk looks the other way.

Michaelmas passes unnoticed now, though the flowers that carry

Michael's name bring glorious colour to his special time. He was a glorious saint himself, riding full tilt at the powers of darkness on his great white horse. We could do with a few like him to canter about the world today, with shield and spear. With his blessing on boats and horses, his appeal to the Celts is clearly seen in the Mounts of Brittany and Cornwall.

As his day fell at harvest time, it was celebrated in the West with the baking of rich bannocks and the riding of wild, bareback races. If these communal festivities were engaged in today perhaps we should progress more slowly, but more surely towards the goals we set ourselves. We would look around to see where we were going. At any rate, let us cheer the memory of Michael and be glad there were once folk who took time off to fête him.

Autumn can come in now when it pleases. It has been making a few signs—a leaf blazing red here and there, a yellowing of the bracken. But the birches are still green and only an odd bramble is ripe for picking.

We do not need an Indian summer this year, for the real one was so splendid. Its goodness is sealed in honeycomb and clamp. It will pass safely into legend and raises a flag for life, putting the manufactured ills of the world into their shallow perspective.

III
THE LAND

THE CLEARANCES—1970

As the establishing of at least one large-scale industrial complex on the fringe of the Highland area is a much-discussed question in the north at the moment, I think it is appropriate to consider what such an undertaking will really contribute towards a solution of the Highland 'problem'—the 'problem' being how to make large areas of neglected, but potentially fruitful land, maintain a healthy population.

But first, why would a foreign firm decide to set up production in these parts? Not, obviously, in order to fit in with any overall plan for the improvement of conditions in the whole of the north, but only if they get what they want—building land, roads, houses, transport, labour—on terms which will make it possible for them to earn bigger profits here than they could in the more competitive conditions of the south. And where will the profits go? Big business only occasionally even pretends to be philanthropical.

So they start off with the ball at their feet. And then what will happen? The glens and straths to the north and west will be drained of the young men and women who have so far, in the hope of finding some betterment at hand, resisted the call to make for the industrial centres of the south, but who now find the bright lights glittering along the shores, say, of the Moray Firth. What else they will find there is obvious—the Bingo halls, the pubs, the varied devices that will help rid them of their pay-packets, the gangs and rackets of urban life. And, sooner or later, the pay-off and the frustrations of industrial living.

Meanwhile, what of the situation in the home areas they have left? There, a depression deeper than any so far known will have settled as landlords find their clearances ready-made again and set briskly about re-appropriating every available acre, enclosing as they see fit and developing their playgrounds. The tired business giants will need spaces where they can relax—fishing, shooting, sailing and breathing some unpolluted air, so as to renew their energies.

Why is it that any plan for industrial development is considered bold and forward-looking, whereas the idea of developing agriculture is accused of being a backward-looking, sentimental dream? To re-plan the use of land is surely the most forward-looking thing one can do. To let it stagnate is to condone and perpetuate all the mistakes and injustices of the past.

I sometimes wonder if the planners for the Highlands have ever really lived in the area, got to know the people or even the places for which they plan. To the Highlander, his country is anything but a 'Shangri-la'. It is, for better or for worse, the part of the world where he belongs. His love for it is tough and resilient, compounded of awareness of its quirks and drawbacks and a fierce devotion to its mastery. The Highlander is still one of the most civilised men in Europe.

With a road, electricity, the telephone and plumbing, remoteness need no longer mean backwardness. There are lives being lived in the glens today which are richer, fuller, infinitely more satisfying than many lived in urban areas. The quality of living still counts.

There is time for hospitality and understanding. Honest dealings and courtesy are still in fashion. The material benefits of modern times are there, without the drawbacks. There is the library book and the record-player, but no Bingo halls or slums.

So many more could live these lives if the planners would make plans to fit the people and the land, and not expect the people to conform to the plans. If land were allotted so that every glen and strath were fully inhabited, there would automatically be a variety of work for everyone. Fully-planned land use means outlets for the young men as shepherds, foresters, tractor-drivers, stockmen, mechanics, agricultural advisers, research assistants, according to their desires and capacities. Young women can and do enjoy work in agriculture, in the dairy and poultry sides, or they can train as teachers or nurses or work in shops or offices in their nearest small town.

It is always tacitly assumed that youngsters prefer urban life. As long as there are plenty of them, they thrive on country ways. One has only to go to a meeting of a Young Farmers Club to find this. The pursuits are so various, the get-togethers so gay. The glamour of urban life soon fades for most of them.

Emigration was, and still is, due to outside pressures. Of course, when families were big and crofts ridiculously small, one had to 'get out to get on', if one weren't actually forced to do so by one's superiors. But little record remains of the thoughts and feelings of those who did go.

What they achieved in the end in the lands into which they were thrust could have been given to their own land, and we might have no problem with us now.

As for looking back, it is, in fact, helpful to glance over one's shoulder now and again. One finds useful scraps of discarded knowledge. One learns, for instance, that balance is the thing. The ancestors had come to this conclusion—that sheep and cattle run very well together in the glens, for the sheep crop close and the cattle trample and eat coarse growth. But the nineteenth-century sheepmen and the cattle ranchers of the twentieth preferred to ignore this precept, in their scramble for markets, and now we find land soured and overgrown.

One can profitably look back. And then one looks forward again, to the time when all the scientific knowledge of today is really applied to the Highlands—when fish-farms can be established and new crops tried, when the climate of the west, which can produce gardens like Inverewe, can be harnessed to make possible the growing of all kinds of fruit and vegetables, when trees will provide shelter for sheep and not deprive them of grazing. All this is planning, too.

It is evident to anyone who look and thinks that the potential for food-production in the Highland area is vast, and that to ignore it is folly. Before large-scale industrialisation on the fringe of the area takes place I would ask the planners to consider what is at stake for the generations to come.

Give them industry and you give them some easy money, glamour and boredom and all that follows. Give them their own land and a modern plan to work it, with the natural development of diversified trades and small industries in balanced centres of population, and you allow them a quality of living which could be unique in human history.

LAND REVOLUTION IS NEEDED NOW

On a journey through the far north and west of Scotland, the Easter traveller feels a tremendous lift of the spirit. Where else on earth, he thinks, can there be such light, such colour—thirty-seven shades of blue, he reckons—such grace of outline in hill and moor, such exuberance in racing water and flying cloud.

Then, as the spring dusk falls, and a curlew's call trembles in the distance, he feels the sadness in the air. Who could fail to feel it? It is there. It is in the emptiness of the spaces.

The traveller makes quickly for the first beacon of light and warmth, for the sound of voices and the look of a smile.

This is the land, he has been told, of the glens and the hills and the heroes. He has seen the glens and the hills, but where are the heroes? The tale of their going has been told often enough. It is time now to speak of their return to the land that bred them.

You cannot drain a land of its life-blood and expect it to prosper. Its life-blood is in people. There has been so much begging of this basic question. Surely now we must face the fact that there has been, and still is, an antipathy to real development of the area. There has been a wish to keep it underdeveloped, as a playground for the few. This is a death-wish. And of course the living have fled before it.

Shepherding, stalking, gamekeeping will not keep many, even though some wives are allowed to accommodate the tourist with 'bed and breakfast.' It is so easy to dismiss the area as unproductive. We simply do not know its potential, for modern methods, used by modern people, have never really been given a chance to prove it. What is needed is a gigantic and comprehensive plan for the development of all the natural resources of the whole of the north lands.

Reports and surveys have been made piecemeal. An enormous amount of scientific knowledge about climate, soil, drainage, fertilisation, has been accumulated. Small-scale experiments have been carried out in re-seeding, fish-farming, alternative cropping. Much tentative groundwork has been done. It is time now for the drawing-up and putting into action of a really big and really bold plan for the natural development of the whole area.

Development does not mean exploitation. To exploit is easy and ruthless. It is largely a matter of quick returns and scant regard for the quality of life, now or in the future. The world is only too eager to play it that way.

To develop needs understanding, patience, cooperation and respect for humanity. A plan for the whole Highland area would take into account the subtle differences of temperament, springing from ethnic differences, between, say, the peoples of east and west, as well as the obvious contrasts of climate and terrain. Plans must fit. People are slow to change.

But change in the land and what it will produce can be effected unbelievably quickly. We have seen already what re-seeding can do in the islands of the west.

The planting of shelter-belts, such as are used in southern France to protect fruit crops from the bitterly cold 'mistral' wind, could make some of the barren isles richly productive of vegetable crops. Drainage and fertilisation can transform a mainland strath as though by magic. I have seen corn growing at close on the thousand-foot contour, where only rushes and bog-cotton previously flourished. Bulldozers and au-tomatic drainage units are the giants that accomplish miracles today.

A well coordinated plan would ensure that developments did not conflict. Thus the planting of trees would be done in smaller parcels than at present and in places where they would provide shelter for beasts and crops and in high regions where only they will prosper. The proportion of tillage and grazing, as well as afforestation, would have to be adjusted. It is all too easy to exploit land agriculturally, to exhaust and ruin it. The test of a landsman's integrity is to keep it in good heart. He should be encouraged to do so.

The resources of the area include those of the waters round the whole coast-line, as well as of the rivers and lochs. The potential of these as sources of first-class food has never been fully realised. And what of the other sources that reared the fighting men of the past—the deer and the game. These will flourish on ground too poor for sheep or cattle.

Venison, salmon, trout and grouse are luxury foods which could be produced in appreciable quantities and exported fresh. With refrig-eration and transport by air, this presents few problems. Alternatively they could be canned or processed in the area—and at once employment would be created—especially for women.

The cutting and processing of peat, of which there are vast deposits in the area, is another enterprise with a potential which has never been fully explored. It requires very much less capital investment than coal-mining. And its transportation by rail could well be a means of keeping the line to the north working economically.

Plans only serve to clutter the shelves of offices if no action is taken on them. And drastic action of the kind needed to revitalise a whole land will have to hurt here and there. Some rocks must be riven.

There is a glen in Sutherland which is cut across by the marches of four different owners of land. Sutherland, as is well known, is a paradise for the stalker, the fisher and the shot. Sutherland has also been a hell for the small, faithful people she has bred. Their sons went off to fight Napoleon with promises of land on their return. Those that did return found not only no land but the smoking ruins of their former homes. Social injustice, inflicted with or without the sanction of the law, must leave a scar on humanity. It is not too late, even now, for reparation.

The scattered Jewish people were allowed to claim their promised land and we know what they are making of it. Give a young man a settlement and the means to work it in cooperation with his kind—a pool of modern machinery, expert advice and an initial grant of livestock—and you have a plan in action. And let us get away from the image of the thatched roof, the peat fire, the heather in the ears.

Today's settler needs a snug, neat dwelling, with basic mod. cons., so that he and his wife can devote their energies to the hard work they have to do. The heroes are waiting. Many already have their names on a register. So many like them opened up Canada, New Zealand, Africa. They should be allowed, now, to pioneer their own land. To pioneer is to look forward. It is to push back the frontiers of hunger, which is surely the urgent necessity of today.

Once the natural resources are being fully worked, with care and understanding, along the rhythm of the land, a healthy society can be safely born. There is balance. Appropriate ancillary industries—food-processing plants, boat-building yards, agricultural engineering works and many others—come naturally into being, providing work for people of varying ranges of ability—manual, clerical, technical, administrative and so on. The professionals will fit naturally into the scheme—the teachers, doctors, nurses, vets, lawyers. The minister will know his flock again. This is the kind of setting which produces balanced people, with roots.

Balanced people, eager to take responsibility, confident and secure in their communities, will get things done. They will shout for better roads until they get them. They will shout for adequate transport facilities and modern schools and training centres and the appropriate industries they want and get them, too. Confident people, sure of their identity and purpose, can and will move mountains.

The traveller through a truly regenerated north land would find a valid lifting of the spirit. The light, the colour and the contours would be as glorious as they are today. And the sadness would be gone.

There would be the sound of voices, children capering, tractors roaring and in the evening, the lighted windows, the feel of companionship and purpose, the feel of life. The heroes would be back, taking their rightful place as producers of the basic necessity of the human race—food. It would be a country to inspire the travellers of the world. They would carry home tales, not of a playground, but of a land that worked.

It can be done. It will not be easy because we can count only on ourselves to bring it about. It will not be easy but it can be done. It must be done.

WHY THE RUINS?

'You don't really live here, do you?' That was the question, compound of bewilderment, exasperation and ironic humour, put to us some time ago by a city friend as he stumbled to the door of our hilltop croft house, clutching his hat against the fury of an April gale.

The answer, then, was to bring him in to a seat at the log fire, to shed our working gear of gumboots, balaclavas and oilskins and to serve him tea with cream and buttered scones with bramble jelly. We hadn't long to sit with him, for there were cattle to be seen to and a stint of ploughing to be finished before dark and the round of the lambing ewes to be made. At that time we were working our acres for a living and every hour of the spring days was crammed. When he left, warm and rested, the exasperation and the irony had gone and only a little, I think, of the bewilderment remained.

The answer to the same question, fifteen years later, is still 'yes'. True, it isn't put now with quite the baffled tone in the voice, for we no longer live in the croft house tucked away off the road in a fold of the high strath called Caiplich. Our home is the schoolhouse, in its acre of wild garden. Tenancy of it is part of my reward for teaching daily in ten-miles-distant Inverness and my husband runs a minute Post Office and library in the outer porch.

'But how do you manage the hill in winter?' every other visitor asks, looking at our small van parked in the playground shelter. To be honest, there is a week or two, most winters, when the thought of a warm bungalow in town, safely accessible in all weathers, is not altogether anathema. But the mood is only a flicker. On the worst mornings, their faces stiff with cold, but splitting into grins as their snowplough triumphantly reaches us by 8 a.m., the county roadmen fling gravel on to the ice-bound slopes with more than the courtesy of Raleigh.

If a storm blows up later in the day, then there's no undue hardship in leaving the van in the shelter of the old quarry by the main road and climbing the mile and a half on foot. The tonic effect of filling the lungs with the cold hill air does away with tiredness, lifts all the worries of the day and brings everything back into perspective.

Perspective is, I think, what close on twenty years of living in the heights has brought us. Perspective does give some sort of a shape to life. The old people of these uplands had it and the feel for it is still there, in the steady eyes bequeathed by the generations, in a turn of inherited speech, in the set of a pair of shoulders.

For us, no place compares with these bare, high spaces. Our daughter, a much-travelled modern language student, comes home from a study spell in France or Italy, or from a summer's work in a kibbutz by Jordan, takes a great breath of the hill air and renews the strength of her beginnings. She is a child of the strath and the welcome she gets on every croft threshold never fails to thrill her. Her initials are there, carved on the walls of the playground shelter, along with those of the other generations. But in the empty classrooms she feels sad.

They are filled only occasionally now with the sound of young voices and young feet, when a party of town Scouts or Cadets comes to spend a few days in the open. To see them exploring the burn, trekking through the birch wood and up the hill makes one feel happy, yet deeply sad.

Why should they be allowed only so brief a glimpse of their natural inheritance? Why should there be these empty schoolrooms? Why the ghostly initials? Why the ruins? Why are the rushes choking the pastures by the burn? Why is the heather creeping back when so many hands struggled to keep it at bay, once? Why are the people in the small places only part-timers now, having to travel miles to work on distant building schemes, wearing out the strength which they long to use on their own acres? Why does the enjoyment of a modest prosperity, gained in the production of basic necessities, in the incomparable natural surroundings of the Highlands, have to remain a dream?

It is not for lack of strong young people willing to live and work here. There is a hunger for such living. We have seen it in the eyes of many who have spent their annual release from the industrial treadmill wandering in these parts, and have called at our home to ask if we know of any small farm to rent. One young man, in particular, we shall never forget. He had the firm shoulders and the strong hands and a sort of desperation in his eyes and voice.

'Surely there must be somewhere,' he said, looking at the empty crofts. 'I could make it fine. And my wife...she's from the west and she'll be happy only in bare country like this.' They speak plainly, from the will and the heart. But we can't help them.

Of course, they have no capital, these youngsters. But they have the hunger and the energy and the will. They are practically dauntless. And they don't think in terms of colour television and a new car every other year. 'These could be bonny acres,' they will say. And they are right. The earth is there. It is very patient. It doesn't, as in parts of Norway, have to be carted and built into fields. Nor do the sheep have to be housed and hand-fed all winter. It is not such a bleak and barren land. But why is it still and empty?

To fill it with tourists is not the answer. Hotel-keeping is bound to be seasonal and is a precarious and not a satisfying trade. It involves huge expenditure on roads which are used only in short spells. Build roads to the isolated crofting areas and they will be used all year and every year.

The weather is not attractive to the short-term holidaymaker, who has not the time to appreciate its glorious shifts and quirks. The licensing laws and the midges are the final irritants to which the tourist does not have the time to adjust!

Afforestation is only a partial answer. It can help, by providing a certain amount of employment and creating shelter in some of the bleakest areas. But a proper balance must be kept. Trees do not feed the multitude. And is all that amount of paper really necessary?

Large-scale industrialisation is not the answer either. I don't think anyone really believes that it is. The man of the north never takes kindly to clocking in and clocking out and standing all day and all night at the conveyor-belt. And that, after all, is what it comes to. But give him some acres, and a boat if he is in the west, and happiness is his.

A happy man works round the clock and doesn't notice it. And he doesn't need recourse to drugs to beat boredom. Whisky was never a curse before the Clearances. A dram was for a wedding or a wake or a welcome to New Year, but not a soporific and so a curse.

No. The question has been begged long enough. There are the Highland spaces. There are the young lives waiting to be lived in them. There is the wide world shouting desperately to be fed. Common sense, not any political dogma, surely makes it plain that these three factors point to one thing—that the land must be made available for a vastly increased amount of real production.

There must be draining and reseeding of barren hill-land on a huge scale. There must be schemes, as there were during the war, for the hiring of heavy equipment at cheap rates. Loans must be procurable on minimal security.

The natural bent of the land and the people must be followed. Throughout the world Scotland has a reputation for producing excellence —incomparable beef, mutton, fish, wool, whisky. Increased quantity need not mean a decrease in quality. Why could not the rivers teem with trout and salmon instead of yielding a costly few to the rods of the American tycoon and the Spanish grandee?

If the land were fully used so much else would follow. The establishment of ancillary trades would allow the growth of small, balanced centres of population where there would be room and need for the professionals—the teachers, doctors, dentists, lawyers, and vets. The small schools could be reopened. Many people could be full-time countrymen again.

Children brought up in a country which needs them grow into true contentment. They take enjoyment in their stride and don't let it rear into a god. An afternoon playing shinty or football, a day's fishing, an evening learning about dressmaking or photography, the Saturday night dance, the summer barbecue, the winter ski-trip—and there's still time to read and swim and lie on the hill doing nothing. They have time. They have time to grow real. They are waiting to be born.

The land has waited a long time. There are acres facing me as I write which are still covered in virgin growth. A couple of miles up the road three fields, recently won from the heather, are bright green with new-sown grass. This is the greenprint on which to build.

Robert Southey, in his *Journal of a Tour in Scotland in 1819*, wrote: 'The restoration of the forfeited estates has produced no good in the Highlands...Far better would it have been for the country in general, and especially for the poor Highlanders, if the estates had been retained as Crown lands, and leased accordingly, or even sold to strangers. The Highland Laird partakes much more of the Irish character than I had ever been taught to suppose. He has the same profusion, the same recklessness, the same rapacity: but he has more power and he uses it worse: and his sin is the greater, because he has to deal with a sober, moral, well-disposed people, who, if they were treated with common kindness, or even common justice, would be ready to lay down their lives in his service.

'Some fifty land-Leviathans may be said to possess the Highlands: for the number of smaller heritors, or rather the land which is occupied by them, is comparatively a mere nothing. A few of these are desirous of improving their own estates by bettering the condition of their tenants. But the greater number are fools at heart, with neither understanding nor virtue, nor good nature to form such a wish. Their object is to increase their revenue, and they care not by what means this is accomplished.

'If a man improve his farm, instead of encouraging him they invite others to outbid him in rent, or they dispeople whole tracts to convert them into sheep farms. Whereas if they would offer beneficial leases to their tenants, as Evan Baillie is doing, to men who are willing to bring it into cultivation, such is the disposition of the Highlanders (manifested by them, wherever they have opportunity to manifest it) that in half a century the Highland vallies would be as well cultivated as any part of England.'

That was written more than 150 years ago, by an outspoken man of perception. Have things changed very much since he saw and wrote?

IV
AN ENDING,
A NEW BEGINNING

AN ENDING

The pages of this Diary were written almost fifty years ago, when we were working that croft in the hills above Loch Ness, then latterly living in the old schoolhouse, and when we were lucky enough to have the company of the last of the native crofters. They have all gone now, all those good people, taking their skills, their memories, their laughter even in the face of despair, their stories, their song, everything that gave their lives purpose and meaning and in which we were able in small measure to share.

They will not come again, those days of struggling with soaked sheaves of corn, of spending long summer hours with bands of neighbours at the peats, of carrying that limpid water in swaying pails up the track from the well, of savouring lamplit winter evenings when the roof beams shudder in a north-east gale. But new times will come, and they can be good. The young are waiting to inherit and are looking afresh to the old ways of tending the earth, feeding it naturally, discarding what a former generation called the 'artificials'. That, they realise, is the way forward. And they realise, I think, that greed does not pay. Take too much out and you lose everything.

Frank Fraser Darling, that great ecologist, who really understood the Highlands, in his book *The Future of the Highlands* says: 'While the Hebrideans were dependent on the environment for their whole subsistence a very beautiful ecological adaptation to circumstances took place... When a culture is beginning to break down, its disciplines of existence also begin to fail and the empirical conservation of habitat at which the people had arrived breaks down to exploitative attrition of natural resources.'

'Exploitative attrition' can be avoided. 'Why would a man possess more than he needs?' was the wondering query of an American Indian a hundred years ago, when he found the white settlers destroying his environment.

Lately, in the crofting areas, there has, perhaps, been too much dependence on the running of sheep. Sheep are greedy eaters and sour the ground. The over-dependence on the potato led to famine last century, when the crops failed. Lamb can be imported from many other parts with the sophisticated freezing techniques of today. Wool, that

194

superb body-warmer, has been ousted by synthetic fabrics which do better in the washing-machine.

Cattle always kept the ground in better heart, trampling coarse growth, not over-grazing, manuring richly. The sward is still bright green at the old shielings. The beasts that were taken up there to recover from the winter on the sweet grass of the high pastures did not need the injection of hormones to promote growth. They, like the crops, were reared organically.

Even the houses, in very old times, were built organically. The materials were to hand—stone and turf for the walls, branches to hold the roof of heather thatch, a floor of earth or clay. These houses were shaped to withstand storm and seemed almost to grow out of the ground. Thatch, discarded when the house was re-roofed, was ploughed into the fields. Impregnated with peat-reek, it made excellent fertiliser.

Before the introduction of those 'artificials', the chemical fertilisers, dung was the essential feeding for the ground. Sheep dung was scattered far and wide, but the dung of winter-housed cattle was accessible and precious as gold coin. Lime was a great improver and it was found locally and freely applied. Some old kilns are still to be seen.

For people in the islands and on the coast there was another source of wealth—seaweed. It was invaluable in the making of the 'lazy-beds', the tiny strips of ground among the rocks where potatoes and maybe enough oats to make the family's morning brose could be grown. Seaweed also made a nourishing dish which is still enjoyed today. The old lairds of the eighteenth century knew what they were doing when they sent many of their evicted tenants to the coast to develop the kelping industry—the burning of seaweed to produce alkali used in the manufacture of glass, soap and other things. They made small fortunes out of it, though the workers only reaped rheumatism and other illnesses.

The intuitive wisdom of the native people—those born to crofting life—kept them in a right relationship with their land and its resources, grateful for what it could give, putting back more than they took. Their relationship with one another was also on this seemly level. The house door was never locked, a welcome was assured. Help for the sick, the old, the injured was spontaneously given. The ceilidh turned relaxation into a renewal of the spirit, with its own source of inner energy and delight.

Perhaps, with the millennium, this land of hill and moor, of river and loch, of forest and seashore and deep glen, may cease to be a wilderness and a playground for the rich, may revert to its original destiny, to be a place where those who love and understand it may come together to work it with the regard it needs and to enjoy that unique way of life which is their real inheritance.

A NEW BEGINNING

With reform in the system of landholding at the top of the politicians' agenda there is surely hope, now, that the crofters' tenuous grip may be strengthened and crofting may be enabled to progress, to take its rightful place in the scheme of things. It was always more than a business enterprise. It represented a unique lifestyle, its long-held customs and traditions promoting a healthy form of cooperation, of working together, in which everyone, young, old or infirm, was valued and had a part. Hospitality was taken for granted, an open door could save a life. Courtesy of manner was part of the code. Can such communities come together again? I believe they can. The signs are there.

The Crofters' Act of 1886 gave crofters security of tenure in their

A young 'Croft Entrant' family

197

holdings. They could not be dispossessed at the whim of a landlord. But their holdings were pitifully small, much of their grazing ground given over to sheep and, later, to deer. It had always been intended that the crofter would find waged work to supplement the subsistence provided by the croft, originally in the kelping industry or on the estate and so on. Now there are plans to allow certain estates, or parts of them, to be bought by crofting communities, with the help of funds raised from various agencies. For the past number of years it has been possible for crofters to buy their individual places at a reasonable price. Many have chosen not to do this as they feel adequately protected by the terms of the Act and by the existence of the Land Court to which they can take any grievances, and of the Crofters' Commission. This agency is actively engaged in promoting the development of crofting, issuing leaflets explaining the benefits available, the grants for housing, fencing, draining and so on. It has plans for the improvement of livestock by the hire of pedigreed bulls and rams. Advice on many matters is always available from the Commission or its local representative. It is proposed to simplify procedure, to cut red tape and to reduce the amount of form-filling.

Lately the Commission, in association with Scottish Natural Heritage, Highland Council Education Department, Comunn na Gaidhlig and Highlands and Islands Enterprise, has issued a pack for schools which aims 'to develop children's knowledge and understanding of the agricultural, cultural, environmental and economic aspects of crofting'. It is intended for use with the first two years of secondary schooling or the last stages of primary work. It is most attractively produced, well illustrated, with work-sheets, teachers' notes and descriptions of crofting life by young people living on crofts in different areas.

The Commission's most important stand at the moment is against the absentee landlord who allows the ground to degenerate, and in favour of a new 'Croft Entrant' scheme, whereby a crofter no longer able to work would grant the tenancy to a younger person, he himself being allowed, if he wishes, to stay on in the house, with garden ground.

Having acquired a tenancy with a house—the original one or one newly built and grant-aided—and livestock to provide his family's essential needs, the new crofter can look to many interesting diversifications to supplement his income. Total dependence on inshore fishing and sheep culture is no longer possible. The exchange rate, the imposition of quotas, the collapse of markets, many factors have brought about changes. Wool has gone out of fashion. The Russians have to manage without imported sheepskins.

The members of Abriachan Community Woodland Trust

One resource for island and coastal mainland communities, a re-source renewable if harvested wisely, an asset waiting to be fully explored, is seaweed. It has long been known as a valuable fertiliser and foodstuff, full of essential minerals. The Welsh people, in particu-lar, have always used it widely. Now, in Orkney and elsewhere, it is being made into many health-giving dishes. It is also used medicinally and in the making of cosmetics, toothpaste, ice-cream and other things. It is hoped that a drying facility can be built in one of the islands so that transport costs to mainland factories can be reduced. The weather in the west, being largely dependent on the beneficence of the Atlantic drift, would seem to make ideal conditions for the development of horticulture. Shelter-belts of trees, as well as plastic tunnels, could pro-vide protection from the winds. With the increasing numbers of people catering for tourists much produce could be sold locally. If freight charges could be reduced much could be transported quickly by air to Glasgow and other centres. I've tasted carrots grown in a croft garden in Harris and can vouch for their succulence and size. And that hardy and perhaps undervalued winter green—kail of the famous 'yaird'—can survive any kind of weather. A start has already been made with

199

the production of vegetables on crofts in Skye.

With the ever-growing number of people everywhere turning to vegetarianism and looking desperately for organically-grown food a market would be assured. The islands, in their state of comparative isolation, would seem to be the ideal place in which to promote the organic production of food of every kind. Cattle, sheep, pigs, poultry could all be reared in this way. With increased production, prices could level out, though many people are even now prepared to pay more for what they really want. And the producer can qualify for a premium. Having once tasted a 'free-range' egg, who would go back to the others? Those 'free-range' lambs straight off their high hill-grazing are surely organically grown. Scottish food is already held in high repute. To have it organically produced would ensure it an even higher profile.

From the small island of Lismore locally produced cheese has found a market world-wide. The goat, that much-maligned creature, produces, on a meagre diet, milk which can be made into cheese of a special variety. Ewes' milk, too, can be used in this way.

I have heard lately of a mainland crofter who is planning, after

Cattle grazing on the machair

waiting several years for his ground to be 'de-toxified' of chemicals, to produce organically grown vegetables for the local market, such is the demand.

Flowers, also, especially those grown from bulbs, could find a niche in the croft lands. Anyone who has seen the early summer flowering on the machair will understand the potential there. The gardens of the west are glorious, Inverewe world-famous.

Crofters are now being encouraged to plant trees on part of their land. It would certainly be a great thing to reverse, even in a small measure, the effect of the depredations made over later centuries, when the cutting-down was ruthless. Forests had always held great significance for the Celts. The Druids reverenced groves of sacred trees. To cut down the oak or the ash was a crime. The life of trees mirrored that of human beings. They grew in woods, many species together, strongly rooted in the earth, their hefty trunks reaching upward, gaining sustenance through their leaves from light, air and water, enduring the seasons as humans do.

The creation of natural woodland means the planting of the old native trees—ash, alder, willow, rowan, hazel, holly, apple, even oak—all of which had valuable uses, and that most beautiful of trees, once regarded as a weed, now a protected species, the birch. An early alphabet was based on the names of these familiar trees. Grants are to be made available for planting and advice given about contacts with various authorities and similar matters. Partnership is vital.

One community, in Abriachan, near Inverness, has formed a trust and managed, with funding from various sources, to buy an area of forest, once hill-grazing, now planted with conifers, from the Forestry Commission. They plan to transform it into native woodland, using natural seed, and to make it accessible to people, on a modest scale. It is rich in plant and wild life. It will also, in time, provide employment for several local men and women.

Crofters in various areas have, over the last years, been able to buy and manage the land they live on. Assynt was first in the field, then the island of Eigg, now Knoydart and Valtos in the island of Lewis. The people can see their own ideas for development—in local industry, environmental projects, tourism, improved social facilities, marketing—come to fruition with the help of the 'Crofting Township Development Scheme', which is run by the Commission. This fosters a communal approach to developments of all kinds and co-operation with the various agencies involved and can help with advice, incentive payments for approved plans and so on.

There are, potentially, many forms of diversification for the crofter today. The oil industry can provide working conditions conducive to the management of a croft. An employee can spend two weeks off-shore, on a rig, and two weeks at home, which allows him, especially if he has a cooperative wife and family, to cope with croft work. Wives and families have always been an essential part of crofting life!

If wind and wavepower could be satisfactorily harnessed—and I believe some new ideas for this are on the move—small industrial centres could be established. Some crafts now worked on a small scale could be put on a commercial basis. And surely the production of the world-famous tweed should not be allowed to perish.

With modern developments in telecommunication it is possible, now, of course, to conduct business of any kind from the most remote situations. At the press of a button or the turn of a switch one can be instantly in touch with the world of commerce out there and all its ups and downs. One room in a croft house can become a well-equipped office, its occupier commuting only from the kitchen. And he or she has the assurance that the croft is always there, providing a safe background of housing and the means of subsistence. There is happy cooperation in the Western Isles between crofters and Scottish Natural Heritage in various measures to protect the environment and wildlife. One such is a scheme to help the corncrake, small grants being made available to compensate for adapting the timing of crop-cutting to suit the nesting habits of the birds. The renewed use of seaweed as fertiliser is also being encouraged. This involves heavy handling, but its worth is recognised. To work with the earth, learning its ways and the ways of the livestock you can manage to rear on it, on the intimate scale of a few acres and some rough outrun, this is to learn real respect for the environment, the environment of nature—of hill, rock, water, plant—of animals, of people. In older times, with the understanding inherited through the generations, the ground was tended with almost reverential care, as the sustainer of life. With wildlife there was an affinity that engendered respect. People were valued above all. This harmony between the land, the animals and people had been the foundation of the Celts' spiritual attitude to life.

With people living and working on the croft lands again the social life of the communities would be assured. The school would be re-opened, the minister of religion could hold services and attend to his flock, the shop, with a Post Office, that essential focal point, could survive. The ceilidh would come into its own again, in welcoming houses everywhere. There would be gatherings in the hall or the schoolroom on festive occasions. The sense of solidarity would be renewed.

Culture, that many-faceted concept, expressed in the magic of a people's poetry, in the flying movement of dance, in the long-told stories that bring the generations to life, in song that can stop the heart; culture, with its inheritance of tried values, lying deep in the age-old customs of courteous welcoming and care, all this is waiting to be repossessed.

In a world looking for actual reality, as opposed to the virtual kind on the flickering screen, the crofting way of life, with its sense of inter-dependence, its scope for human abilities and skills of many kinds, its openness to the new ideas that evolve from the old traditions, could well be a way forward for the generations to come.